MYTHOLOGIES

MYTHOLOGIES

A POLITICAL ECONOMY OF U.S. LITERATURE, SETTLER COLONIALISM, AND RACIAL CAPITALISM IN THE LONG NINETEENTH-CENTURY

Joel Wendland-Liu

INTERNATIONAL PUBLISHERS, New York

CIP data available from Library of Congress

ISBN 10: 0-7178-0031-8   ISBN-13 978-07178-0031-5
Typeset by Amnet Systems, Chennai, India

Table of Contents

Acknowledgements

Portions of chapters 1-3 appeared in earlier forms in the following publications: "Conversion, Assimilation, or Sovereignty: Native Shape-shifting and Settler Colonialism in James Fenimore Cooper's *The Oak Openings*," *Journal of the Midwest Modern Language Association*, Vol. 20, Spring 2021; "Black Republicans, Natives, and Anti-colonial Resistance in James Fenimore Cooper's *The Oak Openings* and Andrew J. Blackbird's *The History of the Ottawa and Chippewa Indians of Michigan*. *Interdisciplinary Literary Studies*, Vol. 23, no. 2: 267-287; "Orientalism and the U.S. Empire: A Reading of Royall Tyler's *The Algerine Captive*," *Nature, Society and Thought*, Vol. 20, no. 2, 2007, 161-189; "'Mutual Dependence' and Subversive Work: Exploring Dialectics of Race, Gender, and Labor in the Antebellum United States," *Nature, Society and Thought*, Vol. 16, no. 1, 2003, 5-31.

The author expresses gratitude to each journal—its editors, editorial assistants, copy editors, reviewers, and all of the workers responsible for publication—for their work in bringing out the original and their consent to adapt them for this format. In addition, the author thanks the following people for their years of comradeship, intellectual and political mentorship, and professional support: Azfar Hussain, Gerald Horne, Joe Sims, E. San Juan Jr., Delia Aguilar, T.V. Reed, and Patrick Johnson. Deepest devotion is offered to Yilin Wendland-Liu.

MYTHOLOGIES

Introduction: Entry points

1619, arrivals

> And one amongst the rest did kill his wife, powdered her, and had eaten part of her before it was knowne, for which hee was executed, as hee well deserved; now whether shee was better roasted, boyled or carbonado'd, I know not, but of such a dish as powdered wife I never heard of. This was that time, which still to this day we called the starving time.[1]

In the closing months of 1610, the people who launched a colony that would within 180 years become the homeland of a "white," slaveholding republic were hungry. There are no less than five accounts of English cannibalism during the "starving time" at Jamestown. As offspring of noble families who despised work, they preferred hunger over the labor of cultivating needed crops. Disease and laziness caused many to perish; others attempted to survive by resorting to such acts described above. Recently, historians have grown skeptical of these accounts, which seemed to use extreme tales to justify the colony's early failures. Nevertheless, some of the first untranslated English-language writings that might be called "American" are a body of literature on murder, a rudimentary political order, European transitions to imperialism and colonialism, cannibalism, labor, political chicanery, and, above all, class struggle.

Less than a decade later, a ship's sail was spotted on the horizon. It was a Dutch war vessel that had just met an English ship and had taken on about two-dozen enslaved Africans. John Rolfe, tobacco planter and one-time husband to Pocahontas, wrote:

> About the latter end of August, a Dutch man of Warr of the bur-
> den of a 160 tunnes arriued at Point-Comfort, the Commandors
> name Capt Jope, his Pilott for the West Indies one Mr Marmad-
> uke an Englishman. They mett wth the Trier in the West Indyes,
> and determyned to hold consort shipp hetherward, but in their
> passage lost one the other. He brought not any thing but 20. and
> odd Negroes, wch the Governor and Cape Marchant bought for
> victualle (whereof he was in greate need as he pretended) at the
> best and easyest rate they could.[2]

The Dutch vessel had found Jamestown accidentally and sold its human cargo for supplies. As the *New York Times* 1619 Project authors note, "this began slavery in America."[3] Of course, the spatiality of "America" and U.S. imperialism today disturbs easy conceptualizations of "America." The exchange between the English and Dutch ships was part of an ongoing European-controlled slave trade that had already kidnapped thousands of Africans for labor in the Americas. Neverthe-less, the account of this arrival introduced racial slavery to the tobacco plantations owned by lazy English gentlemen who had accused one another of eating their kin. Slavery was a solution to labor problems.[4] Racial slavery would be founda-tional to the U.S. nation-state, its capitalist development, and the racist contradictions in its democratic political system.

1781, republican threshold

In his only book, future U.S. President Thomas Jefferson described the state of Virginia. He claimed to have penned *Notes on the State of Virginia* as a response to "a foreigner" who had posed to him a series of questions in 1781,[5] while the insur-gency against the British had not fully been resolved. Indeed, British proclamations, such as the Philipsburg Proclamation which expanded the Dunmore Proclamation, granting free-dom to escaped enslaved people who joined the British cause, remained British military policy.[6] The foreign friend had made copies of Jefferson's initial notes and shared them around. Given the popularity of that document, Jefferson decided to publish it as a book. The book surveys and assesses his home state's geography, laws, economic development, and people. A few things stand out. He remarks on the confiscation of lands and property of British loyalists who refused to pledge loyalty to the new country.[7] He defines agrarian republicanism, a theory of social organization for which he would become famous. Decrying the "mobs of cities," Jefferson writes:

> Those who labour in the earth are God's chosen people, if ever he had a chosen people, whose breasts he has made his peculiar deposit for substantial and genuine virtue. It is the focus in which he keeps alive that sacred fire, which otherwise might escape from the face of the earth.[8]

Though expressed in non-racial language as a universal, it is evident that Jefferson believes such laborers, these "chosen people," are not the toiling enslaved Africans. Jefferson's supposed scientific explanations for racial differences between white people and Black people would clarify this distinction and serve as a basis for who is defined as "chosen." The clear racist difference in Jefferson's mind marks his universalizing language of "those who labour in the earth" with its obvious boundary of racial whiteness. It establishes white identity and white supremacy by elevating whiteness to the category of the universal. Whiteness signifies chosenness, a virtue rooted in the white person's direct proximity to work and the earth. The structural identification of racial superiority and land ownership: invokes a second contradiction. Jefferson, a wealthy owner of land and people, holds no necessary closeness to either labor or the land. His presentation is of an ideal type of racial purity linked to skin color, work, and class, but above all, racial identity was an immutable biological matter. Jefferson muses with apparent scientific authority:

> Whether the black of the negro [sic] resides in the reticular membrane between the skin and scarfskin, or in the scarf-skin itself; whether it proceeds from the colour of the blood, the colour of the bile, or from that of some other secretion, the difference is fixed in nature, and is as real as if its seat and cause were better known to us.[9]

This biological difference could not be altered. It signaled a massive civilizational gulf between Black people and white people.[10] It justified "white prejudice" and the establishment of legal, cultural, and territorial boundaries between the two. It justified the white ownership of Black people.

The exclusion of Black people from this ideal human type is presented in his discussion of laws revised after the establishment of the white, agrarian republic. He expresses a hope for the abolition of slavery and the removal of Black people from the state. By 1781, when he first compiled his *Notes*, the effects of British abolition policies saw at least 20,000 Africans enlist in the British military. Thousands more had fled from enslavement to British lines, foreshadowing the "General Strike" during the Civil War, which W. E. B. Du Bois documented in *Black Reconstruction in America*.[11] Historians have shown that many large plantation owners in Virginia (including Washington and Jefferson) saw the numbers of enslaved laborers diminished as a result. Even as Jefferson attempted to respond to his foreign friend's queries, Virginia's property relations and productivity were largely disrupted. Enslaved property had not yet been recaptured; Tory property confiscations had not been settled. As the mediator of bourgeois conflict, the state stood in serious disarray.

For Jefferson, the rationality of private property lies close to the heart of racial differences. Thus, in its discussion of securing individual private land ownership, *Notes* distinguishes white civilization from Indigenous societies and Africans (who are themselves property) and republican political forms from feudal ones. Jefferson offers a description of the process of making land purchases in the new regime thus:

> Since the establishment of our new government, this order of things is but little changed. An individual, wishing to appropriate to himself lands still unappropriated by any other, pays to the public treasurer a sum of money proportioned to the quantity he wants. He carries the treasurer's receipt to the auditors of public accounts, who thereupon debit the treasurer with the sum, and order the register of the land-office to give the party a warrant for his land. With this warrant from the register, he

goes to the surveyor of the county where the land lies on which he has cast his eye. The surveyor lays it off for him, gives him its exact description, in the form of a certificate, which certificate he returns to the land-office, where a grant is made out, and is signed by the governor. This vests in him a perfect dominion in his lands, transmissible to whom he pleases by deed or will, or by descent to his heirs if he die intestate.[12]

That Jefferson describes this process with such detail suggests that it is not yet a universal principle but is relatively new. This bureaucratic procedure establishes a legal and political connection between property owners, the state, and the racial order. This trifecta of social positionality defines the basis and limits of social and civil rights. Like skin color and supposed racial purity, property is transmissible to the biological offspring. Here, contradictions overflow. Jefferson is known to have fathered seven children by Sally Hemings, an enslaved woman counted among his property and compelled to live with him for 37 years.[13] Sally Hemings could not inherit his property or become a legal family member. Following the one-drop rule of racial identity and legal status following the mother's condition, his children would presumably be subjected to his plan for forced evacuation with the rest of the enslaved population. Despite the inheritance of race and property, these children were biologically incapable of being his equal, were his property, and could not inherit his capital wealth, including, except under peculiar circumstances, their very own bodies.

While most of *Notes* focuses on the internal conditions in Virginia, a discussion of Indigenous people transcends state boundaries, exploring the continent and hemisphere. This special imaginary travelogue suggests the particular importance of the question for the author. Jefferson creates an expansive historical-spatial narrative, musing on the origins of Indigenous people, testing the "land bridge" hypothesis and the relation between Asian and American indigenes. He notes the plurality of Indigenous nations across the continent, exploring perceptions of languages, cultures, and values, even attempting a census of Indigenous nations near and far. As for Virginia,

Jefferson downplays the role of conquest and genocide in eliminating or removing Indigenous people.

> Spirituous liquors, the small-pox, war, and an abridgment of territory, to a people who lived principally on the spontaneous productions of nature, had committed terrible havoc among them, which generation, under the obstacles opposed to it among them, was not likely to make good. That the lands of this country were taken from them by conquest, is not so general a truth as is supposed. I find in our historians and records, repeated proofs of purchase, which cover a considerable part of the lower country; and many more would doubtless be found on further search. The upper country we know has been acquired altogether by purchases made in the most unexceptionable form.[14]

Such individual transactions can only be contracted legitimately between equals. Thus, individual land purchases between a white person and an Indian were unthinkable and illegal. Jefferson explains, however, that collective land purchases between white governments (British or U.S.) and Indian tribes represented legitimate bargains, despite threats of genocide via war, disease, or other forms of harassment and punishment. Racial or civilizational transactions were acceptable, but racial difference foreclosed Indigenous participation in civilizational bureaucracy on an individualized scale. Indigenous proximity to the earth, to labor in the land, thus, does not include them among "the chosen."

Jefferson's mental survey of Virginia justifies Indigenous elimination rooted in a supposed biological difference, white civilizational superiority, and political and economic dominance of the U.S. nation-state.[15] This latter is carefully marked also by racial boundaries that define its naturalized inhabitants as white people. *Notes on the State of Virginia* is, by any measure, a white nationalist document. And while Jefferson calls for the end of the enslavement of Africans (eventually), his utopian vision of the state mapped a racially pure terrain. It excludes Black people through deliberate expulsion, would be bereft of Indigenous people via a "natural" process of population decline, and is founded on laws of private property and the agrarian republicanism of the white, small-scale landowner. Ironically, Jefferson also envisions his own erasure from Virginia's future landscape, not just with his individual, physical death but that of his class of plantation owners whose capital was based on the large-scale theft of Indigenous lands and African enslavement.

1831-1840, settler-colonial rhetoric

Jefferson published *Notes* in book form the year after he co-authored the Northwest Ordinance, a law that organized the territories of Ohio, Michigan, and Indiana. Notably, the law carried out his preference for a ban on slavery (putting into motion the central contradictions that led to the U.S. Civil War 74 years later). It also created a rationalized system of land surveys that divided the territories into large squares that would shape the geographies of those future states. The invasion, occupation, and Euro-American settlement of the territory was a violent process marked by imperialist conflict, war, genocide, economic crisis, and racial formation.

In the two or three decades subsequent to the passage of the Ordinance, Euro-Americans had still not yet fully mapped the Northwest territories, and many Indigenous nations still controlled their land. European tourists Alexis de Tocqueville and Charles Beaumont, who visited Michigan territory in 1831, referred to it as "the extreme limits of European civilization," claiming a racial affinity to the Euro-American republic.[16] The two men explored the Saginaw Bay area before returning to Detroit and traveling to Mackinac Island via the river and lake system. Unlike Jefferson's musings on removals, wars, and plagues that had all but destroyed Indigenous populations, de Tocqueville and his companion claimed to be entering an empty land with no memory of how genocide had occurred. "The Indians ... are gone I know not whither, beyond the Great Lakes; the race is becoming extinct; they are not made for civilization—it kills them." De Tocqueville depicted a land that essentially had been deserted. "An ancient people," he intoned, "the first and legitimate masters of the American continent, melts away every day from the earth, as snow before the sun, and disappears." This vanishing act justified invasion. As he adds:

> Another race rises up in its place with still more astonishing rapidity; before this race the forests fall, the marshes dry up; vast rivers, and lakes extensive as seas, in vain oppose its triumph and progress. Deserts become villages—villages towns. The American who daily witnesses these marvels sees nothing surprising in them. This wonderful destruction, and still more astonishing progress, seem to him to be the ordinary course of events. He considers them as laws of nature.[17]

De Tocqueville's fanciful account seemed to mourn the loss of Indigenous control of Anishinaabewaki, the land of the Anishinaabe who inhabited and claimed the territory surrounding the Great Lakes, and justify the violence of U.S. imperialism.[18]

White-authored reports, scholarly papers, and travel accounts conceded that much was unknown about the western interior portion of the territory. However, they also tended to craft a scientific, historical, and popular discourse that diminished Anishinaabe peoples into caricatures of their complex social organizations. Ranging from sympathetic, liberal humanitarianism to hostile, aggressive militarism, this literature talked about Indigenous peoples in ways that could be called a racial project.[19] Representing a humanitarian point of view, Rev. Isaac McCoy, a career missionary to Bodéwadmi and Odawa peoples of Southwest Michigan, claimed that Anishinaabe people had been "left in a state of nature." They lay outside of the general progress that characterized human evolution and the development of civilization among even their "Asiatic" ancestors.

Lacking literacy, recorded forms of institutional memory and knowledge, and an education system, McCoy's stereotypical Indians sought only to subsist in the natural world. "They are in their original state," he writes in his 1840 autobiographical account of his mission experiences. "[T]hey never had been more civilized than they were when we first became acquainted with them," he insists. He contends:

The world before them afforded room for them to obtain subsistence chiefly or entirely from the spontaneous productions of
the earth and the waters, and they never adopted any mode, or
invented any thing [sic] which was not essentially necessary in
their mode of obtaining subsistence.... They did not study the
improvement of mind, because the man would be as expert a
hunter if left to grow up to maturity under the guidance of his
necessities, as if he were trained to the studies of a philosopher.[20]

In this theory of "race," the material condition of subsistence
restrained human evolution, subjecting Indigenous people to
a made-up existence without memory or intellectual specu-
lative life or future. McCoy, who had maneuvered to secure
a federal Indian missionary contract in 1823, wheedled a
federally-funded position as a surveyor in 1828, and oppor-
tunistically shifted to Jacksonian anti-Indian politics after the
1828 election, never questioned the superiority of white civilization. "The aborigines are a barbarous, uncultivated people,"
he wrote.[21]

Unlike Jefferson, McCoy advocated an environmentalist
explanation for the condition of what he viewed as a uniform
Indian society and "character" rather than a biological or
racial explanation. "The world is too much inclined to suppose that there are some traits in Indian character peculiar to
that race, and which might not exist with others, though they
were placed in similar circumstances," which he refers to as a
"morbid taste for the romantic." Rejecting this assertion as an
error, McCoy insisted, "[f]acts declare that the Indians are only
what others would have been, had they been placed in similar
circumstances." He argued, "there is naturally no difference
between the natural propensities of the white and the red
man." Indeed, this reality should forestall a moral judgment
on their condition and propel humanitarian efforts to civi-
lize them. Some aspects of civilized life—the habits of seizing
Indigenous land and militarism—are harmful to Indigenous
people in their "original state."[22]

McCoy's repudiation of biological explanations of the differences between Indigenous people and whites coincided

with his recognition of Native title to the land they historically occupied. Unlike almost all of his contemporary opinion-makers and colleagues, McCoy rebuffed the dominant claim that productive cultivation and improvement lay at the base of rightful ownership. He acknowledged that Native peoples had always cultivated some land, even if it was not the fundamental pillar of their economic life. Indeed, in their relations with whites, Indians were more generous, as "they often furnished supplies to the Europeans when in want." In fact, on occasions when his own family needed food, he could count on the generosity of the people on whose land he lived to share.[23]

McCoy's "racial project" differs from that which appears in Jefferson's writings and policies significantly. Jefferson highlighted biological and natural differences that demanded complete physical separation (despite the contradictions of a slaveholding republic he had helped to found). McCoy's missionary project enables settler colonialism and justifies a project of elimination through assimilation cloaked in the fabric of a Christian mandate to save the pagan.

Despite his modification of biological-racial discourse, McCoy emphatically accepted a removal policy. He thought it was an excellent way to coerce Indigenous people to accept Euro-American demands to assimilate. His environmentalist explanation for cultural difference suggests that "a change of circumstances would be followed by a change of habits."[24] This view rested on the necessity of Euro-American leadership and benevolence. For this reason, Indian removal demanded the guidance of civilized intervention and supervision (managed, of course, by federally appointed missionaries and officials). Without this intervention U.S. policies would condemn Indigenous people to extinction.[25] He described this intervention as "the most important business of his life."[26] As one historian notes, McCoy's credentials as an Indian missionary, his advocacy of "Indian rights," and his sympathetic treatment of Indigenous issues in his writings made him the perfect tool for the Jackson administration to provide political cover against the controversial 1830 Indian Removal Act. Endorsement by the likes of McCoy gave the policy a veneer of humanitarianism.[27] Even a liberal approach to Indigenous culture, as McCoy's was, buttressed the systematic expropriation of Indigenous lands.

1870, models

Fast-forward to 1870. About six dozen Chinese men were brought from California to the industrial town of North Adams, Massachusetts. A shoe factory owner brought them because he saw them as a solution to his company's labor problem. Before the arrival of the Chinese workers, all of the Sampson and Chase shoe factory workers were Euro-Americans. Initially, the large majority had been Irish immigrants. They had organized a union called the Knights of St. Crispin. Together, they demanded better wages, shorter hours, and union recognition. The factory owners refused and fought the union by hiring French Canadian migrants as scabs. The Irish workers and the French Canadians, however, joined forces. Worker unity proved only a short-term setback for Sampson, who enlisted the Chinese workers as his next tactic. He chose them, relying on stories of how Chinese railroad workers had competed at racially suppressed wages with Irish laborers for jobs. Because they were not white, he believed, Chinese workers would be docile, and he could pay them much less. He estimated a more considerable profit margin due to the racial division of labor.[28]

The thought of Chinese workers replacing them in the factory angered the shoemakers who had struggled for months to win concessions. According to one newspaper report, thousands of area residents, some out of curiosity, others with ill-intent, greeted the men at the train station:

> Upon their arrival at the depot here a scene ensued to which the people of this town are strangers. Fully 2,000 people, men, women, and children, assembled to catch a view of the Celestial strangers, and, although some indignities were offered, they were discountenanced by the mass of the citizens. A few such as are always in spirit for the recurrence of a holiday in the absence of other excitement, indulged in hoots and cheer as the

dusky procession, in couples, headed by Messrs. Sampson and Chase, and flanked by a posse of a dozen policemen, marched toward the manufactory. When they were nearly there, one man threw a stone and another struck one of the new citizens, but they were quickly arrested and locked up.

Many newspaper accounts positioned the "Coolies" versus the "Crispins." They characterized the new arrivals as "docile," intelligent, hard-working, and models for the stubborn Irish and French-Canadian shoemakers, initiating a "model minority" discourse that was solidified about a century later.[29]

The Knights of St. Crispin, after this nasty welcome, continued to threaten the Chinese men with violence. On the one hand, they claimed a right to the jobs they had held and demanded recognition from their employer. On the other, this anger shifted to the Chinese, whom they viewed with contempt not just because of the circumstances of the strike but because they were non-white foreigners. Some of their actions and words drew on Jeffersonian rhetoric, forging a relationship between their white national identity and their possession of jobs. They understood that the employer had deliberately chosen to bring Chinese men into the workforce as a strategy for breaking their class solidarity. That had been the purpose of hiring the French Canadians, and they had responded with solidarity. In the new situation, however, their racial-national rhetoric strove for Chinese exclusion from their community of solidarity.[30] As the strike continued, they walked back some of their hostility, offering the Chinese workers union membership but only as segregated auxiliary members. They simply could not share full solidarity with brown-skinned men from China. In the end, the union was defeated. The original workers (now in full possession of their white identity) returned to the job without pay increases, a subjugated, humiliated group. The Chinese workers were discarded, and many were forced to return to California. Thus, the racist division of labor marked the Chinese migrant workers as racially inferior, offering more profits for capitalists and diverting consciousness of an inclusive concept of class struggle to the dead-end of white racial supremacy.

Anti-Chinese sentiments centered on three elements: 1) the presence of Chinese people threatened racial purity and white superiority, 2) Chinese migrants to and within the U.S. were "coolie labor," potentially reigniting the slavery question, and 3) petty-bourgeois/middle-class Euro-Americans deployed anti-Chinese racism to criticize simultaneously emergent monopoly capital-dominated class relations and to realign with that dominant class on terms of racial affiliation. In other words, imperialism drew Chinese migrants into the U.S. division of labor to intensify the expropriation of surplus-value through the manipulation of existing racism to divide workers.[31] Once there, however, large numbers of Euro-American workers conditioned to love white supremacy made racial hate a regular feature of everyday life by positioning themselves as victims of the migrants as much as being exploited by capitalists. Further, petty-bourgeois elements, who felt intense class pressure from monopoly capital, targeted Chinese migrant workers as the leading edge of monopoly capital's strategy to destroy their economic aspirations.[32]

As Marx showed in *Capital*, the worlds of Jefferson, de Tocqueville, McCoy, and Sampson—a world of racial slavery, systematized expropriation of Indigenous lands, and emergent global imperialism—created the basis, the logic, and the structure of U.S. capitalist development and its integration into a world system rooted in class processes of exploitation and white supremacy. Marx wrote:

> The discovery of gold and silver in America, the extirpation, enslavement and entombment in mines of the aboriginal population, the beginning of the conquest and looting of the East Indies, the turning of Africa into a warren for the commercial hunting of black-skins, signalized the rosy dawn of the era of capitalist production.[33]

These events and sites are the bloody, fertile grounds on which U.S. literature was imagined, written, and read. It is the reality that conditioned the possibility of imagining an "America" *and* resisting dominant ideas of what that means. As the 19th century drew to a close, that fertile ground persisted. The

U.S. ruling class combined the massacre at Wounded Knee, the invasion of the Philippines, the subversion of a legitimate government in Hawai'i, the denial of nationhood to Puerto Rico, and the institution of Jim Crow as a legal doctrine to reconstitute white supremacy as the logic, the motives, and the forms of U.S. imperialism and global modes of capital accumulation. It is this contingent, shifting arena of struggle into which this study of U.S. literature turns our attention.

Marxism, myth, and ideology

Mythologies is situated in the field of American literary studies. It examines a broad swath of U.S.-originated literature that variously submit to the hegemonic order, offer revisions or reforms, or demand revolutionary social transformations. Literature can be viewed in its broadest possible sense, including autobiographical texts, speeches, novels, poems, reports, essays, and other forms of imaginative writing. The texts above here serve as markers of crucial moments in a period of U.S. letters before the full flowering of U.S. imperialism. They identify moments of opening, of initiations of this settler society on the cusp of racial self-reinvention, a capitalist social formation eager to exploit and subjugate non-white people, anxious to define their world by lines of racial purity, to master a world of peoples they regard as non-beings. The accounts of arrivals, introductions, and openings to racial formations signal and symbolize capitalist development in the geographical spaces of what became the U.S. Each of these moments in the pre-history of U.S. imperialism indicates the ongoing processes by which Euro-Americans remade race in their settler-colonial society as the basis for the accumulation of racial capital in land, bodies, cash, and culture. They tell us how chains of human movements (forced and voluntary) functioned in a search for labor, surplus-value expropriation, and capital accumulation.

This reference to the space and time of the pre-history of empire is not intended to register as a teleology of inevitable "manifest destiny." However, many Euro-Americans imagined their future in that way. What I am suggesting is that we take those Euro-Americans at their word. Their goal was conquest, enslavement, elimination, and accumulation. They sought empire; their ideology of white supremacy, capitalist processes of accumulation, and willingness to enact violence to achieve these ends indicate nothing otherwise. Following literary critic Aijaz Ahmad, I read U.S. literature through a Marxist lens that unearths the material conditions that overdetermine the possibility of its existence and meaning.[34] Marxist analysis reveals the "dramatization of the play of social forces in motion," as scholar E. San Juan Jr. argues.[35] In exploring the conditions of literary possibility, his book looks for the relationship of literature to the U.S. social formation. By doing this, as Barbara Foley states, we find "the fundamental contradictions informing" the society that operates through and among those texts.[36]

The accumulation of these symbolic assets comprises an array of hegemonic meanings in "American" literature. While the disjunctures and continuities in the systems and ideologies of racial formation, settler colonialism, and imperialism within U.S. literature comprise this book's central focus, it does not comprehensively survey a representative overview of U.S. literature. It shows how racial projects functioned for different purposes in different places and times.[37] Instead, *Mythologies* inventories a sample of an accumulated balance sheet and documents its contradictions, disruptions, omissions, and openings as a methodological approach to studying U.S. literature and its contexts. In addition, it documents points of resistance against and antagonism with that dominant order.

The four chapters of this book explore, digest, and interpret four major mythological themes that recur in the long 19th-century of U.S. literature: the culture of victimization, the progress of capitalist development, settler colonialism and the "frontier," and the "self-made man."[38] Each frames the meaning of its theme as it is imaginatively and ideologically constructed in many literary formats (novels, poetry, speeches, autobiographies, and essays).

Marxist theory defines ideology in several ways. In one way, it is a saturation of a social formation with inaccurate, false, mystifying, or distorted ideas, information, and methods of knowledge production that present us with only partial explanations for why things are the way they are. The outsized power of the ruling class and its hegemonic bloc (its control of social institutions, coercive apparatuses, employment and means of survival, land, treasury, and international relations) enhances its ability to mobilize ideas rapidly as material forces. Thus, the most widely circulated and accepted ideologies typically derive from it.

Ideology also articulates class struggles and people's struggles for liberation, which is its second form. Exploitation, oppression, and a general condition of inequality cause dissonance between ruling-class ideas and the experience of everyday life. Thus, some ideological formations attempt clearer, more truthful, or materially grounded forms of communication, social practices, or more comprehensive analysis of concrete situations in historical and spatial contexts. This version of ideology is most closely associated with revolutionary formations, such as communist or national liberation movements. In these first two definitions, ideology should be regarded as "a social practice, not a transcribed 'false consciousness.'"[39]

In a third form, ideology can be a mechanism of deliberate self-delusion or self-deception, producing psychological pleasure in denying reality as the evidence reveals it to be.[40] This latter can be encountered among confused middle strata profoundly shaped by economic struggles, tenuous associations with civic and social power, and a fervent adherence to comforting racial, national, religious, or patriarchal cultural codes that seem eternally under threat. They face immediately and regularly a choice between committing to the painful attempt to understand the source of contradictions or the much smoother path of accepting ruling-class ideas. Self-delusion, then, may satisfy the urge to resist the latter without conceding to the former. The power of any of these three categories lies in their capacity to create a "common sense" resonance. Material conditions—political contradictions, unemployment, war, pandemic, inflation, forms of access to social institutions, shifting international balance of forces—profoundly shape receptions of ideology. Indeed, re-shaping, exposing, or manipulating myths can also alter ideology's impact.

Literature and myth function ideologically to prompt an orientation to one of the three major responses listed above. Such responses can occur with or without the specific intention or partisanship of the author or reader. Marxist literary criticism is an analytical process of drawing the most direct relationships of a text to its conditions of possibility. We may regard the conditions of possibility as the totality of social relations through which meanings are legible to an audience, to the literary traditions and historical contexts in which it imagines a world. Marxists achieve this analytical feat through a class struggle maxim. Under capitalism, exploitative class processes—the extraction of surplus-value, the commodification of labor, and uneven distribution and development—define social relations. Marxists interpret literature through the totality of political and economic struggles, contradictions, and conflicts that constitute the differences among social forces related to productive (and reproductive) activity. Thus, cultural, political, and economic events shape class struggle (locally and on the level of the imperialist world system).

Marxist literary critics orient the reader and text toward the second ideological option. They do so by showing how a text works within the limits of the first or third options in seemingly commonsensical ways. For example, in chapter 1, a Marxist reading of the Revolutionary War-era novel *The Algerine Captive* shows how its structure, plot, and impact powerfully link ideas about the fear of tyranny to the dominant view of white supremacy as natural. In this plot, a fictional Euro-American man enslaved by North African Muslims elicits a dramatic emotional response against the unnatural order in which countries led by non-Christian people of color might assert dominance over white people. This text, thus, elevates a myth of victimization as a core concept of dominant Euro-American cultural identity, normalized and imprinted on what it means to be "American." This myth is repeated across the next two centuries to mobilize political and class forces to achieve particular aims. The restoration of white supremacy in the South after the Civil War, the Chinese Exclusion Act, and countless justifications for U.S. involvement in aggressive wars for empire are just a handful of examples.

While any potential reader might be able to quickly and repeatedly encounter multiple examples of Euro-Americans—to stick to the example of white supremacy—performing in less than exemplary ways, even acting brutally (e.g., murdering Indigenous neighbors, enslaving Africans, forcing citizens into concentration camps, resisting desegregation), they might choose a path of self-deception to accept as normal or natural the idea of white supremacy despite a few bad apples or entertain beliefs in the justice of such violence. They might even apply their racial supremacy theory to a global setting and deny freedom from foreign tyranny to non-white, non-Christian nations, societies, and people. A person or group who holds such an ideological point of view may be aware of the idea's relationship with imperialism and war. They also accept the delusion that such interventions are humanitarian or democratizing. *We are not imperialists! I am not a racist!* With the saturation of such points of view, the repeated habits of mind operate as material forces. These forces shape, condition, limit, or deny the ability of the second form of ideology—class struggle-based counter-hegemony—to achieve without intervention a considerable influence.

For this reason, as Lenin argued, a revolutionary subjectivity is necessary. This subjectivity is produced and cultivated in collective struggle. That struggle is propelled through the vehicle of an organization whose ideas and policies aim to transform the totality of capitalist social relations of production through the negation of its internal contradictions. Presumably, the literary critics who claim to be Marxist are accountable to such a movement. Otherwise, they practice formulas and ritual incantations that serve no liberation. I hope this book enables a habit of reading all literature through the second revolutionary vehicle for ideological struggle.

Notes

1. Quoted in Rachel B. Herrmann, "The 'tragicall historie': Cannibalism and Abundance in Colonial Jamestown," *William and Mary Quarterly*, Vol. 68, no. 1 (2011): 47-74.
2. Quoted in Engel Sluiter, "New Light on the '20 and Odd Negroes' Arriving in Virginia, August 1619," *William and Mary Quarterly*, Vol. 54, no. 2 (1997): 395-398.

3. "1619 Project," *The New York Times Magazine*, 14 August, 2019. https://www.nytimes.com/interactive/2019/08/14/magazine/1619-america-slavery.html. See also Olivia B. Waxman, "The First Africans in Virginia Landed in 1619. It Was a Turning Point for Slavery in American History—But Not the Beginning," *Time Magazine*, 20 August 2019. https://time.com/5653369/august-1619-jamestown-history/.

4. Edmund Morgan, *American Slavery, American Freedom*, (New York: W.W. Norton, 1975).

5. Thomas Jefferson, *Notes on the State of Virginia*, (Philadelphia: Prichard and Hall, 1788), i.

6. Gerald Horne, *The Counter-Revolution of 1776: Slave Resistance and the Origins of the United States of America*, (New York: New York University Press, 2014), 220-221.

7. Jefferson, 166.

8. Jefferson, 175.

9. Jefferson, 147.

10. Nell Irvin Painter, *The History of White People*, (New York: W.W. Norton and Company, 2010), 110-113.

11. Maya Jasanoff, *Liberty's Exiles: American Loyalists in the Revolutionary World*, (New York: Knopf, 2011); W.E.B. Du Bois, *Black Reconstruction in America, 1860-1880* (New York: Touchstone, 1992). Karen Cook Bell documents the experiences of escaped enslaved Africans in this period. But by emphasizing how the discourse of "freedom" ignited by the insurgents captured the imaginations of Black people most, she assumes African loyalty to the yet-to-be-perfected Union. See Bell, *Running from Bondage, Enslaved Women and Their Remarkable Fight for Freedom in Revolutionary America*, (Cambridge: Cambridge University Press, 2021). More convincingly, Gerald Horne shows that enslaved Africans, by a large majority, recognized the greater possibility for freedom in siding with the British. Horne, *Counter-Revolution of 1776*, 125.

12. Jefferson, 145.

13. Annette Gordon-Reed, *Thomas Jefferson and Sally Hemings: An American Controversy*, (Charlottesville: University Press of Virginia, 1997).

14. Jefferson, 101.

15. Gerald Horne documents the formation of "pan-European" racial identity in the course of international events that shaped the U.S. Horne, *The Apocalypse of Settler Colonialism: The Roots of Slavery, White Supremacy, and Capitalism in Seventeenth-Century North America and the Caribbean*, (New York: Monthly Review, 2018), 22.

16. Alexis de Tocqueville, "Fortnight in the Wilderness," in *Memoirs, Letters, and Remains of Alexis de Tocqueville. Translated from the French by the Translator of Napoleon's Correspondence with King Joseph*, Vol. 1, (Boston: Ticknor and Fields, 1862), 139.

17. De Tocqueville, 139-140.

18. Anishinaabewaki is the territorial area and the "social formation" of the Anishinaabe people, the Ojibwe, Odawa, and Bodéwadmi. It covers a vast expanse of land surrounding the Great Lakes, crossing international borders between the U.S. and Canada, as well as multiple states and provinces. Michael Witgen, *An Infinity of Nations: How the Native World Shaped Early North America*, (Philadelphia: University of Pennsylvania Press, 2012), 19.

19. A racial project is the set of social practices (ideological and material) that groups within concrete conditions adopt to define the meaning of race. This idea is based on the original concept developed by Michael Omi and Howard Winant, Racial

Formation in the United States, 3rd ed., (New York: Routledge, 2015). Those projects usually define white racism, but may also construe colorisms, or function as collective salutary responses to oppression, such as "Black power." See Joel Wendland, *The Collectivity of Life: Spaces of Social Mobility and the Individualism Myth*, (Lanham, Maryland: Lexington Books, 2016), xiii.

20. Isaac McCoy, *History of Baptist Indian Missions: Embracing Remarks on the Former and Present Condition of the Aboriginal Tribes; Their Settlement within the Indian Territory, and Their Future Prospects*, (Washington: William M. Morrison, 1840), 14, 18.

21. McCoy, 30.

22. McCoy, 19, 21, 23.

23. McCoy, 29-30, 191.

24. McCoy, 21.

25. James M. McClurken, *"We Wish to be Civilized": Ottawa-American Political Contests on the Michigan Frontier.* Unpublished dissertation, Michigan State University, 1988, 104; McCoy, 257.

26. McCoy, 197.

27. Mary Hershberger, "Mobilizing Women, Anticipating Abolition: The Struggle against Indian Removal in the 1830s," *Journal of American History*, Vol. 86, no. 1 (1999): 29-30.

28. Ronald Takaki, *A Different Mirror: A History of Multicultural America*, rev. edition, (New York: Back Bay Books, 2003), 140.

29. "The Chinese," *Chicago Tribune*, 14 June 1870.

30. "The Celestial Shoe-maker: The Chinamen at Work in North Adams," *New York Times*, 9 July 1870; Takaki, 141.

31. Kornel Chang, *Pacific Connections: The Making of the U.S. Canadian Borderlands*, (Berkeley: University of California Press, 2012), 54; William Wei, *Asians in Colorado: A History of Persecution and Perseverance in the Centennial State*, (Seattle: University of Washington Press, 2016): 18; Jennifer Brooks, "'John Chinaman' in Alabama: Immigration, Race, and Empire in the New South, 1870-1920," *Journal of American Ethnic History*, Vol. 37, no. 2 (2018): 9-10.

32. On "coolie" rhetoric, see Moon-Ho Jung, *Coolies and Cane: Race, Labor, and Sugar in the Age of Emancipation*, (Baltimore: Johns Hopkins University, 2006), 28; Elliott Young, *Alien Nation: Chinese Migration in the Americas from the Coolie Era Through World War II*, (Chapel Hill: University of North Carolina Press, 2014), 21-58. Post-Civil War sugar planters in Louisiana saw Chinese migrants as potential super-exploitable replacements for newly freed Black workers who tried to reconstruct social relations on a new basis of land ownership and political power. Similar rhetoric provoked anti-Chinese hatred and violence in Arizona. See Grace Delgado, *Making the Chinese Mexican: Global Migration, Localism, and Exclusion in the U.S. Mexico Borderlands*, (San Francisco: Stanford University Press, 2012), 29. For a study of similar capitalist accumulation strategies in Alabama, see Brooks, 5-36. On the anti-Chinese violence led by the small business owners and losers in the capitalist competition, see Charles Williams, "Labor Radicalism and the Local Politics of Chinese Exclusion: Mayor Jacob Weisbach and the Tacoma Chinese Expulsion of 1885," *Labor History*, Vol. 60, no. 6 (2019): 685-703. Find a survey of labor union and petty-bourgeois alliances based on anti-Chinese violence in Alexander Saxton, *The Indispensable Enemy: Labor and the Anti-Chinese Movement in California* (Berkeley: University of California Press, 1971). Euro-American hostility contrasts with inter-ethnic class solidarities among Asian and Pacific Islander nationality groups and Mexican workers. See David Struthers, *The World in a City: Multiethnic Radicalism in Early Twentieth-Century Los Angeles*, (Urbana: University

of Illinois Press, 2019), 65-80. Hunton discerns a similar phenomenon in his study the South African mining districts in the 1890s. While capitalist mine operators prevailed upon imperialist authorities to pass laws that allowed them to force Africans to work for artificially suppressed wages under racist circumstances, they "passed responsibility for [the system of racist labor management] to the white workers, the government, and to society in general." Racist segregation, super-exploitation, and abuse were normalized and enforced by whites of all class standings. See W. Alphaeus Hunton, *Decision in Africa: Sources of Conflict*, (New York: International Publishers), 44.

33. Karl Marx, *Capital*, Vol. I, (New York: International Publishers, 1973), 284.

34. Aijaz Ahmad, *In Theory: Classes, Nations, Literatures*, (New York: Verso, 2000).

35. E. San Juan Jr., *Working through the Contradictions, From Cultural Theory to Cultural Practice*, (Bucknell University Press, 2004), 85.

36. Barbara Foley, *Marxist Literary Criticism Today*, (London: Pluto Press, 2019), 13.

37. For such a survey of larger parts of U.S. literary history, see Annette T. Rubinstein, *American Literature, Root and Flower*, Vol. 1, (New York: Monthly Review Press, 1955).

38. We often think of myths as "lies" that give fanciful explanations for social or natural phenomena. Instead, they are pervasive and persuasive cultural themes that mobilize origin stories as a powerful, exclusive cultural identity. They function as commonsense shorthand, organize emotional responses to events, and demand loyalty. If ideology is the social practice and form, then myths are its content. See Joel Wendland, *The Collectivity of Life: Spaces of Social Mobility and the Individualism Myth*, (Lanham, Maryland: Lexington Books, 2016). James Loewen explores a similar concept he calls "social archetypes" in *Lies My Teacher Told Me: Everything Your American Textbook Got Wrong*, 2nd edition, (New York: The Free Press, 2007), 42-43.

39. E. San Juan, *Hegemony and Strategies of Transgression: Essays in Cultural Studies and Comparative Literature*, (Albany: State University of New York Press, 1995), 54; Barbara Foley, *Marxist Literary Criticism Today*, (London: Pluto Press, 2019), 62.

40. Lewis R. Gordon, *Fear of Black Consciousness*, (New York: Farrar, Straus, and Giroux, 2021), 58. Hunton described this phenomenon as a condition of maintain "comforting illusions." See Hunton, 18.

Chapter *1*

Victimization

Racism, orientalism, and nation

Anti-Black racism and national oppression of Indigenous peoples have long histories. They are foundational for the U.S. nation-state, its original and current political frameworks, its capitalist development, and its position in the imperialist world system. Likewise, anti-Muslim and anti-Arab attitudes in North America are not recent inventions of the U.S. government, the Cold War, or the West's global "crusade" against Islamic terrorism. Indeed, anti-Muslim hate is as old as the country itself. In 1785, just a few years after the United States separated itself from the British Empire, Virginia governor, slaveholder, and land speculator Patrick Henry ordered the deportation of three people under suspicion of being spies. According to accounts of the event, the three people—one woman and two men—were found in possession of Hebrew-language documents. Though Virginia authorities could not identify or read Hebrew and discern the contents of the documents, they ordered the three strangers deported back to their country, "wherever that was."[1] They apparently believed the documents were written in Arabic.

Their misapprehensions reflected larger patterns of fear about the Middle Eastern and North African countries. That same year, Algeria-based pirates captured a handful of U.S. vessels. They intended to warn the new government about its responsibility to pay tribute to the Algerian government to do business in the Mediterranean. To exert their control over the Atlantic and Mediterranean trade, the British and

French promoted hysteria about the escapades of the "Barbary Pirates." Fears of invasion in the U.S. prompted draconian alien and sedition laws at the state and federal levels, giving the executive authority to deport suspicious foreigners, especially those aligned with Muslim-led countries. Xenophobic views of North African Arabs and fears of infiltration converged with and contributed in no small part to the construction of a consensus on who could be considered a "real" American. The 1790 Naturalization Act defined the U.S. as a socially harmonious and racially homogeneous society. It allowed only "the worthy part of mankind" who could prove their good character and racial whiteness access to citizenship.[2]

This anti-Islamic and anti-Arab hysteria was both fed by and prompted the orientalist themes in emergent U.S. literature. In the first two decades of the new country's life, a spate of books about captivity in Islamic countries (mainly in North Africa), as well as novels like *The Algerine Spy in Pennsylvania* by Peter Markoe,[3] disturbed the American consciousness of itself as a nation and a perceived need for tight control over its racial, religious, and civilizational boundaries. Markoe's tale pretended to be authored by an Algerian spy reporting on the U.S. state of affairs to aid Algeria in exploiting the new country's vulnerable shipping industry. Along with the more critically acclaimed and financially successful *The Algerine Captive*, published by Royall Tyler in 1797, it was among the first original North American novels with major anti-Muslim and anti-Arab themes.[4] North American literary experts favor Tyler's *The Algerine Captive* because of its self-conscious effort to promote and develop a U.S. literary culture and because it had an enormous influence on subsequent U.S. writers. This book requires special attention.

The Algerine Captive relates the story of Updike Underhill, the scion of a middle-strata farm family whose ancestry stretches back nearly to the foundation of the British colonies. Expressing the ambitions of the petty bourgeoisie, Updike studies medicine and seeks to secure economic independence. Failing to do so, he takes a position as the surgeon aboard a slave-trading ship bound for Africa. He is subsequently captured and enslaved by Algerian pirates. After several adventures in

Algiers and an unlikely trip to the Muslim holy cities of Mecca and Medina, he wins his release with the aid of an Algiers Jew and returns to the United States. Note that Tyler invented the tale wholly out of travel accounts, other captivity tales, and European histories of the Middle East.

Tyler saturates *The Algerine Captive* with the orientalist ideologies that Edward W. Said studies extensively in his landmark book, *Orientalism*. As Said points out, while the North African country of Algeria may not be geographically "oriental," Islam was a cultural, political, and geographical entity that shaped European notions of East and West. For centuries, Islamic societies had posed "an unresolved challenge" to European imperialism and its cultural sense of superiority. This frustration stemmed mainly from European failures to subjugate Islamic kingdoms and countries for centuries. Islamic empires had until recently controlled large portions of Europe. In general, the proximity to Europe (as with North Africa) and the fact that it continues to overlap with sites of particular interest for Europeans, such as the "Holy Land," also prompted concerns.[5]

Orientalism is a system of thought and institutional practices that produces knowledge about and "creates" the orient. It demarcates boundaries of identity between East and West, civilized and "other." European empires had originated it as a cultural tool in their struggles to subjugate Eastern countries. As a system of thought, it took root early on during the European invasion of North America. As is commonly understood, the name Indian was a sign of Columbus's search for the orient in 1492 and his projection of constructed images of the orient onto the land and the people who inhabited it. Despite notions of freedom and liberation spread during the U.S. Revolutionary War and the country's construction, the English and French bodies of knowledge of Islam and the East became the common curriculum at the great universities of the United States. From political thinkers to novelists, U.S. cultural producers highlighted what they viewed as political, cultural, and religious differences with their former imperial master and Europe as a whole. However, when it came to a posture toward Islam, liberty-loving North Americans sided with the

European point of view out of racial solidarity couched in religious and civilizational terms.

Said argues that the orientalist project practices a self-described scientific and objective knowledge gathering process. It is "anatomical and enumerative" and "engaged in particularizing and dividing of things oriental into manageable parts."[6] *The Algerine Captive*'s fabricated—if perceived authoritative and realistic—presence in Algeria constructs an orientalist posture, despite (or perhaps because of) being built entirely out of the second-hand accounts of European scholars and explorers. These accounts are reconstructed as first-hand experiences. During his enslavement in Algiers, Updike Underhill, the novel's perceived first-person narrator and protagonist, details different aspects of the city's culture, mainly discovered through eavesdropping or unnamed informants. In one case, a European convert to Islam speaks of the city's mysteries to Updike in Latin. In other chapters, *The Algerine Captive* presents a systematic fictional discourse on the basic tenets of Islam, descriptions of both Arabic and the vernacular language, and an analysis of the demographic makeup of the population of Algiers, including an anti-Semitic detour on Algerian Jews. The narrator sketches the city from information "obtained on the spot,"[7] outlines the country's history and geography, and surveys its political system, cultural customs, and economy. The narrator offers supposedly precise images of Algeria and Algiers, even down to the military defenses of the city. The overall effect is the production of an omniscient overview mimicking the encyclopedic knowledge of the Western scholar rather than the subjugated slave, reinforcing for the reader their own subjective relation to this civilizational and racial position of superiority.

In addition to dissection the orientalist "makes the Orient speak," an effort that proceeds out of imperialist first causes and interests. The production of the "Algerine" image, as Updike makes clear, proceeds out of the practical needs of the United States, otherwise, it would have remained invisible. The problematical trade relations between the U.S. and Algeria (the piracy issue), the loaded contrast between Islam and Euro-American Christianity as a means of illuminating the trade issue as a domestic problem, the difference between a "despotic" and decaying Islamic civilization with a vibrant, liberty-loving Christian society are Tyler's central purposes for taking up this subject matter. Underhill's return to the United States encourages in him feelings of the need and the ability of the United States to unite and use its strength "to enforce a due respect among other nations" (*AC*, 226). Into the competition for empire and the exertion of dominance over the orient, Tyler cast the new American.

This new American is only partially constructed in opposition to an imaginary Algerian "oppressor." A close reading of Tyler's novel uncovers its orientalist project. The text reveals ideological links among European representations of threatening "Islamic and Arab worlds," the genocide of Indigenous peoples for land, the enslavement of Africans, and class conflict. Because each of these processes fractured the imaginary social harmony of the new country, they demanded textual resolutions. *The Algerine Captive* represented a point of view that regarded this trail of atrocities as a necessary feature of modernization and European and Euro-American-centered progress. The scholarly works Tyler studied to produce this novel adopted orientalist postures. They asserted imperial power and white supremacy through knowledge production, transforming the object of study into something less than human through the projection of comprehensible and manageable images. Centuries of European orientalism and its fraught struggle for domination of the East informed Tyler's view of U.S. national identity and the peoples subjugated within its social and physical geography.

Relationships of domination and subjugation, however, do not leave the colonizer innocent and unchanged. In *The Hidden Heritage*, Marxist cultural critic John Howard Lawson astutely notes, "[n]o one in an exploitative society is truly ignorant of its character. The pretense of innocence is itself a symptom of moral sickness."[8] "Pretense of innocence" is at the heart of claims of victimization at the hands of the "other." It generates the habit of speaking for the societies, communities, or nations that the colonizers seek to dominate. It serves as a cultural thread that runs through the history of the U.S. empire. Here, I define "victimization" as deep emotional anxiety about the perceived reversal of power relations. Members of dominant classes, nations, or racial groups assert that conditions other than their collective dominance register as a condition of victimization at the hands of subordinate groups or individuals. This pretense was ingrained in the first literature produced in the newly minted United States. It continues to resonate today. Over the past two decades, humanitarian (and arrogant) pretense dripped from the lips of U.S. presidents. The "pretense of innocence" has allowed them to deny, conveniently forget, or find weak excuses for the Iraq war atrocities, the invasion of Afghanistan, bombing campaigns in Syria and Libya, and waves of hybrid war, sanctions, and interventions globally.[9]

The republication of Tyler's book in 2002, within months of the events of September 11th, seems particularly appropriate for this context. The "pretense of innocence" and the construction of victimization as an emotional response to critical challenges to Euro-American dominance in all matters is a core habit of mind that a book like *The Algerine Captive* constructs. It creates a closed, totalizing psychological and ideological reversal of reality that justifies the atrocities and violence of colonization. We can call this the foundational moment of a Euro-American culture of victimization, i.e., the emotional reaction to a perceived potential reversal of a supposed natural order of white supremacy.[10]

The exploited and oppressed talk back to and struggle against the brutality and domination of the empire. While imperial authority claims that "[p]eople condemned to servitude or destruction can have no valid past, no culture worth saving, no enduring social achievement," Lawson argues, it cannot silence them forever. Lawson continues:

> The people of the abyss are not literally separated from the exploiters: on the contrary, they are present and indispensable. Their history and culture are ever-present. For example, the Negro is so much and so threateningly a presence in the South that he has shaped and possibly dominated the consciousness of Southern whites. The continuing exploitation of the Negro

has an incalculable effect on attitudes, ideas and arts in the Northern United States.[11]

In other words, imperialism, settler-colonialism, racial oppression, and the exploitative class processes that define U.S. capitalism constitute its political forms and institutions. Those systems condition the dominant cultural ideas and modes of creative and imaginative expression, which structure the totality of that system. They shape the culture of the colonizing nations and dominant groups. In his book, *The Cancer of Colonialism*, Tony Pecinovsky documents how anti-colonial fighters like W. Alphaeus Hunton, Lorraine Hansberry, and Angela Davis articulated the relationship of imperialism and colonialism with authoritarianism and political repression in the country of the colonizers. Internalized repression expressed in dominant cultural production signaled ruling-class fears that a radical systemic criticism could undermine its power.[12] Scholar E. San Juan Jr. saw this U.S. culture of repression of dissent as producing a "deformed liberal-democratic order" in which the "persistence of an authoritarian ethos" pervades U.S. letters, educational institutions, and the culture industry. "Are the writings of Emerson, Faulkner, Hemingway ... a force of repression or a catalyst for liberation?," he wonders.[13] Interpretations of these canonical authors aligned with dominant systems of power, exploitation, and oppression serve the former but cannot erase aspirations for the latter.

Tyler's imaginary world of Euro-American victimization at the hands of non-white violence and terror launched a cultural formation that defined the U.S. by a supposed racially pure whiteness and justified its future global aggression. However, such desired purity remains unfulfilled as imperialism ironically produces resistance that denies the colonizer the desperately sought monopoly on voice, ideas, thoughts, and actions. In a speech delivered in early 2006, the late Cuban National Assembly President Ricardo Alarcón also noted the global interpenetration of imperialist relations. Capitalism creates a boundary-breaking international process of exchange and circuits of money, commodities, people, and ideas: "The third world penetrates the first. The latter needs the former and at the same time rejects it. In Europe and North America appears an undesirable protagonist, a mute guest that demands its rights."[14] While it is impossible to impose the implications of such terms as "Third World" onto the 18th century, the global processes Alarcón describes had already begun.[15] Alarcón's point is that imagined essential boundaries between cultures and identities have been eroded by exploitation, oppression, and struggle and resistance. Understanding that process allows a more precise observation of how U.S. imperialism and capitalism were constituted by its capitalist development and (dynamic) positioning within the imperialist world system.

Tyler's background and social context

Royall Tyler inherited a substantial fortune made in the import business (mainly in trade with England) in Boston, Massachusetts. According to Tyler's biography, Tyler's father was a politically conservative proponent of the U.S. revolution. He relished exploiting his workers and advocated imprisoning the homeless in workhouses, but loved to pretend to share their interest in social mobility and liberty. Tyler was a bit of a profligate for the times. He fathered a child out of wedlock, failed to win the hand of future U.S. President John Adams' daughter through his laziness and his inability to keep his nose clean, squandered his inheritance, and anonymously authored pornographic poetry. Few of these qualities would necessarily earn him much social disapproval in the modern age. Still, his lifestyle departed from the time's professed ideal morals and character.[16]

Tyler spent a brief period during his college years as an aide to a minor Revolutionary War commander and eventually aligned himself with the conservative Federalist Party after the war.[17] Tyler's claim to political fame was his role in bringing an end to the notorious Shays' Rebellion, launched in Massachusetts in late 1786. Daniel Shays led an armed uprising of indebted farmers who sought relief from the economic depression. Widespread indebtedness and regressive taxation forced many farmers to lose or sell much of their property, undermining or risking their political rights and independent identities. Many viewed the credit system as means by which land speculators forced smallholders into selling out. This deliberate process consolidated larger landholders' wealth and power and drove proletarianization in the early industrial period. It enabled the expanding settler-colonialist drive to demand new property in Indigenous territories.[18] Tyler served as a go-between for the authorities and the rebellion's leaders. While pretending sympathy for Shays and his cause, Tyler convinced neighboring states not to provide aid or refuge to Shays and his band and eventually forced his capture.[19]

Shays' uprising was part of a wave of armed protest in Massachusetts, several neighboring states, and as far south as Virginia. In Rhode Island, for example, an army of debtors took over the legislature and printed and distributed paper money (an attempt to reduce interest rates and stimulate economic activity). In response, the central government and wealthy elites financially supported the suppression of these rebellions. The threat of violence from the rabble convinced the Federalists (and Tyler) that, instead of reexamining the credit and taxation systems to ensure a degree of equality and fairness, a more potent, more conservative constitutional form of central government that reserved the lion's share of power to the wealthy was in order.[20] Fear of insurrection was so intense that some aligned with the Federalists talked of installing a military-backed dictatorship.[21] Federalists were suspicious of democratic forms of government and favored the rule of the wealthiest property holders. While it contradicts current popular views of the egalitarian character of life in the early United States, this perspective was fueled by stark class differences and interests. Historical studies show that a small class of landholders owned most of the property. Social ills such as unemployment, indebtedness, homelessness, and absolute impoverishment were commonplace.[22]

The wave of violent protest in late 1786 and early 1787 against exploitation and the rule of the wealthy that included Shays' Rebellion was not the only conflict that rocked early U.S. society. Five years before Shays led his ill-fated movement, authorities charged Samuel Ely with treason for leading an armed uprising in Massachusetts against the unfair debt system and taxes.[23] In 1794, a group of whiskey makers in western Pennsylvania blackened their faces or dressed as Indians and assaulted federal government tax collectors. A force of 15,000 U.S. troops ordered into action by President George Washington put down the rebellion. The conflict lasted three years. Residents sympathetic to the uprising were angry about tax collection and the failure of the federal government to defeat and expel Indigenous peoples. Again, land acquisition appeared to disproportionately favor the wealthy, and many landless or small-holding whites expressed their class hostilities with attacks on Indigenous settlements. Wealthy land speculators and other ruling class agents saw attacks on Indigenous land sovereignty as a way to access new tracts of land and to alleviate lower-class anger. As one historian has shown, "even as their personal ambitions were frustrated, their land hunger, as well as their labor and misfortune, served an ascendant empire." Despite the dangers posed by internal armed conflicts, the U.S. government would deflect the class anger of the poor and marginalized small landholders toward the outer edges of the nation. The "settlers operated as agents of colonization, killing Indians, importing slaves, and clearing large tracts of land."[24]

Despite Jefferson's pretense (as noted in the Introduction), conflicts with the Indigenous people who claimed the invaded territory typically resulted in bloody violence and genocide. The act of transgressing racial and civilizational boundaries by dressing as Indians or Africans during the revolt should be read as more than a simple disguise.[25] It was the performance of a temporary identity with the most marginalized populations in America to indicate what taxation, debt, and landlessness do: they make free people into enslaved people or outcasts. Thus, racist language and performance became a vehicle for expressing a critique of exploitative class processes. Implications of victimization crafted and enacted by those defined as "the people," the sole legitimate civic basis of the newly formed nation-state, were derived from the logical structure of the Declaration of Independence. This culture of victimization, especially articulated in racial terms, spilled over into the post-revolutionary war period into the ideological frame used to construct the slaveholders' republic. It shaped Euro-American political culture, in the main, in relation to its ruling class, other nation-states, Indigenous societies, the Africans they participated in enslaving, and different real or imagined racial-national-cultural groupings perceived at a distant global scale. But it was also an implicit hint at the ferocity (and justice) of resistance by these marginalized or colonized others whom the white rebels sought to emulate and invoke. The culture of rebellion, racial transgressions and identities, and class politics would force their way into Tyler's literary work. In other words, the "people of the abyss" could not be silenced by this conservative advocate of fictional social harmony.

Harvard-educated Tyler studied and practiced law. Despite several terms on Vermont's Supreme Court, Tyler spent his days relying on the charity of his neighbors. Apart from his disastrous private life and his dull and less-than-lucrative professional career, Tyler wrote financially and critically successful drama and novels foundational to U.S. literature. In her study, literary scholar Cathy Davidson notes that writing and reading novels in the late eighteenth century should be considered a subversive act. Highbrow culture rejected the novel as a trite form of expression filled with immoral and lurid images that weakened morals and devalued a culture.[26] That Tyler chose such a genre for his most accomplished work signals an overt rejection of aristocratic British tastes by transforming a subversive medium into a conservative tool for bourgeois cultural hegemony. His choice of form reveals his own contradictory relation to political conservatism and authoritarianism, his inability to adhere to dominant cultural norms and values, and his financial instability. Writing a novel may have offered financial rewards while giving expression to his own salacious tastes.

Social harmony or conflict?

In the preface to *The Algerine Captive*, the narrator comments on the rise of books "designed to amuse rather than to instruct" in New England. Noting that English novels promote either "vice" at worst or "an erroneous idea of the world" that puts North American culture in a bad light, Underhill wants to portray New England values positively. In his mind, this is a critical function of emergent literature published in North America for a North American audience. Though Underhill reproduces the commonly held belief that women, the primary consumers of novels, are victims of the moral perfidy inherent in English novels, he also imagines a society of readers composed of men and women. In this setting, "the worthy farmer," "Dolly the milkmaid," and "Jonathan, the hired hand" have discarded highbrow European culture for books of "amusement." This market of readers, a female inhabited social space, could be invaded, captured, and colonized by North American authors and publishers, a decidedly masculine social space, suggests Underhill. Such changes in the publishing market could establish and promote the new country's unique culture. Benedict Anderson's well-known thesis about the link between the rise of print capitalism in Europe and the emergence of nationalism and national cultures clarifies Tyler's understanding of the potential innovative role of print capitalism in fostering U.S. national identity (AC, 5–7).[27]

But this identity is, from the outset of this novel, imagined through a bourgeois lens. The social conflict and Native American genocide on the frontier, the class rebellions, and the presence of hundreds of thousands of enslaved Africans are erased or silenced in this fictional social harmony of readers. *The Algerine Captive*, combining the two main genres of books for amusement—the novel and the travel narrative—is consciously aimed at this "imagined community" of readers to replace esoteric European culture and foster what literary critic Kenneth Burke once called "identification."[28] Tyler's challenge is to create a new North American literature that cultivates identification of his readership with a set of values and customs that he claims to be peculiar to New England, and that eliminates or silences the dissenting voices. The genre of the novel is a tale of coming to self-consciousness of a character. In this case, its main character explicitly identifies himself as an imagined normative New Englander. Thus, it establishes the frontiers of North American identity in a manner that anxiously restores order out of chaos and social peace out of violent conflict.

In conformity with his choice of subversive literary forms, Tyler invents the novel as the ideological myth of bootstraps.[29] In contrast to the author's own experience, Updike Underhill is the son of a struggling farmer with signs of intellect. His promise attracts the attention of his schoolmaster, a local minister, who convinces Updike's father to allow him to tutor Updike, especially in preparation for higher education. Eventually, Updike studies medicine and alternates between earning his living as a schoolmaster and a doctor. Neither occupation initially offers the economic security he imagines, but ultimately his indecisiveness leads to his travels, eventual captivity, and future career as a "man of letters." It is a social trajectory marred by instability and setbacks, but it is a far cry from the ditch-digging jobs poverty threatened to consign him to in the novel's early pages. The novel's effect leads the reader to expect that his fortunes will be settled and secure once Updike has reconciled with the social harmony—the united, ordered, imagined national community.

Despite employing several "hired men" on the farm, Updike's father initially pleads poverty when approached by a local minister who wants to tutor Updike. The father yields and borrows significantly to pay for Updike's education. The minister teaches Updike Greek for four years. Although the beauty and poetry of the language "move Updike," people around him are unimpressed. This account of Updike's initial experience with education humorously treats the divide between overeducated intellectuals and ordinary folk.[30] In a series of episodes that project the narrator-protagonist as the prototypical ally of the laboring classes and give life and authority to a practical Yankee identity, Updike deploys his knowledge of Greek in settings inhabited by working-class people. On his father's farm, Updike occupies his mind with the poetry of Homer, where this preoccupation "eradicated love for labour" (*AC*, 29). In a local tavern, Updike's Greek diversions cause a profound misunderstanding among the "young men of the town" who found his "descant upon

Xanthus" during a discussion of racing horses incomprehensible (*AC*, 32).

Updike's obsession with Greek also produces disaster in his interaction with women. Invited on one occasion to mingle with local young women, Updike "thought this a happy opportunity to introduce Andromache," a pedagogical effort met by a "stupid stare." Updike's attempts at elevating his peers are derailed by more youthful entertainment. As the evening winds down, Updike believes that one of the young women might be interested in having him walk her home, but Updike turns down the offer because he cannot think of the precise courting sentiments in Greek (*AC*, 32–33). On another occasion, an older woman, "attempting to ward off the invidious appellation of old maid," expresses interest in Updike by borrowing and reading his books "with astonishing rapidity." Initially, Updike is impressed with her eagerness to learn. Still, after she requests a book using a pornographic reference rather than its scholarly title ("Rolling Belly Letters" instead of Rollins's *The Method of Teaching and Studying the Belle Lettres*), Updike rushes out of her house in a panic, ending his efforts at romantic love (*AC*, 54).

Having obtained essential esoteric knowledge, Updike takes a position as a schoolmaster. He looks forward to elevating the thoughts and character of the local children. Unfortunately, his students have little interest in what Greek has to offer. In addition, the wages of a schoolmaster fail to provide "independence," and Updike is forced to collect his livelihood in the form of "a half of a peck of corn or rye" from local families (*AC*, 34). Updike quickly comes to "sorely regret the mispense [sic] of time" in learning Greek (*AC*, 33). His father, by contrast, "a plain unlettered man, of strong natural abilities," questions the value of education that fails to provide practical knowledge. He admires more the person "who invented printing, discovered the magnetic powers, or contrived an instrument of agriculture, that should abridge the labour of the husbandman" (*AC*, 27).

This gentle mocking of the impracticalities of higher education serves the specific purpose of disguising the class basis (and its incumbent power differential) of higher education through a rhetorical elevation of the wisdom and culture of the ordinary folk. (Ironically, much of the basic information for this novel required access to English- and French-language studies of Islam, North Africa, and the Middle East since the narrator's claim to personal experience was fabricated.) Tyler's rhetoric of the common folk contrasts sharply with a typical view of the people held by many Federalist political leaders and opinion-makers. For example, Alexander Hamilton, in describing the "imprudence of democracy" and calling for rule by the wealthy, wrote:

> The voice of the people has been said to be the voice of God; and however generally this maxim has been quoted and believed, it is not true in fact. The people are turbulent and changing; they seldom judge or determine right.[31]

Is Tyler simply a more democratic-minded person than Hamilton? Davidson suggests that the loss of his inheritance and the instability of his career late in his life may have influenced Tyler to more expansive views of "the people." Whatever Tyler's fortunes later in life, his literary sympathies when the novel was published are belied by textual evidence. He massages class antagonisms and openly calls for social harmony within the existing social framework. This novel's message, themes, and plot trajectory serve the same project that Hamilton pursues, but through "identification" and imagined community and without the overt coercion implicit in Hamilton's outlook on maintaining social harmony. *The Algerine Captive*'s discourse consciously strives to acquire the consent to be ruled by the worthy farmer, Jonathan, the hired man, and Dolly, the milkmaid.[32]

Genocide as motif

A conservative, reactionary construction of class hostilities is not the only influence on Tyler's novel. Few of Tyler's real New England readers would have misconstrued the racial identities of Tyler's imaginary readers—the worthy farmer, Jonathan, the hired man, and Dolly, the milkmaid. While the military defeat of large-scale Native American armed resistance to the land-hungry U.S. empire would not happen until a century after Tyler, Indigenous people in the geography of Tyler's novel are confined to a spatial-temporal wilderness past. The fact that this captivity narrative—in contrast to several prominent, widely read Native American captivity narratives—takes place in North Africa is a comment both on the forced disappearance of many Indigenous nations in New England and the silencing and marginalizing of the events that caused that disappearance. Early in the story, the narrator relates his mother's dream that Indians had kidnapped him. About this recollection, Updike remarks, "she had the native Indians in her mind, but never apprehended her poor son's suffering, many years as a slave, among barbarians, more cruel than the monsters of our own woods" (*AC*, 23). The irony in this remark suggests the dangers posed by Indigenous resistance have been supplanted by the imminent potential for abuses at the hands of Algerians. The transposition of one danger for the unlikely other indicates the emotional power of the culture of victimization wherein the Euro-American protagonist's civilizing agenda is perpetually under threat and demands immediate attention and action.

By the turn of the 19th century, an estimated 2,000 members of various Indigenous bands, tribes, or societies remained in New England in real life. Forced expulsion, genocide, forced assimilation, and disease were the leading causes of this disappearance of whole peoples.[33] Fears accompanying the resistance of Indigenous nations to the U.S. empire derived mainly from frontier violence. By contrast, powerful Indigenous nations would not be forcibly removed or decimated in the South until the middle part of the 19th century. This fact, with its profound civilizational and racial uncertainty, may have given the South, in Tyler's mind, a more amorphous, uncertain geographical quality, described mainly as "southward" (*AC*, 74, 79) than his New England home.

Updike is the descendant of Captain John Underhill, who came to Massachusetts in 1630 and eventually accepted a leadership position in the Massachusetts militia during the Pequot War of 1637. After his role in the deadly encounter with the

Pequot nation, Captain Underhill was chastised by the Massachusetts elites for "liberal" religious views and adultery and banished from the colony. Captain Underhill admitted to looking at a woman who had holes cut into her gloves to make using tobacco more convenient. Still, this charge appears to have been made to add weight to the more severe charge of heresy and sedition for criticizing the religious leaders of the colony. Updike Underhill spends several pages addressing the unfairness of these charges and the eventual punishment of his "honoured ancestor" and even reproduces a letter explaining his deeds written by Captain Underhill addressed to the Massachusetts court.

There is a puzzling imbalance in this portion of the narrative. The incidents and Underhill's subsequent trial took place immediately after the Pequot War. The detailed description of Captain Underhill's adultery charges and defense, alongside a slight reference to one of the deadliest conflicts with an Indigenous nation that claimed large swaths of territory desired by British settlers in Massachusetts. That the matter also deeply implicated imperialist interests and multiple local and global alliances is significant if suppressed in the novel. At the time of Captain Underhill's religious trial, the Pequot nation was a thriving, numerous, and powerful people. Its economic strength and control of local trading routes formed the basis of its regional hegemony. By the 1620s, the Pequot nation aligned with the Dutch, fearing growing numbers of British settlers. The rival Narragansett nation aligned with the British colonies in Massachusetts and Connecticut. Both the Narragansett and the British sought control of the Pequot trade system and aimed to drive the Dutch out of Massachusetts. Using the fabrication that members of the Pequot tribe had killed two English sailors, the Massachusetts militia attacked Pequot towns and trading centers. Encountering heavy military resistance, the English forced the Indigenous armies to surrender by murdering hundreds of noncombatants in a massacre at Mystic River in 1637, a tactic deliberately designed to terrorize the Pequot nation into defeat. The atrocity even shocked the Narragansett allies of the English militia.[34]

The narrative's emphasis on one person's sins and trials while ignoring this international conflict during which British atrocities propelled their local dominance distorts the historical forces that shaped the foundations of Underhill's world. This stunning imbalance in the narrative erases a critical historical confrontation between the British Empire and a thriving and populous Indigenous nation. The outcome of that confrontation was far from inevitable or preordained when it began. The record of events is distorted as if it were a relatively minor detail in an unimportant conflict caused by a persecuted if overzealous Christian community. This discursive erasure, mirroring Jefferson's similar dismissive attendance to Indigenous issues in *Notes* (see the introduction), was part of the narrative creation of a vast, empty, and "savage wilderness" (*AC*, 19) tamed by well-meaning, if sometimes brutal, people. In his effort to recover the good name of Captain Underhill, not from the un-Christian act of mass murder but from being erroneously accused of adultery and for speaking out against the injustice of the town leaders, Updike opines:

> Who ever reflects on the piety of our forefathers, the noble unre-strained ardour, with that they resisted oppression in England, relinquished the delights of their native country, crossed a boisterous ocean, penetrated a savage wilderness, pestilence, Indian warfare, and transmitted to us their sentiments of inde-pendence, that love of liberty, that under God enabled us to obtain our own glorious freedom, will readily pass over those few dark spots of zeal, that clouded their rising sun (*AC*, 19).

Thus, genocide is chalked up to mere overzealousness; a necessary evil to protect the civilizing mission. It seems less important than an incident of a wrongful accusation of and punishment for adultery. When this episode is read against Updike's ruminations on his return after his captivity in Algiers, a deeper erasure and absolution that extends beyond his personal experiences to the collective history of the whole nation occurs. His return from captivity to the bosom of his family and North America and its rights and privileges makes him feel "a rich compensation for all past miseries" (*AC*, 225).

In the end, the business of enforcing social harmony and getting on with building the republic are worthy enterprises. Updike insists that the wretched history of the Euro-American relation to Indigenous nations and the atrocities committed against them were temporary but worthwhile sacrifices. Complete erasure, however, could not be accomplished. By recalling his mother's vision at his birth that predicted his capture by Indians, Updike discourses on the credibility of such visions citing the authority of no less a personage than the colonial Puritan intellectual and theologian Cotton Mather. Mather's major historical work, *Magnalia Christi Americana*, details denominational disputes such as that which befell Captain Underhill and the more infamous Salem witch trials and the destruction of the Pequot nation. On the latter, Mather described the war as a battle between God and the Devil. Regarding the treaty that ended the war, Mather wrote: "in little more than one hour five or six hundred of these barbarians were dismissed from a world that was burdened by them."[35] Mather, too, offers more concern for potential disruptions of European unity than with his people's mass atrocities.

Updike's appeal to Mather's authority on the meaning and veracity of visions is ironic, given that Mather's history of New England was an important source of information for his account of the period in which his ancestor lived. This reference functions as a device for developing Updike as a humorous and unfortunate character with an inflated sense of his intellectual powers. It also ties the novel to a discourse on Indigenous people as both present and absent savage characters occupying a wilderness requiring the Christianizing and civilizing influence of the European immigrants. In a scene at the Harvard Museum, Updike laments the absence of artifacts from this Native past, which he describes as "wretched, bauble specimens" unworthy of such an esteemed institution. These "specimens," indiscernible by region or Indigenous nation, signify a dead people defeated by the superiority of the civilized community. Updike sees their presence as mere objects in an institution of civilized learning as essential to understanding the history of the imagined U.S. national community, not the living history of Native Americans and their resistance to empire, and criticizes the small size of the collection (*AC*, 61). *The Algerine Captive* is saturated with ideas concluding that Indigenous nations and peoples must be erased by violence or assimilation and forgotten. Pages of details about adultery and heresy overwhelm brief and distorted references to genocidal wars against Indigenous nations. Embedded within the psychology of this overblown claim of complete conquest, Euro-American fears of Indigenous revenge and war tremble unuttered.

In his introduction to a collection of writing by Indigenous activist and minister William Apess, Barry O'Connell argues that "[t]o be remembered is to be valued." The treaty signed by the surviving Pequots after the 1637 war included the provision that their nation would be forever dissolved and "forbade the use of their name forever." According to O'Connell, "[m]emory of them was deliberately suppressed." This action was not simply a punishment for having lost a war. It was a "historical veiling, the deliberate forgetting in the dominant culture, of individuals and events that might encourage and legitimate a revival of defiance and rebellion at another time."[36] Through this condition of genocidal forgetting, the erasure of a people through violence, and the legal discourse of a coerced treaty forced Apess to adapt his use of English literacy and his relation to the ideas, philosophies, and religious values of Euro-Americans. This narrow escape from absolute erasure that enables Tyler to construct the imaginary world of *The Algerine Captive* also creates the conditions for Apess's ability to craft oppositional literature and social critique intelligible to his American audience.

Indeed, not every Pequot could be exterminated physically; the memory of this war and its atrocities could not be entirely erased. Apess, who was born just a year after Tyler's novel appeared in print and eighteen years before it was again widely republished, invokes in a sermon the history of genocide, the hypocrisy of its perpetrators, and the memory of resistance:

> [W]hites seem almost to forget the corroding sorrows of the poor
> Indians—the wrongs and calamities that were heaped upon
> them. Follow them into the deep recesses of their wilderness

solitudes, hear their long and loud complaints, when driven by the pale faces whom they had kindly received, and cheerfully, in the fullness of their friendship, sustained through days and months of sorrow, and want, and affliction, from their happy homes, the resting place of their fathers. Can you wonder, friends, that they should have resisted, manfully, against the encroachment of their white neighbors?[37]

A year following this speech, Apess became active in what was known as the Mashpee Revolt of 1834. Isolated on a reservation, the Mashpee rejected a Massachusetts Supreme Court ruling that they were "the unfortunate children of the public" and the object of religious charity as a basis for political domination by Euro-Americans.[38] In public protests, resolutions, legal battles, and appeals to the state authorities, the Mashpee asserted their right to self-determination. When members of the tribe prevented two Euro-Americans from stealing wood from the reservation, a common practice, local authorities described "the revolt" as violent and prepared for armed retaliation. They framed the Mashpee protests against territorial incursions as a victimization of Euro-Americans which demanded violent responses. (Incidentally, during these events, local authorities reported their fears of an interracial insurrection composed of Black people and Indigenous people.) The Mashpee won wide recognition for their cause, especially in the Boston liberal and abolitionist press, and claimed the right to choose their elected officials. For his part in the nonviolent uprising, Apess was arrested for instigating a riot, briefly imprisoned, and fined. Throughout his career as an activist and minister, Apess rejected the narrative of dissolution and forgetting found in Mather's and Tyler's texts. Instead, Apess challenged the political and cultural hegemony of the dominant culture imposed through the erasure of Indigenous societies. His is the struggle for voice, presence, and power.

The Algerine Captive's totalizing narrative imagines a manageable class, racial, and civilizational hierarchy. It seeks to produce limits around the white, slaveholding republican ideal by suppressing or eliminating from its territory and memory the voice, action, and even presence of Indigenous, African, and non-Christian people, ideas, and cultures. Its ideological function is to evade the responsibility for genocide by constructing an inverted history that elicits a self-delusion of sacrifice and danger for Euro-American invaders. This discourse of a pioneering spirit and the repression of dissent becomes not only a basis of U.S. literary culture but a material force in mobilizing the solidarity of racial whiteness in the new republic.

Gesturing Africans and white ventriloquism

If erasure and displacement in memory and fact mark Tyler's representation of Native Americans, the enslavement of Africans in the new North American nation invoked another discourse of race and racism also linked to the "Algerine" question. *The Algerine Captive* is an antislavery tract that follows a style used by opponents of slavery such as Benjamin Franklin, the diplomat David Humphreys, poet Joel Barlow, and others. In fact, Barlow, Humphreys, and Franklin have parts in Tyler's novel. In New England magazines, poets, fiction writers, satirists, polemicists, and others frequently linked their antislavery views to the Arab countries of North Africa.[39] Typically in this genre, slavery in North America was contrasted with slavery in the Islamic world.

One such text was authored by Benjamin Franklin, titled "On the Slave Trade," and appeared as a letter to the editor of the *Federal Gazette* in March 1790. Franklin constructed what scholar Mukhtar Ali Isani describes as a "fictional African" to put forward Franklin's views on slavery. Franklin compares U.S. proslavery views to the opinions of the fictional Sidi Mehemet Ibrahim, a supposed member of the government in Algiers, who gave a speech defending the enslavement of Christians in 1687. Ibrahim responded to a petition by a dissident sect in Algiers calling for the end of piracy that had targeted European and North American shipping and the enslavement of prisoners captured. "Who are to perform the common Labours of our City, and in our Families? Must we not then be our own slaves?"[40] Carefully paralleling the argument of North American slavery advocates, Franklin's Ibrahim uttered the lament that manumission would cost slaveholders valuable property and wealth and forewarns that freedom would create a new class of outsiders unwilling to work posing an existential threat to racial purity. Formerly enslaved people, Ibrahim says, echoing eighteenth-century slavery advocates, would become beggars and thieves and would refuse to return to "their Countries." If expelled from the country, they would be preyed upon by other countries in the area and be unfit to care for or protect themselves. Also contrasted with the decidedly uncivilized Islamic Algeria were the hypocrisy and brutality of self-proclaimed Christians who profited from and politically supported the North American system. But those who refuse conversion are treated with "Humanity" and live in the "Light" of civilized Islamic society. Civilization, social order, and religious precepts all require the maintenance of the slave system, concluded Ibrahim.[41]

Franklin's imaginary discourse was meant as irony. It did not reflect first-hand knowledge of North Africa, the Middle East, or other regions where many people practice Islam. Franklin's character suggested that the capture and enslavement of Euro-Americans (and Europeans) in Algeria were political tactics to assert Algerian rights over control of shipping in the Mediterranean rather than an economic system of property and labor.[42] In terms of treatment and prospects for freedom, slavery in North America (and throughout European imperial possessions) compared unfavorably with Algeria's. Like many other writers who used Islamic countries and Islam itself to highlight threats of tyranny, despotism, barbarism, and anarchy,[43] Franklin made a faulty comparison, implying that Islamic society in North Africa was identical to the North American system of racial slavery. Such comparisons with the proslavery advocates were not intended to elevate the Islamic civilization or register as cultural relativism. Instead, anti-slavery sentiment served as an indirect foil to hint at a need to extirpate the worst elements of the West with similar hatred felt broadly for the East and its civilizations, kingdoms, philosophies, and global influence. In other words, Franklin's anti-slavery views were underpinned by the idea that the ideas and actions of U.S. supporters of enslavement were not unlike abominable North Africans of decidedly inferior racial and civilizational origins.

In creating these narratives, Franklin and others produced fiction in which "the black appears merely as a transparent persona intended not to serve as a believable character but as a means of broaching the subject of slavery."[44] North American opponents of slavery spoke in voices disguised as Africans and frequently opined on the inhumanity of slavery, delivering extensive descriptions of brutality and violence and threats of slave insurrections (à la Toussaint Louverture in Haiti in 1791). Antislavery writing typically, however, insisted on the rigidity of racial boundaries between Black and white, identifying the former with slavery and negativity and the latter with freedom and privilege. In no way were these characters imagined as contesting from within the imagined social harmony of a racially pure, Christian national culture.

This veritable tumult of ventriloquistic writing provided Royall Tyler with the form for expressing his views about North American slavery in *The Algerine Captive*. But it was the work and experiences of an "authentic" African, Olaudah Equiano, who provided the content. Tyler initiates the novel's treatment of slavery in an unnamed Southern state,[45] in a church where Updike Underhill observes a minister, after severely beating an enslaved person for a minor infraction, proceeds to give a sermon on the Fourth Commandment. Ironically, the Fourth Commandment requires adherents to keep the Sabbath as a holy day and rest; it also requires servants to be given the day off. The minister keeps his discourse to an efficient eleven minutes and then hurries to the weekly horse races (*AC*, 80).

Sympathy for the condition of the enslaved, however, does not imply equality, shared humanity, or a welcome into the fold of civilization. For example, in his Southern travels, Updike fails in medicine and is forced to consider accepting a position as a schoolmaster, but under indentured conditions similar to an enslaved person—"So that to purchase a school master and a negro was almost synonymous [sic]." Updike states that he would "have prefered labouring [sic], with the slaves on their plantation, than sustaining the slavery and contempt of a school" (*AC*, 83). While this assertion portends the great irony of Updike's eventual enslavement in Algeria, it also resonates with the predominant discourse on racial identity and its relationship to liberty and slavery. As shown above, the privileges of citizenship and civilization were constituted both legally and culturally as white possessions. Tyler's imagined consumers of emergent national U.S. culture were white. The laws that governed slavery (in both the North and the South) defined the institution by race. Working-class discontent and rebellion were often couched in symbols and language in which exploitation and oppression were identified with Black people, and by contrast, freedom and rights with Euro-Americans. Tyler invoked this discourse and complex of institutional practices in his popular 1787 play, *The Contrast*, in which Jonathan, a hired man, is "mistaken" for a servant. Jonathan replies angrily: "Servant! Sir, do you take me for a neger—I am Colonel Manly's waiter."[46] Tyler understands that discourses of independence and racial identity were closely linked in the minds of his audience and deliberately fosters a linked national and racial identity predicated at least partially on social distance from Africans and enslaved people.[47]

Thus, when he writes a scenario that hints at a condition much like enslavement through being economically indebted to a community, such as the work conditions of the schoolmaster offered to Updike, he is not saying that being a schoolmaster would require the same punishing labor or the same physical brutality as that meted out to enslaved people among whom he "prefered labouring." The racial difference between Euro-Americans and African-descended people makes the economic relation of dependence seem as brutal for the white as violence and punishment are for Africans. This particular contrast of race and condition of labor would reemerge in the pronouncements of white workers less than two decades later struggling with the contradictions of the racial makeup of the "agrarian republic" and the emergence of industrial capitalism and their incorporation into it as "wage slaves." Capitalism had withdrawn the promise of independence and political power through land ownership; now, all they had was their racial identities as a source of collective political power. First uttered by Jonathan, the mythical Yankee character of U.S. literature, and then repeated by Updike, his complicated descendent, this discourse of racial identity promotes social distance and difference between white and Black rather than asserting essential humanity and equality. Using racist and orientalist discourses to deny the humanity of some Euro-Americans who profit from and advocate slavery is the limit of Tyler's critique.

The contradiction between the "humanism" of opponents of slavery and their actions is highlighted when Updike bumbles his way into a position onboard the slave ship *Freedom*. Offered economic security, the essential component of liberty, Updike accepts a position as surgeon on board this aptly named vessel heading to London before undertaking the trip to the African coast as part of the North American slave trade. After a brief stay in London, Updike boards the ship *Sympathy* with its cargo to be traded for enslaved Africans.

At this point in the novel, Tyler adds a twist to the racial ventriloquism practiced by his contemporaries. From the moment Updike sees Africa, the narrative borrows heavily without citation from *The Interesting Narrative of the Life of Olaudah Equiano*, published in 1791. (Citing Olaudah Equiano's work might have called into question the realism of the tale. However, the novel's frequent use of scholarly conventions to cite European sources of information on other matters suggests a refusal to accept Equiano's authority.) Equiano's descriptions of the "cleanliness" of Africans in their everyday habits, the "complexions" of the Portuguese slave traders, and the medical inspections of newly purchased enslaved people echo in Tyler's text. Indeed, many of Equiano's descriptions of the conditions in the hold of the ship, perceptions of the attitudes of enslaved people to their condition, and the treatment meted out by the sailors appear to be lifted directly into Tyler's novel (*AC*, 94–101).[48] But Equiano is silenced. Indeed, all of Tyler's enslaved Africans, other than inarticulate "frequent shrieks," "tears," or one who "gathered all of his strength, and, in one last effort, spoke with great emphasis and expired," or have their "expressions" translated through "the linguist," are little more than gesturing people (*AC*, 98).

For example, before the ship sets sail to return to the West Indies, Updike convinces the captain that rather than beating recalcitrant enslaved people to death, he should bring the sickest ones to land to provide them medical assistance and restore them to health. (Ironic that "yankee [sic] humanity" helps preserve the profits of the slave-trading captain). The captain agrees, and within days the sick Africans are healing and, naturally, appreciate Updike's help. Through "signs," they show their affection for Updike, they clap with joy, signify their desire to be free, and make him "comprehend" their preferences for freedom, but they refuse to leave Updike. Tyler imagines gesturing fools who love their "humane" captor and naturally serve him. Who does not believe that victims of enslavement, presented with a chance to escape, would not retaliate against a man who aided in their capture and enslavement rather than stay and await the return of the slave ship? Tyler's African images are of a child-like figure less threatening than the rebellious Toussaint or even the African who talks back, such as Equiano. Equiano is a silent, invisible (but real) African presence that haunts Tyler, enabling his self-discovery and conscious identity, as novelist Toni Morrison proposed would become a recurrent theme in American literature authored by Euro-Americans.[49] Tyler's images are designed to render the African harmless but not an equal deserving the privileges of citizenship or humanity, and certainly not as a participant in a hybrid, highly contested North American culture. Tyler's Africans are silent figures used to present political views rather than imaginatively constructed humans with views of the world, aspirations for liberation, and goals for social development.

Tyler's caricatures function as a racist gesture meant to degrade the artistic work of his contemporaries—poet Phillis Wheatley, scientist Benjamin Banneker, or A.M.E. Church founders Absalom Jones and Richard Allen—and to silence calls for freedom and equality by antislavery and equality activists such as Equiano, Lemuel Haynes, and Prince Hall. In her poem "To the Right Honourable William, Earl of Dartmouth," penned in 1772 to a British official overseeing the North American colonies, Wheatley notes that her reasons for opposing tyranny come from personal and community experience of enslavement and racism. "I, young in life, by seeming cruel fate/Was snatch'd from Afric's fancy shore. ... Such, such my case. And can I then but pray/Others may never feel tyrannic sway?"[50] Wheatley's voice and experience starkly contrast with the gesturing imposters invented by Tyler or the ventriloquist dolls of Franklin and others.

Ironically, most commentaries on Wheatley's poetry identify her as a "patriot" sympathizer with the Revolution and its ultimate establishment of a white slaveholders' republic, typically associating the British with oppression and the new republic with freedom. However, her earliest poems addressed to British colonial officials appear in a time frame before such a notion even existed. Indeed, the poem cited here is dedicated to William Legge, Earl of Dartmouth, assigned to head the British colonies in North America to mend hostile relations between the colonists and London after the landmark *Gaspee* Affair and the *Somerset* decision. Dartmouth's reputation as an abolitionist preceded him, and Euro-Americans viewed even his most conciliatory interventions with hostility. The *Gaspee* Affair was a violent armed conflict against British authority spurred by colonial resistance to London's efforts to curtail the illegal smuggling of enslaved people and the use of an African's testimony in a British court to convict whites accused of insurrection. *Somerset* was a legal case that resulted in the abolition of property in humans in the British Isles. Each event signifies what Gerald Horne has called London's "incipient abolition."[51] In 1773, after Dartmouth's arrival, many enslaved African-descended people, including Wheatley, may have regarded London as moving toward the abolition of slavery and, conversely, that the growing colonial rebellion stood as a roadblock to that venerable goal.

Most importantly, Tyler's representations provided an alternative version of "the African" to the image conjured by the shocking overthrow of French imperial rule of Haiti, an event seared into the mind of the slave-trading nation. W. E. B. Du Bois notes in his study of the slave trade that the revolution led by Toussaint Louverture in 1791 "contrived a Negro 'problem' for the Western Hemisphere, intensified and defined the anti-slavery movement." The Haitian rebellion "rendered more certain the final prohibition of the slave-trade by the United States in 1807."[52] Indeed, driven by a fear of slave rebellion and the presence of a Black republic near its shores, Euro-American political leaders in the earliest years of the constitutional republic pursued contradictory and even deadly policies of perpetuating slavery, attempting to limit the importation of enslaved people, and managing a growing crisis of internal and external insurrection.[53] Slave rebellions, rumored or factual, swept through the United States from North Carolina and Virginia to New York and New Jersey. Conspiracies of armed revolt, violence, arson, destruction of property, runaways, and suspicious gatherings of Blacks haunted the minds of Americans—North and South.[54]

The "unfurling contagion" of slave insurrection across the Caribbean, as Gerald Horne states in *Confronting Black Jacobins*, propelled to new heights by the Haitian Revolution, strengthened the impetus for abolition in many circles (even in its oblique discourses represented by Tyler and Franklin). Combined with these material forces of insurrection, the Wheatley's, Equiano's, and Apess's literary efforts enable a counter-hegemonic ideology of the true nature of the "slave-holders' republic," its aggressions, and violent intentions. They point to white supremacy and slavery as the essential condition of Euro-American freedom and power. This ideological formation's appeal and moral force fueled the contradictory urge among the Euro-American ruling class to dig in its heels and protect the systemic sources of its power. In political circles and ideological manifestations, a desire coalesced around fostering the solidarity of the descendants of Europe around the psychological value of their skin color, even if with failed promises of social mobility and power in the New World.[55] African resistance and revolt, rather than Tyler's ideologically fraught moral appeals, proved to be the force that ended slavery. Insurrection established the humanity and equality of Africans.

Empire, women, and Islam

Tyler's novel connected the ancient "hysteria about Islam" of the 15th and 16th centuries that propelled a racial sense of

European-ness, its expanded interest in the growing global slave trade, and the earliest contradictions of capitalist relations of production.[56] White victimization through enslavement by an oriental power provided a powerful image that sustained anti-slavery sentiments and the urgent plea for European solidarity against powerful and threatening African and Asian states and empires. Images of victimization produce even deeper emotional responses centered on contrasting fabrications of the treatment of women.

In one of three commentaries on the treatment of Islamic women, claimed to result from his own experience or from "authentic information," Updike describes the women of Algiers as "enjoy[ing] greater liberty than is generally conceived." It is conjectured that "the women take great liberties in this general disguise," referring to wearing veils from head to toe (AC, 175). This language invokes the image of a contrast to the West. It implies that popular Western perceptions of the total subjugation of Islamic women are exaggerated and that Islamic women use their confines to engage in secret, subversive activities. Tyler's remark suggests that concern for the fate of Islamic women weighed on the minds of enlightened Westerners, at least to some small extent. At the same time, this imaginary projection of the orientalized woman encased in a body-length veil performing subversive acts underneath hints of deviant sexuality. In his other encounters with Islamic women, Updike describes them as perpetually hidden behind veils and segregated sections of the house (AC, 121–22; 151–53; 174–75).

Humanitarian obsessions with veiled women in Muslim-majority countries link Tyler's humanism with U.S. imperialism's justifications for interventions, war, and ultimately failed conquest of Afghanistan beginning in 2001. In building its case for retaliation against that militarily weak, economically isolated, and politically divided country, U.S. leaders held onto orientalist views that Tyler had articulated 200 years before. By 2002, growing criticism of the U.S. bombing and invasion of Afghanistan and the subsequently extended occupation, despite an apparent defeat of the repressive Taliban regime, pushed the Bush administration for broader justifications for the ongoing conflict. Speaking, apparently on behalf of the world's women, Laura Bush came forward to rejuvenate the ancient concern for Islamic women. She praised the efforts of the invading forces for saving the women of Afghanistan:

> The plight of women and children in Afghanistan is a matter of deliberate human cruelty, carried out by those who seek to intimidate and control. ...
>
> Civilized people throughout the world are speaking out in horror—not only because our hearts break for the women and children in Afghanistan, but also because in Afghanistan we see the world the terrorists would like to impose on the rest of us....
>
> Because of our recent military gains in much of Afghanistan, women are no longer imprisoned in their homes. They can listen to music and teach their daughters without fear of punishment.[57]

"Civilized people" center the concern for the liberation of veiled women. This humanitarian impulse substituted for the desire for revenge, a decidedly uncivilized motive for imperialist war. The images presented are not those of human equals but rather of silent, passive victims awaiting the power of the U.S. military for liberation. They displace and erase the history of the struggles of democratic forces, including feminists, in Afghanistan, suppressed by religious fundamentalists. In the 1980s, the U.S. empire sided with the fundamentalists against the influence of Communism by imprisoning, deporting, and murdering those women who dared prematurely to demand equality. Now that those repressive forces of terror posed a threat to civilization, U.S. imperialism could turn its benevolent interests to the abused and tortured women of Afghanistan and continue to ignore the democratic struggle there.

This "illusion of benevolence," to borrow again from Said,[58] like its ideological cousin, "the pretense of innocence," attempts to cover the naked power of U.S. imperialism. Just as the imagined veiled woman symbolized tyranny and barbarity that could only be overcome by the strength through unity that resonated with Tyler's 1797 audience, she had become the image of U.S. military power and civilization in 2001. Indeed, the irony of the closing lines of Tyler's novel as the slogan that mirrored the rhetoric of "war on terror"—"BY UNITING WE STAND, BY DIVIDING WE FALL" (*AC*, 226)—only underlines the ties of the present to past. As it was then, Tyler's slogan remains a call for a white racial empire veiled as a crusade.

Notes

1. Robert J. Allison, *The Crescent Obscured: The United States and the Muslim World, 1776–1815*, (New York: Oxford University Press, 1995), 3-6; see also Peter Gottschalk and Gabriel Greenberg, "Common Heritage, Uncommon Fear: Islamophobia in the United States and British India, 1687-1947," *Islamophobia Studies Journal*, Vol. 1, no. 1, (2012): 82-106; and, Mary K. Bloodsworth-Lugo and Carmen R. Lugo-Lugo, *Containing (Un)American Bodies: Race, Sexuality, and Post-9/11 Constructions of Citizenship*, (Amsterdam: Brill/Rodopi, 2010), 7-22; and, Carmen R. Lugo-Lugo and Mary K. Bloodsworth-Lugo, *Feminism after 9/11: Women's Bodies as Cultural and Political Threat*, (New York: Palgrave Macmillan, 2017), 78, 100, 125.
2. Ronald Takaki, *A Different Mirror: A History of Multicultural America*, (New York: Basic Books, 1993), 69-70.
3. Peter Markoe, *The Algerine Spy in Pennsylvania, or Letters Written by a Native of Algiers on the Affairs of the United States of America from the Close of the Year 1783 to the Meeting of the Convention*, (Philadelphia: Prichard and Hall, 1787). The narrative structure positions the U.S. as a victim within the imperial world system. It signals the vulnerability of European domination of that system. The unacknowledged assumption is that North African powers were strong enough to exploit differences among Europeans and the newly formed U.S. Such a tale undoubtedly sparked anxiety and fear in a readership that was still trying to establish a slaveholders' republic based in no small part on the ownership of African people.
4. Cathy Davidson, *Revolution and the Word: The Rise of the Novel in America*, (New York: Oxford University Press, 1985), 85.
5. Edward W. Said, *Orientalism* (New York: Vintage Books, 1978), 71-72.
6. Said, 72.
7. Royall Tyler, *The Algerine Captive, or The Life and Adventures of Doctor Updike Underhill*, (New York: Modern Library, 2002 [1797]), 161. Hereafter cited in the text as *AC*.
8. John Howard Lawson, *The Hidden Heritage*, (New York: Citadel Press, 1968), x.
9. Vijay Prashad, *Washington Bullets: A History of C.I.A., Coups, and Assassinations*, (New York: Monthly Review Press, 2020). While it is easy to conflate periods and project contemporary U.S. imperialism back to 1797, my argument here centers on Tyler's role in creating a cultural basis of victimization culture.
10. The Declaration of Independence likens American subordination to British rule as a form of slavery. The forgotten history of forced expulsion and expropriation of Loyalists in the aftermath of independence served as retribution for this victimization. U.S. invaders of Texas in the 1830s repeated the claim that Mexico's abolition of slavery was an expression of tyranny, legitimizing their illegal coup and subsequent attachment to the U.S. as a slaveholding territory. Euro-American settlers frequently regarded Indigenous resistance as the primary threat,

mobilizing support for genocide, removal, and forced land cessions. Capitalists typically view labor strikes as an assault on their well-intentioned and benevolent actions. Today, Euro-American opponents of affirmative action, defenders of the "thin blue line," and haters of global economic competition frame persistent emotional anxiety about the loss of power in terms of victimization, propelling the overtly racist "tea party" movement and a host of openly neo-fascist formations.

11. Lawson, x.
12. Tony, Pecinovsky, *The Cancer of Colonialism: W. Alphaeus Hunton, Black Liberation, and the* Daily Worker, *1944-1946*, (New York: International Publishers, 2021), 35, 45, and 137;
13. E. San Juan, Jr., *The Philippine Temptation: The Dialectics of Philippines– U.S. Literary Relations*, (Philadelphia: Temple University Press, 1996), 25; Gerald Horne explores similar connections between U.S. neocolonialism and popularly consumed cultural artifacts in the book *Mau Mau in Harlem: The U.S. and the Liberation of Kenya*, (New York: Palgrave MacMillan, 2009), 149-150, 153;
14. Ricardo Alarcón, Opening Speech at the International Conference "The Work of Karl Marx in the 21st Century." *Nature, Society, and Thought*, Vol. 19, no. 1 (2006):17–27.
15. Indeed, Aijaz Ahmad's intervention on using the term "Third World" is worth remembering. Aijaz Ahmad, *In Theory: Classes, Nations, Literatures*, (New York: Verso, 2000), 287-318.
16. Details of Tyler's life are drawn from Caleb Crain, "Introduction to *The Algerine Captive*, by Royall Tyler," (New York: Modern Library, 2002), xvii-xxxiv.
17. Crain, xix.
18. Howard Zinn, *A People's History of the United States: 1492–Present*, (New York: Harper Perennial, 1995), 90-94; Herbert Aptheker, *Early Years of the Republic and the Constitution, 1783–1793*, (New York: International Publishers, 1990), 144-147.
19. Davidson, 192-200.
20. Zinn, 90-94.
21. Charle Beard and Mary Beard, *The Rise of American Civilization*, (New York: Mac-Millan, 1941), 308. As Gerald Horne has shown, fears of revolt drove Southern white politics, which manifested as a dominant motive during and after the U.S. revolution to develop a conservative republic to ensure the existence of the slave regime. See Gerald Horne, *The Counter-Revolution of 1776: Slave Resistance and the Origins of the United States of America*, (New York: New York University Press, 2012). Such fears drove the whole emergent U.S. ruling class, despite its regional and material differences, into an alliance that endured until the 1850s.
22. Gary B. Nash, *Red, White, and Black: The Early Peoples of the Republic*, (Englewood Cliffs, NJ: Prentice-Hall, 1992), 208-212.
23. Aptheker, *Early Years*, 143-144.
24. Michelle R. Sizemore, "When are the People?: Temporality, Popular Sovereignty, and the U.S. Settler State," *South Central Review*, Vol. 30, no. 1 (2013): 7; see also, Thomas P. Slaughter, *The Whiskey Rebellion: Frontier Epilogue to the American Revolution*, (New York: Oxford University Press, 1986).
25. Philip J. Deloria, *Playing Indian*, (New Haven: Yale University Press, 1998), 21-22.
26. Davidson, 30.
27. Benedict Anderson, *Imagined Communities: Reflections on the Origins and Spread of Nationalism*, (New York: Verso, 2002).
28. Kenneth Burke, *A Rhetoric of Motives*, (Berkeley: University of California Press, 1969), xiv.

29. Tyler's narrative includes a visit to Benjamin Franklin, and Updike notes the elder statesman's rise from the lowly stature of "Poor Richard," making the bootstraps myth more explicit.

30. In another piece written under a pseudonym, Tyler described "Syriac" and "Arabic" as "dead languages." See Davidson, 197.

31. Quoted in Zinn, 95.

32. "Jonathan" is a character Tyler's twentieth-century critics have identified as one of the "central myth figures" of U.S. national culture. See Roger B. Stein, "Royall Tyler and the Question of Our Speech," *New England Quarterly*, Vol. 38, no. 4 (1965): 455. Scholar Leo Marx says Jonathan in Tyler's play *The Contrast* "took hold of the popular imagination" for his "intriguing blend of astuteness and rural simplicity. See Marx, *The Machine in the Garden: Technology and the Pastoral Ideal in America*, (New York: Oxford University Press, 1964), 132–33. Updike Underhill could be regarded as a version of this figure with more character depth.

33. Nash, 280-286.

34. Nash, 82-84; Zinn, 14-15.

35. Quoted in Nash, 84.

36. Barry O'Connell, "Introduction to *On Our Own Ground: The Complete Writings of William Apess, a Pequot*, ed. O'Connell, (Amherst: University of Massachusetts Press, 1992), xxiii-xxv.

37. William Apess, "The Indians: The Ten Lost Tribes," In *On Our Own Ground: The Complete Writings of William Apess, a Pequot*, ed. Barry O'Connell, (Amherst: University of Massachusetts Press, 1992 [1833]), 114.

38. Quoted in Donald M. Nielsen, "The Mashpee Indian Revolt of 1833," *New England Quarterly* Vol. 58 (1985): 401.

39. Mukhtar Ali Isani, "Far from 'Gambia's Golden Coast': The Black in Late Eighteenth-Century Imaginative Literature," *William and Mary Quarterly*, Vol. 36, no. 3 (1979): 353–72.

40. Benjamin Franklin, "On the Slave Trade," in *The Heath Anthology of American Literature*, 3rd ed., ed. Paul Lauter, (New York: Houghton Mifflin, 1990 [1790]), 758.

41. Franklin, 759-760.

42. Allison, 107.

43. During the Revolutionary War, agitators used Islamic countries to show the effect of tyranny and despotism. After the war, conservative Federalists used stereotypes about Islamic countries as evidence in favor of a strong central government. Anti-Federalists used Muslim stereotypes to expose the despotic threat of Federalist ideas, Allison, 35-39.

44. Isani, 356.

45. By the time of the publication of *The Algerine Captive*, many Northern states had abolished the slave trade, but census figures indicate that the number of enslaved people in New England stood in the thousands. See W.E.B. Du Bois, *The Suppression of the African Slave Trade*, in *Du Bois: Writings*, edited by Nathan Huggins, (New York: Library of America, 1986 [1895]), 1-396.

46. Royall Tyler, *The Contrast*, in *The Heath Anthology of American Literature*, 3rd ed., edited by Paul Lauter, (New York: Houghton, Mifflin, 1998 [1797]), 1163.

47. Historian Gordon S. Wood notes this conversation and Jonathan's rebellion at being considered a servant. He links it to working-class distaste for being considered lowly and identifies this sense of self-respect with the revolution's discourse of independence and liberty. Wood fails, however, to note its racial dimension. See Wood, *The Radicalism of the American Revolution*, (New York: Vintage Books, 1991), 184. Wood does not discuss how such meanings were made legible by how thoroughly racism

defined U.S. slavery. Horne more effectively explores the relation of racial slavery, capitalist development, and U.S. political philosophy and institutions in *The Counterrevolution of 1776*. Further, he explores the roots of the development in pre-U.S. colonial and inter-imperialist dynamics of the region in *The Apocalypse of Settler Colonialism: The Roots of Slavery, White Supremacy, and Capitalism in Seventeenth-Century North America and the Caribbean*, (New York: Monthly Review Press, 2018).

48. Olaudah Equiano, *The Interesting Narrative of the Life of Olaudah Equiano*, (New York: St. Martin's Press, 1995 [1791].

49. Toni Morrison, *Playing in the Dark: Whiteness and the Literary Imagination*, (New York: Vintage Books, 1992).

50. Phillis Wheatley, "To the Right Honourable William, Earl of Dartmouth." In *The Complete Writings of Phillis Wheatley*, ed. Vincent Carretta, (New York: Penguin, 2001 [1770]). 40.

51. Horne, *Counterrevolution*, 125, 203-219.

52. Du Bois, 74.

53. Gerald Horne, *Confronting Black Jacobins: The United States, the Haitian Revolution, and the Origins of the Dominican Republic*, (New York: Monthly Review Press, 2015), 30-77.

54. Herbert Aptheker, *American Negro Slave Revolts*, (New York: International Publishers, 1993), 209-15. For a discussion of how resistance, running away, or the threat of retaliation haunted capital value in enslaved humans, see Daina Raimey Berry, *The Price for Their Pound of Flesh: The Value of the Enslaved from Womb to Grave in the Building of a Nation*, (Boston: Beacon Press, 2018).

55. Horne, *Confronting*, 49, 52, 76, 101-102.

56. Gerald Horne, *The Dawning of the Apocalypse: The Roots of Slavery, White Supremacy, Settler Colonialism, and Capitalism in the Long 16th Century*, (New York: Monthly Review Press, 2020), 48-49, 69. Oliver Cromwell Cox, *The Foundations of Capitalism*, (New York: Philosophical Library, Inc., 1959).

57. Laura Bush, Radio Address by Mrs. Bush. 17 November 2001. https://georgewbush-whitehouse.archives.gov/news/releases/2001/11/20011117.html.

58. Edward W. Said, *Culture and Imperialism*, (New York: Vintage Books, 1986), xvii.

Chapter 2

Progress

The transition to capitalist social relations of production marks the conditions of the early U.S. republic. A new gendered division of labor, a racial formation rooted in enslavement, and new modes of accumulation founded on settler colonialism consigned feudal relations to the past. This chapter explores these dynamic and interlocking processes through readings of *The Pioneers* by James Fenimore Cooper and *Our Nig* by Harriet E. Wilson in the developing industrial class formation. A materialist exploration shows how, from Jefferson's agrarian concepts of citizenship, commodified labor became a basis of social identity in this emergent social formation. Further, a discussion of the life and thought of Sojourner Truth in connection with the ideologies in those works of fiction contextualizes the resonance of pre-Civil War imaginative literature with social movements.[1] This chapter illuminates foundational literary materials that articulated rebellious acts which nurtured hierarchical transformations. Ultimately, fictional characters, subordinated by inequalities, prefigure more historically significant social changes through corresponding subversions of actually existing social relations. It is commonplace in U.S. mythology to see the endless movement of human society through time as a natural unfolding of social progress. This chapter studies how each of these literary figures positioned themselves against this concept of social progress.

Cooper and Wilson serve as chronological bookends for this period. Cooper's *The Pioneers* and Wilson's *Our Nig* are good examples of opposed ideological imaginings of the structures of the antebellum social formation. Written in 1823, *The Pioneers* romanticizes a crumbling feudal past[2] as mercantile and industrial capitalism began to reorganize social life. In 1827, the year his home state of New York finally abolished slavery and the same year Sojourner Truth claimed her own freedom, Cooper wrote a defense of slavery's constitutionality. He resorted to familiar arguments against abolition. First, because slavery originated with European domination of the continent, it simply could not be resolved. Second, freedom would lead to political equality, which would lead to "racial amalgamation."[3] If Cooper's tale is a backward-looking social imaginary, Wilson's novel accurately represents her present. It depicts a racial formation and gendered division of labor that has become identified as central to emerging antebellum capitalism. *Our Nig* (1859) produces the dialectical negation of the ideological messages of the bourgeois imaginary mobilized by *The Pioneers*. Truth offered true freedom and equality as the only basis for social progress, conditions that Cooper and the majority of Euro-Americans simply were unwilling to accept. Cooper's work moved to the center of American letters while racist circumstances forced Wilson and her writing into obscurity.[4] Meanwhile, though Sojourner Truth has been lodged in the general historical memory, her image and thought remain distorted and out of focus. Inevitably, the social relations that conditioned the possibility of each author's literary production also shaped how we remember and mythologize them.

The Pioneers: Rebellion on the frontier

James Fenimore Cooper's *The Pioneers* is now sometimes read exclusively as a racist, imperialist rendering of the early U.S. frontier.[5] In his biography of William Cooper, James Fenimore's father, historian Alan Taylor draws strong parallels between the Cooperstown of James's youth and "his most powerful memories" retold in the Leatherstocking Tales, especially *The Pioneers*. According to Taylor, Cooper sought to reclaim "his legacy by imagining and crafting an improved past," which alleviated "genteel" anxieties about rapid social transformation in the revolutionary period. He tried to reconstruct a world stabilized by a patriarch whose authority tamed the anarchistic elements lurking at the frontier and within the untamed social spaces of modernity. Like most of Cooper's work, this novel elaborates a class hierarchy, patriarchal order, and racial formation founded on Euro-American male ruling-class authority.[6] The historical William Cooper ("Judge" Marmaduke Temple of the novel) sought a community based on, as he put it, "mutual dependence." By it, he referred to an imagined organic whole uniting all of its members into a single, common cause of production, distribution, and culture-building in the frontier of western New York. Historically this community was founded on the expropriation of Indigenous land and structured by a class hierarchy dominated by the elder Cooper, who, through property law, owned the land and its resources. He rented these resources to settlers, creating various levels of debt peonage and dependence on him.[7] Ultimately, in a sign that capitalist relations had supplanted the supposed permanence of feudal entitles, challengers to Cooper's political authority and competitors for land and resources dismantled his control of the region. They left the son to try to reclaim imagined stability in his father's generation via literary production.

To create his literary hierarchies in which social betters are the protagonists of a romanticized past, James Fenimore Cooper introduces racialized and gendered "others" within his texts. Literary critics typically study Natty Bumppo, Chingachgook, and Elizabeth Temple, the daughter of the wealthy patron. In different ways, these characters have become archetypal for literature, poetry, movies, and other forms of cultural production since their invention. However, for my analysis here, Betty Hollister, a minor "dependent" female character, deserves careful attention. She is a woman dependent on her labor and her husband for her living. Though fixed by a hierarchy of gender and race—through which the novel articulates her class relations and precarity—Mrs. Hollister challenges structured arrangements of station and power. Cooper intends her solely for comic relief that views critiques of power as laughable and easily dismissed, a role she resists (unsuccessfully) as well. In the end, however, her character functions to deny a working-class radicalism, which is based on the dialectical transformation of the social order into a classless formation. Ultimately, she typifies Euro-American rebellion whose racial allegiances and actions foreclose necessary inter-racial alliances.

Her "station" (her social position and its accompanying social power) is determined simultaneously by her gender and race and more directly by her labor as a tavern-keeper. The meanings of social status and station become more evident through relationality, mainly through comparing Mrs. Hollister with Elizabeth Temple, the economically secure daughter of the valley owner, and Louisa, the financially dependent daughter of the minister. Each of these latter two characters, unlike Betty Hollister, are stationed in a confined domestic sphere. They are, however, positioned as higher in their social station and active social authority (though still constrained by the patriarch's public and private authority). Elizabeth's labor is limited to giving directions to servants, as a cultured woman's station was derived from the economic ability to avoid both public labor and the rigors of domestic work. Betty Hollister is married to a petty-bourgeois tavern-keeper, but her gender proletarianizes her in the tavern because she does not own or legally control her workplace or the means of production. Although he may not gain social power by physically subordinating his rebellious, masculine wife, her husband does expropriate her value production for himself.

Mrs. Hollister's reliance on labor and the continuum of her labor's transgression of the ideological and spatial barrier between private and public realms coincides with characterizations of her masculinity, a negation of the appropriate gender division of labor. As the Judge and his daughter make their way through the town of Templeton (of course, named for him) for Christmas eve services, the Hollisters greet them. Mrs. Hollister, with her "masculine countenance" and "masculine strides," stops the Judge's sleigh and speaks first to the Temples, asking for directions on how to prepare for the Christmas celebration. Further, feminine clothing only confuses her manly appearance in this contradictory deference to Temple's authority. The narrator comments that she wore "the mockery of a ruffled cap, that was intended to soften the lineaments of features that were by no means squeamish."[8] "Captain" Hollister, as is customary for his character throughout the book, remains in the background of the scene. The "sargeant" [sic], as Mrs. Hollister refers to her revolutionary-war-veteran husband, is also used to following his wife's directions (TP, 199-200). Later, the Judge's butler refers to the tavern as "Betty Hollister's warm room," confusing legal and patriarchal authority in the Hollister household and business (TP, 234). Mrs. Hollister commands the life of the tavern. She disturbs the line between the separate spheres staked out by the notion of domesticity. Still, marriage and gender restrict her legal power. Her contradictory depiction as masculine, potentially unstable, and abnormal circumscribes her social worth. In this manner, her gender identity, mediated by her class position and laboring condition, resembles normative presentations of masculinity among the subordinated class in the novel's social order.

However, Betty Hollister deploys this masculinity in ways that may disrupt, at least, or rearrange the neatly packaged social hierarchy of Templeton. Masculinity provides her with temporal forms of authority over her workplace and access to public realms, which men dominated at the time. Before the Revolution, women—usually widows—were authorized to own taverns to provide for themselves materially and stay off the public dole. Newly independent American elites, fearful of the potentially socially disruptive nature of the tavern as a political organizing site, sought to exert greater control over tavern ownership. These post-revolutionary laws forced many poor women out of what little control of the industry they held and into publicly funded institutions for their upkeep. In contrast, materially advantaged women found new political power in the temperance movement, in churches, and primarily in the domestic sphere.[9]

Mrs. Hollister refuses to adhere precisely to the rules of the new order. She unapologetically engages her customers in conversation on topics such as religion, law, and the political direction of the Templeton community (TP, 204-12). This gender crossing allows contemporary readers to draw lessons about social order, social station, proper gender division of labor, and the mythology of the Euro-American "civilizing" mission. Mrs. Hollister is a comical counterpoint, an amusing internal opposition to Elizabeth Temple's more appropriate presentation and performativity of feminine womanhood. While the narrator cannot imagine Betty Hollister as a genuine threat to the properly ordered vertical hierarchy of class relations expressed ideologically as "mutual dependence," her characterization and actions do express the narrator's fear of such a possibility—the potential negation of Marmaduke Temple's carefully designed recreation of a feudal order.

From a larger structural perspective, Elizabeth Temple also accomplishes a sort of gender crossing. By helping to free Natty and Edwards, Elizabeth had taken on a masculine role. She had risked both her father's patriarchal authority and the "civilizing" mission implicit in his instruction that "the laws alone remove us from the condition of the savages" (TP, 535). Where then is the difference? Elizabeth's moral rebellion against her father is necessary for the plot's movement towards its climax and the restoration of proper relations. In a genuinely bourgeois catharsis, Marmaduke Temple forgives Elizabeth's rebellion once resolved tensions restore his patriarchal power and unearth her fiancé's true aristocratic identity. Ultimately, Elizabeth's subversion of her father's authority aids the restoration of order and provides genteel justice for highly stationed, though misunderstood, characters. It also renders her potential economic authority impossible. Instead of dialectically negating oppression, Elizabeth's rebellious acts enable a false dialectic. They are negated and subsumed through the restoration of power hierarchies. Against her father's initial wishes, her loyalty to Edwards leads to their marriage and his eventual ownership and control of her father's property through inheritance.

On the other hand, Mrs. Hollister's action in the novel includes leadership of the formation of a failed looting party of "20 curious boys" intent on expropriating a share of the rumored wealth hidden in the mountains of the Judge's property (TP, 605-6).[10] Upon the failure of the endeavor,

Cooper characterizes Mrs. Hollister as a comical character who chastises her husband for his clumsy exploits. She is then rendered invisible throughout the rest of the text. The hierarchical structure of the text contains and renders farcical what could have been an expression of collective struggle to subvert the social arrangements of property and the way wealth is accumulated. Her erasure from the narrative manages her subversion of the gendered division of labor, the performativity of masculinity (through physical appearance, gesture, and social function), and the sanctity of property relations. The novel's complete erasure of Betty Hollister, unlike the elaboration of Elizabeth's central role, reveals a forced intervention to deny a collective, radical overturning of property relations and normative rules of wealth accumulation.

Additionally, the role of Captain Hollister and his relationship with Betty point to significantly divergent gender- and class-based positions and loyalties that appeared in early nineteenth-century U.S. In the British colonies, the militia muster had since the 17th century, served as a basis for rallying Euro-American men of different economic classes to the banner of patriarchy and white supremacy via nationalistic sentiments and calls to defend civilization.[11] By the early 19th century, the militia's leadership fell to the petty bourgeoisie. This modicum of social power effectively enabled a deflection of potential critique of the capitalist class. Additionally, the petty bourgeoisie became economically and ideologically dependent on the emerging capitalist class. Thus, when democratic movements arose threatening the legitimacy and position of the system and ruling-class hegemony, people like Hollister could be counted on to suppress such tendencies.[12] The ruling class would manage its fears about insurgency from below (such as the responses to Shays' rebellion discussed in chapter 1) through settler colonialism (forced acquisitions of Indigenous lands for redistribution through cheap sales to small property holders) and the (re)constructions of Euro-American solidarities in the form of white supremacy. Expropriations of Indigenous land and capital accumulation through enslavement commodified both land and labor. Efficient transactions required both the establishment of the bureaucratic relation to the state, as Jefferson described, and the development of new financial instruments such as credit, debt, insurance, and other instruments of finance capitalism, subverting the feudal imaginary in favor of a capitalist social formation.[13] Capitalism disrupted the imaginary bond between Hollisters and the Temples through a metaphysically ordained chain of being and the ties of place. Instead, a class relation inflected by whiteness and the operation of colonization, mediated through the U.S. nation-state.

Hollister follows this historically assigned task. He forged a powerful economic difference between himself and his wife, reproduced the patriarchal status quo, and comically contributed to preserving class hegemony. Yet Hollister's military role, aside from its ritualistic element of calling out the militia to defend the social order, is unnecessary. According to *The Pioneers'* plot, the legitimacy of the established system of hierarchies is ultimately preserved by revealing the truth about the aristocratic identity of Edwards and his secrets, not Hollister's military prowess. The enlistment of the petty bourgeoisie serves primarily as an act of deference to the entrenched social arrangements of power. Although Judge Temple defers throughout the novel to the law and his powerlessness to go against its dictates (533-35), he alone wields personal authority that can halt the chaos unleashed. He carefully avoids being present at the militia muster to pursue Natty and Edwards (*TP*, 597). He cynically insists that incompetents such as Hollister (and other social inferiors) control the legal forms designed to pretend that democratic justice exists. Despite such claims, it is he alone who "command[s] the peace" (*TP*, 608).[14] Thus, the fragility of Hollister's social position is exposed and further delighted in by his wife. Mrs. Hollister berates her husband for failing to conduct himself bravely and successfully and being "nothing but a shabby captain of malaishy [militia]." Though framed as a failure of masculinity, Mr. Hollister's actions, in Betty's view, point to his class treason. It indicates his impotence under Temple's authority. Her desire for power has been frustrated by the class division and gender loyalties that had fractured the camaraderie presumably formed by their marriage. She suggests his soldierly efforts departed from those of "the raal captain" whose valor in the Revolution was unmatched (*TP*, 605-6). Mr. Hollister's current submission to power compared unfavorably to his rebellious courage of yesteryear.

Women as factory workers

As readers consumed the first copies of Cooper's novel, 1824 saw another kind of collective action in a different historical and spatial frame from that imagined in the book. It was the textile workers' strike in Pawtucket, Rhode Island. Textile manufacturers, to intensify exploitation and raise profits, had cut the amount of time allotted for meals and reduced the rate for unskilled piecework. The textile factories in Pawtucket employed most of the industrial working-class population in the town. Around thirty percent of the factory laborers were women. Further, women were an even larger proportion of the factory population of unskilled laborers affected by the piece-rate cuts. Factory owners wanted to divide their workers along gender lines, incorrectly believing that skilled male workers would not concern themselves with the working conditions of the women.[15] In gender-segregated meetings, the skilled male laborers voted to strike to force the bosses to reestablish the shorter workday, and women workers agreed to walk out until the bosses restored their wages. Collectively the Paw-tucket textile workers took to the streets, closed the mills, and even visited the manufacturers' homes to make their demands known. With broad popular support for the strike, the manu-facturers felt obliged to make concessions and reestablish the usual working hours.

Then the alliance broke down. The capitalists recognized the union and conceded on the working hours issue. The skilled male workers achieved their goal, and they ended the strike when the owners rejected the women workers' demand for higher piece rates. Without this crucial alliance, the unskilled workers were forced to return to their jobs without success. Thus, a vital class alliance was dissolved because intraclass differences in skill were articulated as gender differences. The result was a hierarchy within the newly emerging industrial working class based on the traditionally defined social worth of gender identity.[16]

These definitions of worth were forged via the traditional ideology of domesticity, but contradict the realities of Euro-American working-class women's lives in the mid-19th century. In the early industrial period, working-class women were responsible for domestic reproduction *and* public production to sustain themselves and their families. According to historian Carole Turbin, this position did not have to hinder a united struggle. It provided a location from which women laborers could stand at the forefront of class struggle dialectically linked to struggles against male supremacy, whether in union leadership, as rank-and-file members, or as supporters of union work.[17] These facts demonstrate the concrete reality of the public and private labor continuum. Euro-American working women in Pawtucket's textile mills recognized this reality and deployed active resistance to exploitation and oppression through withholding their labor.

On the other hand, these facts also indicate the persistence of divisions in the alliance of women and men necessary to make an effective movement. Male Euro-American workers exacerbated these fractions through demands for male paternal control over the emerging labor movement. White women workers in this movement deployed a kind of feminist resistance to their male "benefactors" in addition to a class-based opposition to capitalist exploitation.[18] Ultimately, as was the case for some of New York's first union movements, the failure of female labor associations can be directly linked to the refusal of male workers to countenance feminist critiques as necessary to a dialectical understanding of the total structure of exploitation and oppression. As one writer for the labor newspaper *The World* argued, the Working Woman's Association failed because its leaders believed that men's and women's interests were "divergent" and that the feminist goals of the organization were "a perversion of its efforts into indirect and unprofitable channels."[19] In this manner, progressive white male leaders blamed class disunity on social criticism of their male supremacist ideologies. Arguably, the women workers fought for a demystification of what Karl Marx called the dialectical unity of productive and reproductive systems. In *Capital*, he wrote that "[w]hen viewed, therefore, as a connected whole, and as flowing on with incessant renewal, every social process of production is, at the same time, a process of reproduction." Such a viewpoint put into practice would demand equal social value, shared work, and class unity among men and women allotted to a socially constructed gendered division of labor. By staking a claim to equal treatment and pay in the public realm of productive labor, Euro-American women workers asserted a right to shared leadership and unity with male workers in the textile industry. Because they regarded equal relations of men and women as a form of their own victimization, male workers, however, insisted on an affirmation of the social (and monetary) value of the distinction between productive and reproductive labor elevated by the ideology of domesticity.

Although the similarities between the emerging union movement and lower-class revolt in Cooper's *The Pioneers* are apparent in how class insubordination is rendered invisible or ineffectual as a way to preserve white male power, stark contrasts also surface. As historian Alexander Saxton has shown, "the primary thrusts" of Cooper's heroes are imperialist, antiprogressive, and antimodernist, and are concerned "with reaffirm[ing] the politics of deference."[20] The confluence of events set in motion and structured by the novel's social relations reveals contradictions between the feudal social order and the chaos of capitalism' new property and labor regime. As Saxton contends, Natty Bumppo, the protagonist in the Leatherstocking Tales, served as an imaginary popular hero who helped conserve ruling class authority. He paved the way for civilization, reinforced racial hierarchies, and provided a contrast with and critique of lower-class revolt.

Even as Cooper constructed such an ideological stage, the symbolic role of being at the vanguard of U.S. imperialism links Bumppo dialectically to the possibility of revolt symbolized in Betty Hollister. The social space available for her subversive activities is directly created by Bumppo's legitimation of Edwards' older aristocratic claim to property which pre-dates Temple's. She allows racial whiteness to ally her with Bumppo's overarching project of spearheading U.S.

territorial expansion and genocidal destruction of Indigenous societies. This alliance, however, dissolves counter-hegemonic collaborations across race and gender lines.[21] Still, her figurative presence grows and foreshadows the subversion of the feudal economic arrangements and gender hierarchies idealized in *The Pioneers*. While Cooper sought to defend the social order based on deference, his socially subjugated characters ("Jacksonian democrats") and those of the emerging union movement began to dismantle such an ideology.[22] The rebellion against feudal forms of deference that Mrs. Hollister embodied portends the emergence of market capitalism arising in ideological revolt against Cooper's "natural" hierarchical social order. New social relations would also accompany this ideological revolt. The merchant class of small producers would sometimes gain against the large landholders of Temple's milieu, in some cases becoming the new bourgeoisie.[23] Such a class displacement impacted Cooper's father directly, as merchant and finance capitalists whittled away his monopoly control over Cooper's Town.

As the ideologies and practices of patriarchy became differentiated by class and race, another set of textual contradictions appear. The development of public women's labor clashed with the ideology of domesticity. To set themselves apart, emerging middle-class women borrowed the discourse of gender hierarchies, racial differentiation, and economic distinctions to express their new social status. This ideology explained the socially constructed split between the public realm of men and the domestic realm of women. It constructed an assumption of the naturalness of bourgeois social relations and obscured the nagging question of which men and women gained in the new power arrangements. Economically secure women found themselves exempt from performing "productive" labor for a wage. Many found respite from the domestic, unpaid work in their homes because they could afford servants and enslaved people.[24] But most poor women found themselves employed in the "public" sector or who did unpaid "reproductive" labor at home. The ideology of domesticity provided a model of womanhood that affluent white women could deploy for less work. It prevented most working women (white and of

color) from identifying their class interests with male workers and demanded more from them in the household. Further,
employers expected "compliant behavior among women"
workers because the ideology of domesticity contributed to
the view that their jobs were "transient" and their wages "sup-
plemental." They were expected to marry soon and leave the
labor force because their real interests lay at home.[25]

Examining these issues of separate spheres and the site of
domesticity as a location of struggle over class, the meanings of racial hierarchy, and gender difference provide a
unique insight into how working-class alliances are made
and disrupted by articulations of gender and race. Historical
constructions of domestic service as gendered and racialized
in *The Pioneers* point to early industrial hierarchies in U.S. life
and culture. Nonelite white women articulated the ability
to set themselves above the waged and dependent domestic
on the terrain of white supremacy and their racial affiliation
with the ruling class. Both Mrs. Hollister and Remarkable
Pettibone, the Judge's housekeeper, assert racial difference
to secure a modicum of social power arranged through the
"natural" hierarchies. Mrs. Hollister, in describing their African American employee Jude as "the lazy black baste [sic],"
asserts her racial prominence, voiding Jude's ability to participate in any collective identification with Mrs. Hollister as
a laboring subordinate to her husband and the aristocratic
hierarchy in Templeton (*TP*, 200). In so doing, Mrs. Hollister
discursively limits the possibility of Jude's collective alliance
with Remarkable Pettibone based on their common laboring
position. Against this, however, Remarkable foreshadows
the discursive outlines of working-class republicanism when
reflecting on Elizabeth's arrival into the Judge's household.
She finds "the idea of being governed, or of being compelled
to pay the deference of servitude ... absolutely intolerable."
She further articulates servitude and deference in terms of
race: in response to the butler's suggestion that Elizabeth will
be her mistress, Remarkable remarks, "Mistress! ... don't make
one out to be a n----" (*TP*, 231-41).[26] This racialized assertion
of independence precludes alliances based on class with non-
white workers. It assumes the likelihood of class collaboration

with non-working-class whites on issues not immediately discernible as economically in the interest of white workers.

Elizabeth's presence demotes Remarkable from surrogate mother to paid domestic laborer in the Temple household. She also marks such a move as a slip in the racial hierarchy and asserts a racialized characteristic of domestic labor. This "racial division of paid reproductive labor," as Evelyn Nakano Glenn calls it,[27] and the reproduction of hierarchical class-differentiated ideologies and practices point up the difficulty of dialectically understanding the material links between and among racial and gender oppressions that formed significant bases of working-class culture. These links can be interpreted as either the mystifying effects of exchange values assigned to racial positions vis-a-vis labor (i.e., labor assigned both a cash value and a social, racial, and gender value) or as the conscious decision of Euro-American workers to benefit materially and socially from whiteness—probably both.

We can trace these contradictions in critical ways to the republican tradition and contests over its meanings. Bourgeois republicans envisioned a U.S. society that preached political equality but limited such power for Euro-American property holders. As industrializing capitalism produced an unpropertied, proletarianized class of free white men, they reworked this ideology to affirm power residing through possession of male gender identity and racial whiteness. Embedded within this version of republican ideology was the notion of possession and ownership of knowledge, skill, and labor itself.[28] Possession and ownership, the original location of political, cultural, and ideological authority, had been exchanged in the early period of market and industrializing capitalism, to mean not the legal control of real property nor the collective ownership of the means of production but the symbolic property of knowledge and labor within each laborer. White working-class women extended this notion further to elaborate feminine republicanism apart from the middle-class ideology of domesticity and their male class counterparts, though contained usually by white, working-class male paternalism.[29]

At the same time, however, this notion of possession and ownership reinforced the racial boundaries delineated by free and enslaved labor. Euro-American workers, in large part, came to identify themselves as not-slave, not-Black and thus imbued naturally with the political privileges of the republican society. Even the lowliest Euro-American worker could invoke the language of possession and ownership of labor to improve work conditions and have a voice within the political coalitions that dominated electoral politics. Without "necessarily requir[ing] a structural solution," one historian notes, "[w]hite workers could be treated better—reforms could occur."[30] Eventually, economic equality linked to land and to the property of tools and artisanal knowledge in the new republican state was symbolically and materially exchanged for simple possession and ownership of labor, a collective, cross-class, and cross-gender racialized white identity, and, for Euro-American working women, tenuous and short-lived independence from patriarchal versions of women's labor.[31] Under the conditions of dominant industrializing capitalism, whiteness itself became a virtuous and politically enabling republican possession.[32]

Our Nig and its ideological function

The contested possession of labor in the pre-Civil War period served as a primary ideological framework for explaining conditions and the possibilities of resistance to hierarchies of social and political power. When contextualized by this language of white republicanism and bourgeois notions of the ideology of domesticity, Harriet E. Wilson's novel *Our Nig* provides particular subversions of dominant, though structurally differentiated, values. Further, it represents a sustained attack on the whiteness of possession and the republican ideological language that contained the debate on labor in the antebellum U.S.

Wilson's novel tells the story of Frado, a child of mixed racial parentage who, because of her parents' extreme poverty and social marginalization, enters a Euro-American, lower-middle-class household as a domestic laborer. The story's primary thrust blurs the supposed distinction between free Northern labor and enslaved Southern labor as the general characteristic of racialized Black labor. The naming of the story as that of a "free black" upon whom "slavery's shadows" fall fundamentally shapes the irony of a false distinction between freedom and enslavement for Black people when ensnared by U.S. white supremacy.[33] Simultaneously, the novel asserts the contradictions embedded in Euro-American pontifications of Christianity and liberal humanism when structured by the violence of racialized domesticity and the expropriation of surplus value from labor. It, then, imagines the possibility of human liberation unmarked by racial and gender oppression and unbounded by the inequalities of a capitalist organization of labor-power as an expropriated commodity.

These dialectically linked critiques are divulged through the novel's form. This is not to suggest a primacy of form over content but rather to indicate that the material conditions, the social relations, and lived experiences—its content—elaborated in the text necessarily complicate Wilson's use of traditional literary forms. Aside from the content, Wilson's manipulations of form underscore the unspoken, possibly utopian elements lurking beyond the critique. Thus, a critical examination of the novel's form helps organize a reading of its content.[34] The use of the elements of sentimental fiction created by white women in the antebellum period and the blurred use of fictional autobiography, as Henry Louis Gates notes, suggest a particular relation to both forms but with "curious rupture[s]." Combining sentimentalist elements with the slave narrative, the Our Nig relies on the "openness of motives" without negating "aggression or self-esteem" and the will to act out freedom.[35]

Additionally, the novel performs and subverts the formalistic features of the conversion narrative strongly linked to "popular notions of womanhood and domesticity," especially pervasive in the sentimental tradition. Scholar Elizabeth West identifies an "interdependence" between "Christian doctrine and literary constructions of womanhood." She argues that the conversion motif finds its way into the sentimental novel through the salvation of an exposed dependent character. However, because Wilson's protagonist refuses to give in to conversion, the book reveals contradictions between religious ideals and their ideological purposes. West argues that the independence of Wilson's voice, not Christianity, provides the ultimate salvation.[36] An important caveat should be noted. Because, as Henry Louis Gates points out, Wilson's novel is not simply voice or speech but an act of labor embedded in a desperate and ultimately failed gesture to save her son and herself, salvation does not happen, and her voice is ignored until 130 years after she spoke. In this manner, the form of the novel serves to provide a narrative space in which to critique Northern racism without conflating it with chattel slavery. Additionally, the text uplifts the agency of the racialized laboring subject while blasting the hypocrisy of Christian ideological messages interwoven with economically privileged notions of womanhood and domesticity. Since form "ideologically circumscribes" content, Wilson's use and subversion of multiple forms imply a lack of, or at least fractured, ideological loyalty to the "naturalness" or benevolence of U.S. social relations in its emergent industrial capitalist setting.[37]

Beyond these generic forms, the novel performs and contains a series of redundancies. These devices[38] help the reader negotiate a vast space between humanism, embodied in ostensibly good characters, and sadism, enacted by the most brutal characters. This space is neither empty nor arbitrary, however. The careful reader will repeatedly collide with the interactive material processes of racial and gender oppression and economic expropriation of labor's surplus-value and the ideological underpinnings for those social relations. For example, the first of several redundancies that relate to the Bellmont household, to which Frado's impoverished and socially outcast interracial parents abandon her, is the opposition of Mr. Bellmont's "kind, humane" qualities and Mrs. Bellmont's disposition, described as "a whirlwind, charged with fire, daggers and spikes" (ON, 24-25). Although Mr. Bellmont intervenes several times on Frado's behalf–to disrupt extremely severe beatings inflicted by Mrs. Bellmont [ON, 44,47]; retrieve Frado's beloved dog, which Mrs. Bellmont had sold [ON, 62]; allow Frado to attend school [ON, 30] and church against the advice of Mrs. Bellmont [ON, 89]—he is redundantly described as "silent" (ON, 25), as "a man who seldom decided controversies at home" (ON, 30-31), as conspicuously absent during

Mrs. Bellmont's rages (*ON*, 34-35), or simply "unable" to prevent Mrs. Bellmont's cruelty (*ON*, 104).[39] Wilson ultimately reveals the false nature of the opposition between these two characters. In one conversation, Mrs. Bellmont reminds her husband of the "profit" accrued to them from Frado's labor, which Mr. Bellmont gladly accepts (*ON*, 90).

Such episodes are repeated with the "kind" characters: the sons, James and Jack; the lovely but disabled daughter, Jane; and the religiously pious Aunt Abby. Although these characters repeatedly sympathize with Frado's "fate" and sometimes successfully prevent the fullest expressions of Mrs. Bellmont's wrath, their presence in the novel is also marked by various forms of inaction or incapacity. Aunt Abby is unwilling to risk her precarious position in the household through interference. Jane's physical weakness and departure through her marriage prevent her sustained assistance on Frado's behalf. Although he promises to bring Frado with him soon, John leaves the household searching for his fortune. James perpetually promises to take Frado away from his cruel mother, but his sickness and ultimate death prevent such a beneficial action. Notably, Wilson extends the scope of these redundancies to the nonfictional world of "professed abolitionists" who fail to live up to their antislavery ideals by ignoring "slavery's shadows" in the North (*ON*, 129).[40]

On the surface, these recurring episodes of failed attempts at kindness engage the reader's sympathy for the good characters, demonstrating the importance of the humane treatment of dependent individuals. Likewise, they superficially invoke the possibility of the alliance of the protagonists against racial prejudice and brutal treatment, in the process preserving the humanity of the oppressor and oppressed. Why, then, does the narrator describe Fido, Frado's dog, as "a more valuable presence than the human beings who surrounded her"? And, why at the dog's death does Frado "shed more tears over him than overall beside," referring to the deaths of James, whom she loved dearly, and Mary, the cruel daughter of Mrs. Bellmont whose end she celebrated (*ON*, 62, 117)? Wilson purposefully unpacks the myriad of social relations that structure the social formation and simultaneously debunks the ideological formations that obscure those relations, including liberal humanism. The formalistic device of redundancy allows Wilson to propose specious differences among the various characters regarding how they relate to Frado. The subsequent exposure of falsity enables her to show how power and privilege preclude even the most humane protagonists from maintaining a meaningful alliance with Frado (or, in the case of abolitionists, with free northern African Americans).

One significant ideological formation that the story demystifies is the ideology of domesticity in Euro-American households. The achievement of elite status and "true womanhood" rested significantly on a Euro-American woman's ability to avoid paid public labor, be financially able to hire domestic labor, and confine her work to that of household management. (It is this ideologically defined space of labor and value in which Mr. Bellmont rarely intervenes.) Mrs. Bellmont realizes this social value upon Frado's arrival into the household. She quickly injects certain racial assumptions into true womanhood that mark the ideology as economically elitist and racially white. She comments on the value of Frado's learning to do her (Mrs. Bellmont's) work. But then she adds, "I have so much trouble with the girls I hire, I am almost persuaded if I have one to train up in my way from a child, I shall be able to keep them awhile" (*ON*, 26). Mrs. Bellmont suggests that Black women are suitable only for work:

> [Y]ou know these n- - - are just like black snakes; you can't kill them. If she wasn't tough she would have been killed long ago. There was never one of my girls who could do half the work (*ON*, 88-89).

The implication here is that white domestic laborers (which included Frado's white mother for a short period [*ON*, 9]) display a lack of willingness to submit to Mrs. Bellmont's sadistic domination. Unspoken is that the whiteness of a woman worker induces regular payment, specific limits on terms of service, and the likelihood of job actions (in this instance, quitting) in the event of unfair treatment. This way, Mrs. Bellmont's former white employees limited her class authority and ability to perform the role of true womanhood.[41] Frado's membership in the household, though rife with a tendency to rebellion, is unpaid. Mrs. Bellmont assumes the term of service to be eighteen years, and Frado's youth permits training for complete submission.

Further, in the novel's preface, Mrs. Bellmont is described as "wholly imbued with southern principles" (*ON*, preface). Taking in Frado enforced her belief that racially inferior workers can best perform menial labor. Thus, Mrs. Bellmont's social status as a "true woman" derives from her exploitative and oppressive dominance of Frado's domestic labor. In the North, although domestic labor could not be racialized as Black because of the small number of Black women, African American working women almost exclusively could be designated as domestic labor. Phillip S. Foner reports that as many as 80 percent of Black women workers earned their living as domestic servants in some urban areas. Most of the other 20 percent worked as skilled seamstresses, though not fairly remunerated.[42] While Frado's indentured status may not have been typical among African American women in the antebellum North, circumscribed opportunities in other fields of work, meager wages, and the racially devalued status of the labor performed produced similar material effects.

Wilson produces in this narrative a complex picture of a dialectically linked web of social relations characterized by an expropriative positioning of dominance and subordination. Mr. Bellmont allows his wife's domestication of the household to preserve her racial and economic status. But he retains for himself patriarchal authority and ownership of household production. Mrs. Bellmont's control of the domestic sphere means the ability to extract "profits" in terms of saved labor time, higher returns from household products through low wages, and social status as a "true woman." Wilson further implies the generalization of these particular relations throughout the North. Bellmont's liberal attitudes strongly parallel him with "professed abolitionists," who ignored racial prejudice in their own homes and region. Although he attempts specific kindnesses to Frado, he gains materially from her continued indentured status. Other liberals of his class may also have exhibited specific acts of generosity but were actively complicit in a system of racial hierarchies through the material exploitation of the domestic labor of African American women. These social relations linked the Bellmonts to a broader group of households that held shared class and racial interests. Indeed, class consciousness is construed in fundamental ways through highly gendered spaces of the household framework.

Opposition to this common class interest arose through the employer/employee relation. Domestic workers were able to deploy a series of resistances to employer domination. They might have used a racialized working-class republicanism, if they were anything like Remarkable Pettibone from *The Pioneers*. Wilson only hints at this, but her narrative works to point up the limits of this labor-based ideology. As noted above, working-class republicanism centered on the ownership and possession of labor (independence) and the whiteness of the worker. Frado's resistive acts, on the other hand, do not garner her the same gains in the conditions of her workplace as her white counterparts. At the same time, however, those acts provide Frado with brief leisure time, sometimes momentary pleasure in laughter, and on at least one occasion, "the stirring of free and independent thoughts" (*ON*, 105). By feigning interest in church, she gets Mr. Bellmont to agree to allow her time from work to attend church (*ON*, 86-90). Her prankish antics at school and in the fields provide her with laughter, entertainment, and a modicum of camaraderie with her audiences (*ON*, 32, 37-39). And, perhaps most importantly, her threatened work stoppage in response to Mrs. Bellmont's arbitrary violence wins her a momentary victory against a beating and a permanent sense of potentially independent selfhood.

However, as a young adult, Frado despairs escape from the Bellmont household via the socially proscribed avenue of marriage. "She was black, no one would love her" (*ON*, 108). Thus, her deliverance comes by way of finding work elsewhere and "becom[ing] expert with her needle the first year of her release from Mrs. B." (*ON*, 122). After years of sickness and living on the charity of others, she meets a "friend" who "kindly provided her with a valuable recipe" with which she attempts to make a living (*ON*, 129). Although her skill surpasses her instructor's knowledge, it does not authorize Frado's member-ship in a leading role of the labor union movement as skill had done for white male workers in Pawtucket. It does not provide her access to the social benefits of republican citizenship, nor even the fundamental right of adequate social reproduction, as her health fails and her son, sent away to be cared for by public charity, dies without being returned to her (*ON*, 129). In this manner, an outside benefactor helps her secure indepen-dence, though rife with uncertainty.[43]

Ultimately, Wilson envisions the possibility of a humane, moral society. In a discussion of the "economic identities" in *Our Nig*, literary scholar John Ernest concludes that Wilson envisions a society built around a "marketplace economy" that "depends on ... inevitable conflict," and that conflict "may contain the terms of mutual dependence, the demands of col-lective survival." In his view, if entered into by socially equal human beings, that conflict provides the basis of "a genuine and morally secure community of interests," as implicit in the story of Frado's parents.[44] In the final instance, he does not believe that Wilson is critiquing early industrial capitalism under formation in the antebellum northern United States. He bases this argument on what he reads as Wilson's conscious effort to avoid reinforcing the anti-industrialist opinions deliv-ered by proslavery Southern critics of the North who argued that the dialectical synthesis of class struggle was slavery and her efforts to earn a living by entering the marketplace with her product. According to Ernest, she constructs an imagi-nary space of multiple subjectivities in conflict, which would lead to humane capitalism when imbued with an alignment of authentic Christian principles and actions. In this fram-ing, Wilson's politics may be remarkably related to William Cooper's sense of the viability of "mutual dependence."

"Mutual dependence," however, functions as an ideologi-cal mystification of the expropriative nature of early capitalist social relations and the racial prejudice and gender inequality articulated in those relations through the pretense that the pow-erful are equally dependent on the subordinate classes within an organic social order. Wilson, however, is not defending such an ideological practice under early industrial capitalism;

she is dismantling it and revealing its hidden inequality. Contrary to the claims of another scholar, Wilson's intent is not to show "faith" in "the principles associated" with "the northern economic system." *Our Nig* is not an argument for the benefits of participation of individuals as laborers in the capitalist market. While the claim that Wilson favors emergent industrial capitalism based on wage labor may appear to be supported by the narrator's repeated expression of her ability to earn a living, though meager, to enjoy leisure activities provided by limited hours of work, and on the principle that "presumably commits an employer to the terms of a mutually binding contract." Additionally, being free of "slavery's shadows," a reference that includes northern capitalism, would benefit all. A Marxist reading of Wilson's text places her heroine closer to the women of the "community of slaves," to borrow Angela Davis' term, than to white working-class women who used hostility toward enslaved Black women and servants to define their racial superiority and desire for freedom.[45]

Racism and the gendered division of labor within capitalist relations of production and upon which the dominance of those relations depend negate the assumed reduction of the worker to abstract labor units.[46] Indeed, Wilson's text deliberately dramatizes how the gendered division of labor and arbitrary racial segmentation of the workforce deny this abstraction. This distortion of power renders the mutuality of employment contracts a farce, especially for Black women (enslaved or free). While Frado enjoyed the first two of these three "benefits" of labor during her time with the Bellmonts, the latter depends on the labor movement's ability to coerce the employer into such a contract. As was shown with the Pawtucket strike, its causes derived from the arbitrary deviance from the "mutually binding contract"—a perpetual character of capitalism. Further, Mrs. Bellmont's "trouble" with white domestic servants implies the presence of a collective resistance among white women to the kind of treatment she wished to apply. Her resort to hiring a Black woman stems from a desire for total domination of the servant rooted in racial positioning and white supremacy. In either case, Frado realizes that white workers have some social power to deploy collective resistances that exclude her through racialist pro-scriptions. Frado's knowledge of these facts contextualized by her distrust of other social relations reveals how her resort to entry into the market (as a worker and a writer) is at best a pragmatic gesture at survival rather than advocacy of capitalist commodity forms as a source of freedom. While this narrative also reveals a consciousness of labor's collective transforma-tive power through conscious struggle, the overall success of this latter depends on what she shows to be missing across the subordinate working class: multi-gendered, multi-racial alli-ances combined with a more fundamental critique of social relations.

Elsewhere in his otherwise excellent article, however, Ernest argues that "Wilson deliberately and forcefully conflates the economic situations of working-class whites and culturally enslaved 'free' blacks."[47] He fails to follow the implications of Wilson's thought. Wilson links her critique of racism and "true womanhood" with a deconstruction of the language of republican possession and ownership of "whiteness." The pos-session of these social objects is tied explicitly to the hypocrisy of a "free" society constituted by exploited labor with "mutual dependence" as its foundation. In doing so, Wilson negates the ideological tendency toward fragmenting or mystifying the social totality of capitalism, imperialism, patriarchy, and racism. By connecting the product of the individual's labor—i.e., her novel—to the social relations that produced it, Wilson articulates the part to the whole without confusing either.

Because these logics require a structure of expropriation that could not exist in a liberated, truly "Christian" society, Wilson exposes the contradictions that make possible the capi-talist marketplace. She is not merely calling for reform through the abstraction of the racialized and gendered subject. She is not simply trying to make race and gender matter less in the capitalist marketplace. While the narrator imagines herself as unlovable and ugly, she never desires deracination or nega-tion of her complex social identity. Instead, this text exposes the racial formation and sexism that necessarily constitute free enterprise and capitalist relations of production. In other words, she shows how capitalism relies on those features to exist. And by dialectically imagining the early industrial U.S. social totality, Wilson imagines the immanent field of collective opposition, prefigured in her biological parent's relationship based on the absolute negation of privilege (ON, 12-15)[48] and suggested by her call in the preface to her "colored brethren universally for patronage"—a collectivity perhaps fraught with colliding interests, specificities, and experiences but imbued with the potential for a non-expropriative ideology.

Besides their location within specific historical conditions and their contrapuntal treatment of similar cultural and material themes, what do Cooper's *The Pioneers* and Wilson's *Our Nig* have in common? Both imaginatively represent a social whole. Cooper's world is the ideological construction of a patriarchal community delineated by class, articulated by feudal forms of social station and "mutual dependence," contained by patriarchy and white supremacy. Wilson's protagonist encounters a social formation fragmented by social and cultural divisions of labor and anti-humanist hierarchies, which she narrates dialectically into a social whole. But as Cooper's imaginary world expands beyond the text, receding into a romanticized past, Wilson attempts to locate new ground in an unimaginable future. As Mrs. Hollister and Remarkable Pettibone disrupt *The Pioneers'* structural intentions and portend the emergence of market capitalism with its organization of labor strife, Harriet-Frado becomes the text and prefigures enormous possibilities on the cusp of the Civil War crisis and the emergence of new freedoms hindered or helped by new struggles over racial liberation and class inequality. Though forgotten by her oppressors, "she will never cease to track them beyond mortal vision" (*ON*, 131).

Dialectical wholes and utopia

Wilson's novelization of the totalizing project of capitalism via its emergent technologies of white supremacy, male supremacy, and authoritarian labor relations (enabling the transition from the slavery regime) poses a fundamental question that her book and life could not fully answer. How does a precariously positioned Black woman in such a society surmount, transcend, escape, or otherwise avoid the totalizing structure of that exploitation and oppression? Publishing a fictionalized autobiography, self-making resulted in few financial benefits. Like the Pequot Nation's treatment in its surrender treaty with the U.S, her work was forgotten for more than a century. A structured erasure of a life.

Similar distortions of memory have shaped how the life and thought of Sojourner Truth are retained in the popular imagination. In her definitive biography of Sojourner Truth, eminent historian Nell Irvin Painter explores the history of two important but radically different representations of Sojourner Truth. In 1851, Truth delivered what has since become a famous speech at the Akron, Ohio women's rights convention. Because Truth never learned to read or write, her sermons, speeches, and autobiography, when they were recorded, were done so by white writers. These included writer Olive Gilbert (co-author of *The Narrative of the Life of Sojourner Truth*), newspaper editor Marius Robinson (recording secretary of the 1851 convention), and abolitionist and women's rights activist Frances Dana Gage (whose account was published 12 years after the convention). Gage's convention account is most well-known for rendering Sojourner Truth through a stereotypical Southern Black dialect instead of Truth's Dutch-influenced Northern accents.[49]

It is impossible to reproduce precisely how Truth spoke without actual audio recordings. Still, Painter's argument reveals how the famous "Arn't I a woman" rendering registers as Gage's way to emphasize Truth's Blackness and the Southern geography of slavery.[50] Gage published her account in 1863, in the depths of the war over slavery. Each account of her famous speech, however, reflected a particular usage of Truth's words at the moment it was published. And while it is certain that Truth listened to readings of her *Narrative* by objective parties to control her public image, she would not have been able to manage secondary representations of her 1851 Akron speech.[51]

Truth's words should be the crucial source of meaning. However, as Painter further reveals, Truth's experiences as a public speaker were deeply inflected by the total performance of preaching (drafting the words and performing them). Gestures, inflection of voice, looks, and the perceived positionalities of the audience all produced a rhetorical situation with which Truth had learned to masterfully read and interact (even if potential racism and sexism among her audience members distorted their reception and production of the meaning). Those elements are not captured solely by reading a text, especially text recorded by another person. The close relation between bodily enactment and production of knowledge production highlights the value of the body in a primarily oral cultural setting. It closely connects body function to mental and intellectual processes.[52]

Therefore, to discuss the Akron speech, which holds a vital, if unstable, place within American letters, I rely here upon the immediately rendered recording by Marius Robinson, who, according to Painter, "was used to her way of speaking."[53] One notable element of this speech, given by a formerly enslaved Black woman without formal education, is Sojourner Truth's acknowledgment and rejection of the Euro-American culture of victimization. Instead, she frames a reversal of power relations as freeing for Euro-American men. Discarding male supremacy and other oppression will allow them to avoid being burdened by the struggle to hold onto it as an exclusive privilege. She asserts a spiritually ordained human order that dispenses with that fatal and destructive emotional reaction to potential loss of power. The world she envisions dispenses with dominant rules of white supremacy, emergent capitalist market relations, and property rights as signifiers of social and civilizational progress. That spiritually inflected social formation is based on communistic determinations of ownership, production, and distribution, egalitarian types of gender relations, and the complete elimination of racial supremacy. In addition to her rejection of white victimization ideology, Truth also asserts limits on perceptions of social progress under capitalist arrangements of power and relations.

My argument here follows, with some variation, Painter's investigation and analysis, which is based on acknowledging the radical context of the Akron meeting and its participants. After freeing herself from enslavement in 1827,[54] Sojourner

Truth spent large portions of the next 24 years living in intentional communities. Those communities sharply criticized and rejected emergent capitalist modernity. They expressed a radical opposition to U.S. class inequalities, exploitations, and racist and sexist oppression. These motives drove the adoption of separate forms of social organization. Painter's exploration of the communities Truth opted to live in reveals how direct and indirect affiliations shaped her and many of the people who attended the Akron meeting with such ideas. While Painter emphasizes Truth's spirituality and a personal search for community and family in connection with such a movement, I argue that Truth was a utopian socialist, a fact rarely included in popular images of the feminist abolitionist preacher.[55]

With this context in mind, critical meanings within Sojourner Truth's thought emerge more clearly as articulated in this speech. Painter's thoughtful discussion of the speech is worth using as a frame and foundation for some new conclusions. First, as Painter shows, Truth presents three significant metaphors in the short speech to signify social relations of production and the limits of the existing political system: the body, the mind, and Biblical stories. According to Robinson's recording of the speech, Truth spoke of bodily tropes like this:

> I am a woman's rights. I have as much muscle as any man, and can do as much work as any man. I have plowed and reaped and husked and chopped and mowed, and can any man do more than that? I have heard much about the sexes being equal; I can carry as much as any man, and can eat as much too, if I can get it. I am as strong as any man that is now.

As Painter notes, this specific narration of Truth's physical prowess directly references her work as an enslaved person. (Since self-emancipation, Truth primarily worked as a domestic worker in urban settings or communes rather than as an agricultural laborer.) By deploying this context, Truth demands that her audience infer that her enslaved labor-power (undertaken for someone else's profit) and her enslaved body (as a form of capital owned by another human) are intimately bound together in the present.

Because her body is racialized as Black and gendered as female, she refuses a separation of systems of patriarchy, capitalism, and racial slavery. Usage of the term "man" throughout the speech refers not simply to any individual man. It registers as the structural position of enslaver, capitalist, and patriarch who wields the dominant power over a system that denies women equality, owns human beings, and profits from such systems. Truth's discussion of the process of cultivating, harvesting, processing, and consuming ("when she can get it") agricultural products, as Painter notes, stood explicitly and deliberately "as the symbol of [the American] economy."[56] By articulating her Self as a fusion of her labor power and body with the central feature of U.S. economic productivity and claiming the totality of her being within this formation as "a woman's rights," Truth emphasizes her typicality, the dialectical relation of herself with all oppressed people (women, enslaved, exploited). In so doing, she discards the sanctity of property law and dominant social relations of production. She turns to the bodily production of labor power as the source of rights, the claim to political power, and the fountainhead of equal footing with the enslaver, the capitalist, and the patriarch—by definition, a complete subversion and overturning of those necessarily linked systems.

The symbolic gesture harkens back to the notion of republican agrarianism as the idealized version of economic activity in a free society as articulated by Jefferson (see note 12 in the introduction). Jefferson's *Notes* locates property rights, political power, and civilization in a skin-color-based racial identity. He articulates a bureaucratic process of purchasing, creating titles for, and establishing the legal basis of property ownership, rules of inheritance, and other rational modes of social organization. In 1851, Truth subverted this bureaucratized system as the origin of rights in favor of the direct producer—defined as a bodily human—as the source of physical and spiritual power and political and moral power. Her political theory denies the Jeffersonian conceptualization of whiteness, property, and the state as the fountainhead of social rights and power. Indeed, she shifts revolutionary subjectivity to "woman" and, by inference, "Black."

Painter explores Truth's ironic use of the mind and the Biblical metaphors to mock the idea that women are intellectually inferior and that Christian religious doctrine elevates men above women. Truth said:

> As for the intellect, all I can say is, if a woman have a pint and man a quart—why can't she have her little pint full? You need not be afraid to give us our rights for fear we will take too much–for we can't take more than our pint'll hold. The poor men seem to be all in confusion, and don't know what to do.

And, further, referring to the Biblical story of Eve and original sin:

> I have heard the Bible and have learned that Eve caused man to sin. Well if woman upset the world, do give her a chance to set it right side up again. … And how came Jesus into the world? Through God who created him and woman who bore him. Man, where is your part?

Men are confused and unable to think clearly about the problem of equality. Contrary to the dominant discourse, equality is not a matter of male victimization but total empowerment and shared leadership. Surrendering their sole claim on all power, men can find relief and freedom. The "burden" of this power is what victimizes men. In the present circumstances, "man" may be in for troubling times, as "the poor slave is on him, woman is coming on him, and he is surely between a hawk and a buzzard." Further, Jesus, the foundational character of the country's dominant religion, resulted from the co-creative act between God and Mary. If these figurative elements are pieced together with the foundational concept of labor power rooted in an alternative set of social relations of production, Truth's utopian vision emerges.

Truth concisely creates a unity of the body, the mind, the historical construction of humanity (via the Bible), and the revolutionary agency of "woman." This mind-body-spirit unity constructs the basis of her typicality as "a woman's rights." This unity and revolutionary agency are logically on the side

of the oppressed who are threatening "man's" imminent overthrow. In her thought and actions, Truth answers the question
left posed by Wilson. Women, a subjective positionality of all
that is subordinate—exploited, enslaved, racially oppressed
persons—are positioned to solve the ills of the world created by confused men. Suppose men's resistance to equality
forestalls progress. In that case, the alternative will involve
dangers posed by the violent overturning of the social order
(a hint at slave insurrection and civil war). Capitalist markets
and attendant ideological delusions about social progress,
notwithstanding, fundamental social transformation rooted
in a revolutionary subjectivity, a complete reversal of existing forms of power, offers the starting point for actual social
progress.

Notes

1. On dialectical materialism, see Louis Althusser, *For Marx*, trans by Ben Brewster, (New York: Verso, 1999); Louis Althusser and Etienne Balibar. 1999. *Reading
   Capital*, translated by Ben Brewster, (New York: Verso, 1999). As a mode of the-
   oretical production, dialectical materialism enables the imaginative connection
   of apparently disparate, de-linked, or mystified material conditions: standpoints,
   intersections, and possible alliances in struggles against imperialism, capitalism, patriarchy, and racism. See also E. San Juan Jr., *Hegemony and Strategies of
   Transgression: Essays in Cultural Studies and Comparative Literature*, (Albany: State
   University of New York Press, 1995), especially chapter 4.
2. Marxist economist Samir Amin's term "tributary," with its more capacious definition than feudal, registers the transitional moments imagined in Cooper's *The
   Pioneers*. Amin describes the culture of feudalism as the "triumph of metaphys-
   ics." He refers to the hegemonic belief in the sacredness of the ideological order
   that defines explicit class exploitation as both a matter of what God wants and a
   form of mutual dependence between classes of humans. It is also characterized
   by the subordinate class's traditional, generational ties to a particular plot of earth
   (which it does not own but has a limited right of use). Samir Amin, Eurocentrism,
   translated by Russell Moore, (New York: Monthly Review Press, 1989), 28. E. San
   Juan, Jr. "Literary Studies in the Age of Empire's Collapse," *Danyag: Journal of
   Humanities and Social Sciences*, Vol. 14, no. 1 (2009): 10.
3. See Robert Spiller, "Fenimore Cooper's Defense of Slave-Owning America,"
   American Historical Review, Vol. 35, no. 3 (1930), 581. Spiller's article includes the
   original text of Cooper's commentary for a French publication. Cooper argued
   that the abolition of slavery would negate white supremacy and racial purity. At
   this point, we may detect a congruence between Cooper's and Wilson's thought.
   While the former laments its potential loss, the latter despairs it will not come
   soon enough.
4. Wilson's work was re-discovered by Henry Louis Gates. This rediscovery should
   not be viewed as a mere coincidence or accident. It was a function of the struggles

of African Americans for equality and the emergence of African American studies as a field of academic inquiry that developed out of that struggle.

5. Ashwill develops an analysis of counter-hegemonic writings by Native American writers. See, for example, Gary Ashwill, "Savagism and Its Discontents: James Fenimore Cooper and his Native American Contemporaries," *American Transcendental Quarterly*, Vol. 8, no. 2 (1994): 211-27; Sidner Larson, "Fear and Contempt: A European Concept of Property," *American Indian Quarterly*, Vol. 21, no. 2 (1997): 567- 77; Susan Scheckel, *The Insistence of the Indian: Race and Nationalism in Nineteenth-Century American Culture*, (Princeton, NJ: Princeton University Press, 1998). These authors discuss Cooper's use of white perceptions of Indigenous people to develop Euro-American concepts of national identity, property, and value. See Alexander Saxton's reading of Cooper's opus generally in his *The Rise and Fall of the White Republic: Class Politics and Mass Culture in Nineteenth-Century America*, (New York: Verso, 1990), especially chapter 8.

6. Alan Taylor, *William Cooper's Town: Power and Persuasion on the Frontier of the Early American Republic*, (New York: Vintage Books, 1995), 418-419.

7. Taylor, 104.

8. James Fenimore Cooper, *The Pioneers*, (New York: Lancer Books, 1968 [1823]), 155-156. Hereafter cited in the text as *TP*.

9. David W. Conroy, *In Public Houses: Drink and the Revolution of Authority in Colonial Massachusetts*, (Chapel Hill: University of North Carolina Press, 1995) 310-322. While revolutionary leaders had relied on taverns to mobilize political opposition to Britain. Post-revolutionary leaders, including the likes of Samuel Adams, sought to limit the space for such activity. The tavern was a key target. Liquor licensing and the consolidation of alcohol production limited tavern-keeping to politically dependent people. This process helped define and demarcate separate gendered spheres in some crucial ways.

10. The narrator states that this looting party's organization and mobilization took place at the Bold Dragoon, the Hollisters' tavern. Further, textual evidence indicates that Mrs. Hollister led this particular group. Later, when crisis demanded the militia's mobilization, Mrs. Hollister was "too busily engaged with certain preparations of her own, to make her comments" on its preparedness for conflict. And at the mountain, Mrs. Hollister "was followed by 20 curious boys" (*TP*, 597, 605).

11. Kathleen Brown, *Good Wives, Nasty Wenches, and Anxious Patriarchs: Gender, Race, and Power in Colonial Virginia*, (Chapel Hill: University of North Carolina Press, 1996), 137-186.

12. Arno J. Mayer, "The Lower Middle Class as Historical Problem." *Journal of Modern History*, Vol. 47, no. 2 (1975): 414-416.

13. See Edward Baptist, *The Half Has Never Been Told: Slavery and the Making of American Capitalism*, New York: Basic Books, 2014), 229.

14. As observed in chapter 1, however, Temple's establishment of personal authority did not reflect reality, as thousands of troops and years of repression were required to bring frequent rebellion in the new country under control.

15. Gary B. Kulik. "Patterns of Resistance to Industrial Capitalism: Pawtucket Village and the Strike of 1824," in *American Working-Class Culture: Explorations in American Labor and Social History*, eds. Milton Cantor, (Westport, CT: Greenwood Press, 1979), 209-240.

16. Philip S. Foner, *Women and the American Labor Movement: From Colonial Times to the Eve of World War I*, (New York: Free Press, 1979), 29.

17. Carole Turbin, "Beyond Conventional Wisdom: Women's Wage Work, Household Economic Conditions, and Labor Activism in a Mid-Nineteenth-Century Working-Class Community," in *"To Toil the Livelong Day": America's Women at Work, 1780-1980,* eds. by Carol Groneman and Mary Beth Norton, (Ithaca, NY: Cornell University Press, 1987), 47-67.

18. Foner argues that women's unionizing efforts were thwarted by male hostility. Stansell nuances this argument. She shows that class consciousness informed by male paternalism could soften hostility and help male workers form benevolent cooperative relations with women workers. Still, sexist attitudes, such as paternalism, could easily lead to divisions by gender that weakens class power. Foner, 38-54; Stansell, 137-149. See also Dolores Janiewski, "Making Common Cause: The Needle-women of New York, 1831-1869," *Signs,* Vol. 1, no. 4 (1976): 778-86.

19. Janiewski, 786.

20. Alexander Saxton, *The Rise and Fall of the White Republic: Class Politics and Mass Culture in Nineteenth-Century America,* (New York: Verso, 1990), 193-194.

21. Mrs. Hollister to define and enforce the "naturalness" of racial hierarchies by describing her one female employee as "the lazy black baste [sic]" and by assuming the dichotomy of "savage" and Christian when speaking of Indigenous people *(TP,* 200, 204-5).

22. Saxton, 194.

23. As emerging industrial capitalism created "economies of scale." Huge tracts of lands that formed the material basis of a Temple's imagined community with a single family at its head were broken up into smaller sites that produce for markets. Instead of a sacred connection to a feudal lord, an individualized, secular relation to the market is constructed. Capitalist agriculture functioned better through direct links between finance capital and smaller household units, access or the hope for access to a larger racially-defined class of landowners, and a domestic household ideology based on a gendered division of labor. Property owners came into economic relations with one another. They formed social classes based not on aristocratic or familial allegiances but on economic relations set in motion by the market and ideologies that governed social hierarchies. See Paul E. Johnson, *The Shopkeeper's Millennium: Society and Revivals in Rochester, New York, 1815-1837,* (New York: Hill and Wang, 1978), 15-36.

24. Evelyn Nakano Glenn, "From Servitude to Service Work: The Racial Division of Paid Reproductive Labor," in *History and Theory: Feminist Research, Debates, Contestations,* eds. Barbara Laslett et al., (Chicago: University of Chicago Press, 1997); Alice Kessler-Harris, *Women Have Always Worked: A Historical Overview,* (Old Westbury, NY: Feminist Press, 1981), 35-44.

25. Kessler-Harris, 63; Turbin, 48-50.

26. The significant difference in how Remarkable and Mrs. Hollister assert racial ideas implies their constructions of differences between themselves. Remarkable signifies a protest against diminished status in racial terms. At the same time, Mrs. Hollister simply describes her employee and echoes dominant perceptions of Native Americans' status as savages, invoking Christian-based ideological reasons for American imperialism *(TP,* 205). While the first is the articulation of a laborer, the latter is expressed through a social position that assumes a collective identification with her husband and Templeton's elites, which directly benefits materially from territorial expropriation. Thus, prescriptions are forged here on intergender alliance based in class and articulated in terms of race.

27. Glenn, 113.
28. Ronald Schultz, *The Republic of Labor: Philadelphia Artisans and the Politics of Class, 1720-1830.* New York: Oxford University Press, 1993), 4ff; David Roediger, *The Wages of Whiteness: Race and the Making of the American Working Class,* (New York: Verso, 1991), 45; Christine Stansell, *City of Women: Sex and Class in New York, 1789-1860,* (New York: Knopf, 1986), 190; Alexander Saxton, *The Indispensable Enemy: Labor and the Anti-Chinese Movement in California,* (Berkeley: University of California Press, 1976) 37.
29. Stansell, 146-147.
30. Roediger, 73.
31. Roediger, 43-60; Stansell, 151-153. The earliest versions of U.S. socialism articulated theories of common ownership of both labor and the means of production. Some within this tradition also struggled against accepting the benefits of whiteness within the labor movement. See, for example, Saxton, 37-41.
32. The concept of racial possession is also explored by George Lipsitz, *The Possessive Investment in Whiteness: How White People Profit from Identity Politics,* Twentieth Anniversary Edition, (Philadelphia, Temple University Press, 2018); Alyosha Goldstein, "Possessive Investment: Indian Removals and the Affective Entitlements of Whiteness," *American Quarterly,* Vol. 66, no. 4 (2014): 1077-1084.
33. Harriet E. Wilson, *Our Nig: or, Sketches from the Life of a Free Black, in a Two-story House North, Showing that Slavery's Shadows Fall Even Here.* (New York: Vintage Books, 1983). Hereafter cited in the text as *ON.*
34. Terry Eagleton, *Marxism and Literary Criticism,* (Berkeley: University of California Press, 1976), 20-36. Annette T. Rubinstein, "Fundamental Problems in Marxist Literary Criticism: Form, History and Ideology," *Socialism and Democracy,* 11, no. 1 (1997): 3-11.
35. Gates, *Figures,* 126, 143.
36. Elizabeth J. West, "Reworking the Conversion Narrative: Race and Christianity in *Our Nig,*" *MELUS,* Vol. 24, no. 2 (1999): 3, 10-11.
37. Eagleton 26. According to Hazel V. Carby, Wilson's understanding of her existence in southern conditions in a northern situation shaped her critique of domesticity that influenced her decision to "[adapt] literary conventions to more adequately conform to a narrative representation and re-creation of black experience." Hazel V. Carby, *Reconstructing Womanhood: The Emergence of the Afro-American Woman Novelist,* (New York: Oxford University Press, 1987), 45. In contrast to the other criticism cited here, Lovell misreads Wilson's commitment to the sentimental novel as creating a "salutary view of wage labor" in early industrial capitalism. Thomas B. Lovell, "By Dint of Labor and Economy: Harriet Jacobs, Harriet Wilson, and the Salutary View of Wage Labor," *Arizona Quarterly,* Vol. 52, no. 3 (1996): 24-25.
38. The term "redundancy" is borrowed, with some variation, from scholar Barbara Foley. She suggests that this technique helps expose "social forces impelling the protagonist to develop and change" and depict "other characters whose lives intersect with and parallel that of the protagonist." Barbara Foley, *Radical Representations: Politics and Form in U.S. Proletarian Fiction, 1929-1941,* (Durham, NC: Duke University Press, 1993), 331.
39. However, this silence and absence should not be misread as Mrs. Bellmont's ultimate dominance of the family. Bellmont asserts his patriarchal authority on the issues of Frado's education and of his daughter Jane's marriage (*ON,* 60).
40. Wilson uses the term "slavery's shadows" in the full subtitle of the novel.

41. In this way, racial advantage works to the disadvantage of the white woman worker who may be denied a job because of the presumed difficulty she presents to employer authority.

42. Philip S. Foner, *Organized Labor and the Black Worker, 1619-1973*, (New York: Praeger, 1974), 4-6.

43. See also Henry Louis Gates, *Figures in Black: Words, Signs and the "Racial" Self*, (New York: Oxford University Press, 1987), 139.

44. John Ernest, "Economies of Identity: Harriet E. Wilson's *Our Nig*," *PMLA*, Vol. 109 no. 4 (1994): 435.

45. Lovell, 20. Angela Davis, "Reflections on Black Woman's Role in the Community of Slaves," in *The Angela Davis Reader*, ed. Joy James, (New York: Routledge, 2000), 119-128;

46. See Joel Wendland-Liu, "'Indifferent Commodities' and 'Abstract Labor-power': Angela Davis' Critique of White Supremacy and U.S. Racial Capitalism," *Peace, Land, and Bread*, No. 4 (2021): 131-132.

47. Ernest, 431-432.

48. The issue of Frado's parents speaks to the ease with which whites can reclaim the benefits afforded to them by institutionalized racism. Her surrender of Frado signifies this to the Bellmonts as a symbolic gesture "tantamount to selling her into slavery." Katherine Clay Bassard, "'Beyond Mortal Vision': Harriet E. Wilson's *Our Nig* and the American Racial Dream-Text," in *Female Subjects in Black and White: Race, Psychoanalysis, Feminism*, eds. Elizabeth Abel, Barbara Christian, and Helene Moglen, (Berkeley: University of California Press, 1997), 192-193.

49. Dutch was Truth's first language.

50. Painter further highlights how Gage's rendering re-invents Truth's words as a confrontation with an unnamed man at the convention. Painter's investigation shows, however, that the likely culprit was a conservative white woman of upper-class orientation unwilling to accept the radically egalitarian and socialist views of most of those present. Nell Irvin Painter, *Sojourner Truth, A Life, A Symbol*, (New York: W.W. Norton and Co., 1994), 121-131, 164-178. Alice Walker and Lewis R. Gordon are among the prominent writers and scholars who cite Gage's rendering of the speech. Gordon references Walker's discussion of that version to develop her thought on "womanism." in her book of essays, *In Search of Our Mothers' Gardens*. See Lewis R. Gordon, *An Introduction to Africana Thought*, (Cambridge: Cambridge University Press, 2008, 102-103. I do not point out my differences with these scholars to suggest their interpretations are wrong. Instead, I emphasize the diversity of use-values that different versions of Sojourner Truth's speech have in Africana thought, U.S. letters, and political theory.

51. Sojourner Truth and Olive Gilbert, *The Narrative of Sojourner Truth, A Northern Slave, Emancipated from Bodily Servitude by the State of New York in 1828*, (Boston: J.B. Yerrinton and Sons, 1850), 105. The book's front matter notes it was "printed for the author." Narrative, 1. Painter argues that because Truth paid the printer, she was the publisher of her *Narrative*, its primary promoter, and distributor on the anti-slavery speaking circuit.

52. Walter J. Ong, *Orality and Literacy: The Technologizing of the Word*, (New York: Routledge, 1982), 34-35.

53. Painter, 125. Painter reproduced the speech as recorded by Robinson (125-126).

54. As Painter explains Truth's decision to secure her freedom by running away before the final passage of the 1827 abolition allowed her to avoid the 10-year apprenticeship condition imposed on emancipated Africans under the law.

55. *Narrative*, 83-120. Painter, 38-61, 79-102. In these communities, common ownership and emphasis on the role and leadership of direct producers were ideological
and material practices. See Amy Hart, "'All is Harmony in that Department': Religious Expression with the Fourierist Communal Experiments of the 1840s," *Nova
Religio*, Vol. 23, no. 2 (2019): 18-41. In addition to Gordon, others such as Kelley,
Zamalin, and Gaines do not mention this aspect of Truth's thought and life. Kelley
notes Truth's leadership on the campaign to redistribute land but does not reference its connection to Truth's communistic experiences. Mary Helen Washington
refers in passing to Truth's communist experiences, "Introduction: The Enduring Legacy of Sojourner Truth," in *Narrative of Sojourner Truth*, ed. Washington,
(New York: Vintage Books, 1993), x; Robin D. G. Kelley, *Freedom Dreams: The Black
Radical Imagination*, (Boston: Beacon Press, 2002), 28, 113, 137; Kevin K. Gaines,
Uplifting the Race: Black Leadership, Politics, and Culture in the Twentieth Century,
(Chapel Hill: University of North Carolina Press, 1996), 114, 120. Of particular
note is the exclusion of this data from Zamalin's study of Black utopian thought.
See Alex Zamalin, *Black Utopia: The History of an Idea from Black Nationalism to
Afrofuturism*, (New York: Columbia University Press, 2019), 7, 26.
56. Painter, 126.

Chapter 3

Frontiers

James Fenimore Cooper was annoyed that circumstances required a trip to Kalamazoo, Michigan. Traveling by way of Buffalo and Detroit in 1847, Cooper planned to view 18 plots of land he had gained as payment for a loan to a family member and to oversee lawsuits he had initiated against current and former business partners.[1] He arrive just 16 years after de Tocqueville and Beaumont published their account of their trip to Anishinaabewaki. Perhaps a happy literary result of this unwanted trip was the novel *The Oak Openings: Or, the Bee-hunter*, written and published in 1848. In his preface to the book, Cooper alludes to the trip and emphasizes his "[p]ersonal observation" of what to U.S. inhabitants was "Western" territory. He claims that the "fertility of the west" contrasts sharply with "anything that exists in the Atlantic States." Accordingly, he maps an ideological geography of providentially ordained U.S. imperial expansion closely linked to white supremacy and based on Euro-American attempts to eliminate Native peoples through mass killings or forced removal.[2] The novel's title references Anishinaabewaki[3] landscape features near the Kalamazoo River as agriculturally rich with potential, given proper socio-cultural organization, property regimes, technological application, and industriousness.

Cooper also writes that the western locality of the tale spoke back to the "civilized" east. This rhetorical strategy establishes verisimilitude through the recirculation of stereotypes about the "frontier" as un-husbanded "virgin wilderness" in contrast to "civilization," wherein the former registers a diminishing field of existence (including its Indigenous inhabitants).

Cooper imagines a shrinking Native world, in this particular instance, the territory and society of the Anishinaabe, the People of the Three Fires, the Ojibwe, Odawa, and Bodéwadmi. He finds this change pitiable but believes its inevitability signals a historical progression that would cultivate civilization across the continent (*OO*, 7). With these geographical and topographical tropes in mind, *The Oak Openings* functions to document, reproduce, and enforce a textual racial formation that tries to reconstruct and reshape a Native sovereign space of Anishinaabewaki into Michigan, a region marred by its emergent white supremacy and capitalist social relations within the U.S. empire.

Just over a decade after the publication of *The Oak Openings*, Susan Fenimore Cooper, the author's talented literary daughter, published a collection of introductions that hinted at an alternative origin story. Instead of events or sights in Michigan, she revealed, the story was inspired by an incident on Cooper's New York estate. While overseeing the collection and sale of timber, Cooper and his employees had encountered "a stranger with a tin pail," claiming to have lost a swarm of bees nearby. Intrigued, Cooper and the workers joined the search. Both Cooper and the workers playfully mocked the bee-hunter about climbing the tall, limbless trees urging him to resist the temptation to chop down the 500-year-old giants if he discovered the beehives. The stranger indicated he would "call his bees down" instead of climbing or felling the trees. After locating one honeybee, the bee-hunter insisted that he could tell that it was one of his bees by sight and sound. The hunter then proceeded to catch several bees and, using mysterious techniques, to find and "recapture" the lost swarm.[4]

According to Susan, the "little incident interested Mr. Cooper very much," and he "determined that a 'bee-hunter' should be one of the principal characters" in his next novel. This last of his "Indian tales" tells the story of "how the holy and peaceful influences of Christianity are made at length to triumph over that dearest passion of the American savage, the spirit of revenge."[5] Indeed, the bee-hunter's mathematical skills intrigued Cooper so much that he decided to use the incident to demonstrate the collective progress of white civilization. To do this, Cooper was compelled to reinvent the story's origins and foundational elements.

This interaction with the bee-hunter in New York offered Cooper a compelling metaphor for racial and civilizational discourse. Ironically, this episode reveals the geographical mystification involved in discourses of civilization and race. Rather than a mythological frontier speaking back to a decadent east, the "civilized" east was ideologically constructing itself *and* the "savage" wilderness. Further, the truth about Cooper's interaction with the bee-hunter might have served to highlight educational distinctions between the two men. Instead, the distinguished author chose to recast it as a metaphor for fundamental differences between his imaginary "Indians" and Euro-Americans at the level of race and species. The skill that Cooper's fictional Euro-American male character Boden has with bees seems like magic or "gibberish" (*OO*, 22) to Cooper's Indians. Indeed, "it exceeded the knowledge of the red man to make the calculations that are necessary to take the bee by the process described" (*OO*, 312-313). The bee hunter's knowledge was something Indigenous people supposedly could not produce in their cultural system apart from whites. Cooper's retelling sublimates his initial ignorance about bee-hunting through a projection of his own awed ignorance and desire onto his fictional characters.

Bees and social order

The Oak Openings contrasts the rational, methodical bee-hunter and the Indigenous men who observe him, establishing each as typical stand-ins for two supposedly inalterably different races and civilizations. In addition, bees signify blurred lines between apocalypse and a stable social order in the nineteenth-century world. By the first quarter of that century, "the honey bee becomes the entomological marker of the frontier, drawing a bee-line between wilderness and civilization." For Indigenous people, the bee "was a bad omen." Because the honey bee was not native to the continent, the sudden appearance of "the white man's fly" suggested the nearness of Europeans and likely conflict over land and resources. For Euro-Americans like Thoreau, the honey bee symbolizes industry; for Bryant, a "domestic hum," and Irving, a "harbinger of the white man."[6] Bee discourse accentuates the desire for the solidarity of Euro-American racial identity, advanced civilization, capitalistic economic practices, a patriarchal gendered order and division of labor, and collective Western scientific knowledge as distinct from a supposed Indigenous lack of such.[7]

The text shape-shifts the gender of the bees to masculinize the project of white settler colonialism, capitalism, conquest, and the husbandry of the forest. In the epigraph placed at the opening of chapter 2, Cooper includes four lines from Isaac Watts's *Divine Songs*. In these lines, Cooper alters the original reference to the female worker bee to an "it": "it builds its cell/...it spreads the wax" (*OO*, 24).[8] Watts's original hymn used she/her pronouns to attribute gender to the female worker bees in the hive. Male drones, lacking a stinger, try to defend a hive from an enemy predator by buzzing. Fictionalizing and transposing bee genders naturalizes Indigenous "savagery" by highlighting what Euro-American culture regarded as a fatal flaw: balanced Indigenous gender roles. Anishinaabe women, for example, held powerful, independent, and life-sustaining roles in their villages and bands. The "system of balanced yet autonomous male and female roles" proved unintelligible to Europeans, who came to regard Anishinaabe non-adherence to heteronormative patriarchy as a critical indication of savagery.[9] Anishinaabe societies cultivated a balance of power, roles, and sensibilities based on what Euro-American defined as gender. For example, white producers of knowledge on the Indian—missionaries, government officials, and travelers—typically spoke about what they perceived to be racial categories (their own and that of Indigenous people) through a powerful lens of normative genders.[10] Thus, for bees to function as a metaphor for the Euro-American, capitalist, patriarchal social formation, Cooper had to reimagine the female worker bee as "it." Actual bee social organization—if it is even possible to imagine that bee society adopted Eurocentric heteronormativity—would not work: The queen rules, male drones do no work nor even possess weapons of war, and female workers gather the food, build, and defend the hive.

Real bees, "the white man's fly," resemble neither imaginary
Indians nor whites; and this contradiction highlights how tenuous, arbitrary, and fragile the constructed social identities
that gripped Cooper's imagination. Elements of the closely
linked systems of gender, gender identity, and sexuality operate in contradictory ways. For example, Boden's nicknames
are *le Bourdon*, French for the male drone bee, and Buzzing
Ben, directly linking him to the male bee without a stinger.
Cooper amends this confusion of stinger and sexuality, sexual
potency and physical weakness, by shifting the meaning of the
nickname. Boden's French nickname's negative connotations
give way to heroic qualities. He got the moniker because "[h]
e was notorious for laying hands on the products of labor that
proceed from others" (*OO*, 12). A signification of impotence is
transformed into one of power, the exploiter.

Cooper's endeavor to create order also prevails in the novel's
religious theme. He hoped that Indigenous people could avoid
extinction through complete assimilation by Christian conversion. The conversion narrative follows a typically Christian
plot, complete with Biblical cues. The story of how Saul/Paul
participated in Stephen's martyrdom is a New Testament tale
of the Christian conversion ritual. The central character, Scalping Peter/Onoah (sometimes referred to as "Tribeless"), also
bears variations on two Biblically significant names: Peter and
Noah. Noah stood as the second founder of the human race,
the father of all tribes and races, after God destroyed it. Onoah
("said to mean scalp" [*OO*, 175]) will stand as the "tribeless"
founder of a converted people after its similar destruction at
the hands of white civilization. The martyred St. Peter, also
famed for his denial of following Jesus, was characterized by
Jesus as the "rock" upon which the Christian church would be
built (*OO*, 213). Through conversion to Christianity, Scalping
Peter will serve as the patriarchal foundation on which salvation (religious and racial) can be promised. Scalping Peter's
third name, Wawanosh, meaning a bird in flight, is referred to
only once in the novel (*OO*, 214) and is the name of a historical Anishinaabe *ogimaa*.[11] Like the contradictions of gender,
the text intervenes to repress the fluidity of Wawanosh's identity. By transitioning to a Christian conversion narrative and

Christianized names, it attempts to manage conflict and anxiety produced by highly exploitative and oppressive social conditions.

Shape-shifting plots, plot-shifting Natives

Given such contradictions, a counter-reading may document how "[American] literature emerged from Native and settler spaces of contention and interaction." This alternative origins story makes "the work of recovering and re-presenting Native histories [central] to the project of reinterpreting and re-*placing* American literature in Native space."[12] To accomplish this, I borrow from historian Michael Witgen's methodology of reading European-authored sources "without privileging the fantasy of discovery," or the European ideological assumption of cultural primacy in reconstructing Native histories and cultures.[13] Thus, a shift in spatial and epistemological frames authorizes adherence to theorist Robert Warrior's call to account for "what the viewer/reader might see as possible in considering a Native subject."[14] Warrior's critical reading methodology destabilizes a habit of privileging a Euro-American imaginary that naturalizes capitalism, U.S. nationality and empire, and racist hierarchy. With these approaches in mind, Cooper's animal discourse attempts and fails to hold contradictions between the white "knowledge" of Indians and the specific historical realities of Indigenous social formations.

In the opening scene, Boden mystifies the mathematical process of triangulating the location of a beehive for his audience of one white man and two Anishinaabe men. Assuming Native incapacity for rational thought and completely ignoring the fact that the third observer, a white man, also does not understand the process, Boden pretends his actions are magical incantations. When he locates the hive, "[t]he Indians were more delighted with *le Bourdon's* ingenious mode of discovering the hive than with the richness of the prize" (*OO*, 26). However, if the scholarship on Anishinaabe culture bears out, the "ingenious mode" signals to the Native men Boden's relation to the bees' *manidoo*.[15] This kinship relation intrigues them more than the actual gathering of the honey, a potential commodity for a much-needed source of income. If bees are the "white man's fly," the two men may see in Boden's work a potential kinship relation with bees that might allow access to all the honey they could ever need. The Indigenous men respect Boden's ownership of that relation and its power and anticipate possible access to it if chosen for initiation into its secrets. They view Boden's actions through a spiritual lens of ritual that links humans to the power and resources necessary for their survival and happiness.[16] Cooper's logic, by foregrounding magic, attempts to foreclose Native ingenuity for mathematical rituals that enable Boden's ability to accumulate honey.

The narrator and white characters fail to acknowledge practical concerns of Indigenous social relations. Instead, they attribute what they perceive as a lack of interest in the potential value of a commodity (honey) to a persistent Native quality of irrational superstition and racial inferiority. Unspoken is Boden's implicit demand for large geographical spaces to follow the bees, trespassing on Anishinaabe territory, the initial step toward a large-scale invasion threatening Indigenous sovereignty. Such unacknowledged gaps function as part of the "fantasy of discovery" to construct a mythology of the frontier in which civilization and race are an impenetrable boundary across which the two groups cannot encounter each other on common ground. It assumes the only cultural ground worthy of encounter has already been fixed by the science, economics, and power of Western culture. It excludes entirely Indigenous history, culture and society, and ways of understanding and perceiving the world and other people.

The commonsensical pretense of this exclusion causes the narrator's imagined historical trajectory of Anishinaabe society to reinforce the dividing line between Euro-Americans and Indigenous people and lament the inevitable elimination of the latter. The tragedy of elimination in the liberal mind forces the production of a means for metaphorical movement across the boundary from the Native side to the Euro-American side. Because the two social formations are irreparably discordant, they cannot co-exist or even mutually blend in a "middle ground."[17] The racial logic produces an ethical conundrum in the liberal Euro-American mind. If Indigenous people are to retain their cultural identity, territorial integrity, and political sovereignty, their only recourse is to implement Scalping Peter's plan to mobilize an armed force to eliminate the invaders (*OO*, 157).[18] However, if they are to survive physically, they must surrender this terroristic tendency—or right to self-defense—and convert to white ways.

Indigenous history and culture prove unfriendly to the seeming inevitability of this settler-colonial logic. Anishinaabe societies preferred alliances through mutually beneficial relations over violent confrontations. Such relations complicated and undermined rigidly racialist notions of identifying enemies and family. At the same time, Europeans seemed intent on violence, enslavement, genocide, or acquisition that rested primarily on racial or national differences and hierarchy. Cooper found the option of conversion and assimilation the literary choice to ease his pained conscience and to account for the historical reality of the ongoing presence of Native peoples while maintaining the narrative of civilization's geographical advance into the West.[19] Thus, Scalping Peter must abandon his warlike agenda, Onoah must be reconstituted in a New Testament form, and Wawanosh should surely vanish.

Leading a robust network of nations and kinship groups that stretched across the Great Lakes, the Anishinaabe attempted to manage a gradual but decisive shift in the balance of demographics and military power in favor of European invaders by the early 19th century. Deadly smallpox pandemics and weakened European allies (first the French, then the British) meant that Anishinaabe had to alter their strategies for survival, cultural protection, and the maintenance of the integrity of their territory. The evidence shows that the invasion by Euro-Americans and the proliferation of white settlements in Anishinaabewaki, despite its worst atrocities, did not succeed in total physical elimination, removal, or cultural eradication. Anishinaabe people responded to these dangers in culturally continuous ways based on their historical kinship practices. "[T]he cultural traditions of the Anishinaabe peoples were made of far more resilient material" than what modern Euro-American scholars (sharing Cooper's imagination) attribute to them. While devastating wars may have forced the Anishinaabe into retreat militarily and territorially, their cultural traditions centered around the *nindoodemag* (kinship networks) helped them build new conditions of existence.[20] Thus, practices that appear to Euro-Americans as assimilation are centuries-old Anishinaabe diplomatic rituals meant to invoke mutual obligations of political and kinship alliance. For example, wearing the clothing of one's allies was not a symbol of assimilation but alliance and kinship. It is "an ancient cultural practice, rather than an indication of subservience." This performance worked as "visual symbolism to the new recognition of kinship, and therefore alliance, that the transaction confirmed."[21] In other words, displaying or performing the cultural customs of one's kin and allies works as an autonomous signal of the existence of that relationship *and* the obligation both parties held toward maintaining the alliance. In the context of Anishinaabe history, what has been read as subjugation through the supplanting of traditional cultures can also be regarded as the self-determining cultural practice of resilience and resistance to elimination.

In the era of treaties and removal (1819-1855), the Anishinaabe did not merely surrender cultural identity, assimilate, or vanish as the dominant narrative indicates. Despite their best efforts, the devastating and deadly removal and assimilation policies held mixed success for U.S. agencies while still engendering particular constructions of whiteness, indigeneity, and anti-Blackness that conditioned the region. White supremacy, U.S. nationalism, heteronormative patriarchy, and capitalist rule depend on the production and maintenance of binaries of ineffable difference. Thus, crossing, confusing, or erasing these differences could disrupt stable power categories. "Assimilation," then, "[as a performance] undermined the dominance of white status in the racial hierarchy of the United States."[22] While the decision to adapt to Euro-American cultural practices was not optimal, the Anishinaabe enacted this shape-shifting feat as collective self-defense.

Resilience and assimilation as performance are also tied to an Indigenous belief in mimesis, or the process of cultural imitation "to assert control over their colonial encounters with [whites]." Mimesis refers to a sustained and efficacious practice based on "sympathetic magic." This refers to the deployment of "skillful imitation to bend reality." In other words, magicians affect imitation to gain control of the object being imitated and "threaten discourses of authority and control." This process of "bending reality" originates in the transition from the psychological to the material domains. Mimesis may allow one "to exert control over personal/psychological states in difficult circumstances" which extend to their actions in other social contexts. Such power may "allow individuals or groups to direct and/or circumscribe the actions of others within determinate settings." As a deliberate cultural strategy, it "provides an avenue for indigenous communities to actively demonstrate, or gesture, their views on colonial discourses of inequality and to create powerful moments for conjuring transformation and subversion of these discourses." Magic is the realization of intent and desire; it transforms the imagined into the real, in "actions, agency, in and of itself; it is practical to intend causality." However, the outcomes of this conjuration have limits. The magic of mimesis "cannot be understood as something that could transform the structural power of colonialism."[23] In other words, it is not *really magical* but merely symbolic or psychological.

Magic is real

One particular form of Anishinaabe magic relevant to this discussion was shape-shifting. Shape-shifting is a central theme in Anishinaabe mythology and oral tradition. One scholar argues that "the ability to change one's outward shape is one of the most reliable hallmarks of power in [Anishinaabe] oral tradition."[24] Shape-shifting tropes emphasize the imaginative dimension of storytelling, its connection to real life through language, and the production of action that results in the movement or interactions of social beings with "ethical consequences."[25] Grandfather stories such as "Wawabezowin" and "Mashkwashakwong" are replete with characters who take multiple animal forms, or who move easily between the world of dreams and waking, or the spiritual and material realms.[26] These were never just stories; they were also historical records.

Anishinaabe peoples have often shifted shape in response to environmental factors and the necessities of survival.

Historian Michael Witgen's discussion of Anishinaabe relations with the French provides an essential example of shape-shifting at work. One of the key strategies for domination deployed by Europeans was mapping and constructing legible identities of the inhabitants of a territory they claimed to control. The map is not the territory, however. In reality, the legibility of place is determined by human relationships. To hold productive and profitable trade relationships with the powerful Anishinaabe, the French, in the 17th and 18th centuries, had to operate in a manner legible to their trading partners through the performance of rituals and ceremonies of joining one another's families. For the Anishinaabe, rituals produce kinship relations and reciprocal obligations. Those relations and obligations combine on a territory to produce and reproduce the space and social formation of Anishinaabe-waki. Economic activity and trade among *doodemag* and larger kinship groups, along with the politics of relating to one another and sharing a territory, are founded on an exchange of gifts and power within the socially organized mode of survival. These kinship identities were illegible to the Europeans and Euro-Americans, who instead utilized names like Odawa, Sauteur, Cree, etc. to make sense of the people they encountered. Anishinaabe bands and kinship groups adopted these Native "hybrid identities" to allow themselves to be legible to the French. They also retained more flexible terms of their original kinship identities that the French could not quite grasp.[27]

In some sense, more familiar names like Odawa result from this relationship with the French but cannot be understood as French-created. Instead, they have to be regarded as adopted identities within this alliance framework, which moved from transitional and temporary to more permanent forms of self-identification. "Collective identities such as Odawa or Sauteur increasingly functioned as situational identities linked to the places where the French alliance system worked, on the ground, transforming Natives and newcomers into *inawemaagen* (family)."[28] However, in spaces apart from those where they interacted with the French, Anishinaabe groups identified with systems and kinship relation names that operated legibly to them. This complex of names and relations, according to Witgen, resembles the shape-shifter mythological characters. Anishinaabe production of a "new world" through shape-shifting asserts the autonomy and agency of Native peoples to shape their strategic relations and cultures for their sovereign purposes. In this logic, Europeans are afforded no privileged priority in that cultural process but instead appear as another feature of kinship extension rituals or are identified as enemies that potentially threaten cohesion and community life. Further, it suggests that Anishinaabe peoples not only transformed themselves but also caused their allies and new kin to alter, even if only reluctantly or unwittingly so. Shape-shifting was specifically an Anishinaabe "habit of mind" that "meant seeing the potential for beings to transform themselves, and to be transformed by others."[29]

While this mindset registers as weakness and vulnerability for Euro-Americans, who favor immutability and rigid categories of racial identity and civilization, it had long served as a source of power, creativity, and restoration in the Anishinaabe worldview. Shape-shifting is elemental to the production, continuance, and restoration of Anishinaabe story-telling, scholar Margaret Noodin argues. In a study of Anishinaabe literature, she discusses how the practice of story-telling itself functioned as a metaphor for shape-shifting. She writes "[i]f a stone was the first storyteller, perhaps a useful metaphor would be to think about the ways stones themselves changed." Like rocks altered by the forces of nature, Anishinaabe storytellers, if they are competent, add to and re-shape a narrative for purposes necessary to their present context. The storyteller reproduces a communally crafted narrative rooted deeply in cultural traditions, but also generates something new each time. Storytellers "speak of rebirth and conversion, yet like all children, their features and gestures reflect those who came before them."[30] Heidi Kiiwetinepinesiik Stark affirms this description of the Anishinaabe practice of literary production, stating that "stories are alive," reflecting the Anishinaabe "ongoing interaction with creation" that obligates modifications of stories in newer timeframes altered spatial contexts.[31] This deep relation between past and present, traditional and transformative, invokes the creativity and restorative power of the process of Anishinaabe literature.

Boden's Indigenous audience likely hoped Boden would share the power that would allow them access to the spiritual world through bees, a moment which would have signaled a willingness for alliance and kinship obligations—among the bees, the Euro-Americans, and the Anishinaabe. Scalping Peter undertook his conversion to Christianity for specific reasons intelligible to an Anishinaabe man but missed as Cooper's projections of an aching fear of and guilt over Indigenous disappearance erases their humanity and reinterprets their actions through a Euro-American lens.[32] Cooper frames Peter's conversion as stemming from his reaction to witnessing Parson Amen's torture and execution and the minister's refusal to condemn his killers. In a moment of subjection to ritual torture, the parson asks God to bless and forgive his captors. Instead of weakness, the parson's God enables strength. Peter is "profoundly struck" by this spiritual power, thus initiating his conversion to Christianity (OO, 395). While Cooper drew on the Christian canon for examples of how martyrdom causes shame and repentance in sinners, some Indigenous traditions regard the torture of an enemy as a possible way to reveal the victim's spiritual power that may be worth acquiring.[33]

If we read these events from within Native space (rather than solely Cooper's imagination), we may see how Peter's conversion was a specifically Anishinaabe response to the powerful *manidoo* to whom Parson Amen was related. When prisoners were tortured, it was carried out to honor the prisoner and justify and demonstrate the courage of the captors. Torture also provided the prisoner with an opportunity to act courageously in the face of extreme pain and inevitable death. This action also tested the strength of the warrior's personal relations with the spiritual world. Martial actions were dangerous undertakings closely connected to ritualized practices, an obligation based on the need to survive.[34] Parson Amen's possession of a strong relation to a powerful *manidoo*, reflected in his courageous appeal for blessings on his tormentors, influenced the crisis in Peter's own political and spiritual trajectory.[35] While Cooper does his best to corral Peter into the Christian fold, fabricating a "legend" of him as a new St. Paul, the Indigenous origins of Peter's shape-shifting overflow in the text.

Flashforward

The final chapter leaps unexpectedly into the future when the narrator travels to Kalamazoo to visit the story's characters. On a journey from New York to Michigan thirty-six years after the main action of the story, the narrator comments on the once "empty" land's spatial transformation. Technological changes in transportation have compacted the geography of difference between West and East—a week-long journey to Buffalo three decades ago takes less than a day now. This compression of space and time has also altered the experience of the landscape. "Now," the narrator boasts, "the whole of the beautiful region, teeming with its towns and villages, and rich with the fruits of a bountiful season, was almost brought into a single land-scape by the rapidity of our passage" (*OO*, 489-490). Before, the space of the West abounded with "virgin forests," it was "wild" and (supposedly) unpopulated (*OO*, 10-11). The per-ception of natural spaces has altered as well. The "openings" of the past were prairies of rolling grasslands separated by occasional stands of oak trees, creating an impression of space as a series of discrete and unique landscapes. Now, since "[t]he axe had laid the country open," they are peopled, produc-tive, even technologized, and industrialized (*OO*, 499).[36] The Niagara Falls, which serves as a bookending landmark for the novel, appears new. Its power, celebrated in the opening lines of the novel, has been transformed into "sublime softness and gentleness," a "surpassing loveliness" (490). Indeed, a scene that once posed as a reminder of human powerlessness in the face of nature now renders a feminized beauty wherein "[n]ot a drop of the water that fell down that precipice inspired ter-ror" (*OO*, 490). Humans have subdued the great "cataract" by transforming it into a tourist site, a commodity for profit. The narrator's reverie attempts to subdue Indigenous space into the mythology of capitalist social progress.

This shifting experience of nature is reflected in the narrator's encounter with Peter. The narrator sees Peter and Boden's family traveling together on the boat from Buffalo to Detroit. The reader's attention is directed first to the sight of three generations of women, Margery,[37] her daughter, and her two granddaughters. Through descriptions primarily of their speech and modes of behavior, the narrator conveys his perceptions of the four women as Eastern boarding school educated, if "not of a very high social class" and "not sufficiently polished," nor "models of refinement," and certainly do not share the narrator's class and educational background. Despite this distinction between himself and them, which results in a brief digression by the narrator on language, he finds them "charming" (OO, 492-493). The lack of comment on their race or religion suggests that he takes the four of them to be white, a naturalization of whiteness and cross-class racial solidarity with the women upon which he feels no need to elaborate.

While confining his descriptions of the four women to their clothing, general ages, and behaviors, the narrator's first direct encounter with Peter focuses particularly on his body's appearance. His hair is white, and he is evidently more than 80 years old. Despite his advanced age, Peter's tall body indicates "physical vigor," "great elasticity and sinewy activity," and it is "erect." His skin color and "restless, black eye, indicated the Indian" (OO, 493). Peter's phallic body "drew all of [the narrator's] attention" upon stepping onto the ship's deck one morning. "Here, then," the narrator observes, "was a civilized red man ... an ancient child of the forest, who had been made to feel the truths of the gospel" (OO, 493). Ironically, the demands of storytelling and the narrator's omniscience require the preservation of observable "biological" racial differences, despite decades of assimilation. Before speaking to him, and with a single reference to his clothing as "black, and according to the customs of the day," the narrator confidently concludes that Peter is a Christian, suggesting a link between his dress and his religious affiliation.

The narrator, at the beginning of the story, gives two other initial-encounter descriptions of Peter: Boden's and Margery's first meetings with him. Significantly, the preface to Boden's first encounter with Peter is through rumors associated with his reputation, or an imagined encounter, after hearing the name Onoah. Boden knows the name as others had described him as the most "terrible and most dreaded savage" (*OO*, 175). The narrator's three-page physical description of Peter at the first direct meeting with Boden also stresses his attire, but in tremendous detail, down to the figures painted on the man's chest, the size of his teeth, his haircut, his equipment, and the Catholic emblem on his necklace, indicating a political affiliation, but indeed not a genuinely religious connection, to the French and their Jesuit missionaries (*OO*, 178-180). These details emphasize civilizational differences. Still, the shift from pages of scrupulous detail to a single line about Peter's black suit in the final chapter also reveals a semantic subjugation of Cooper's Indian from overflowing "savage" excess to restrained "civilized" minimality.

While terror marks Boden's initial perceptions of Peter, Margery's are inflected by sexual desire. As Peter is introduced to the small group of whites, he barely notices Margery, "a picture of female loveliness." But she stands before him, "her face flushed with excitement, her spirited blue eye wandering [over his body] with curiosity, and her beautiful mouth slightly parted in admiration" (*OO*, 180). Thus, Peter's terroristic, sexualized body remains unchanged from when he first enters the story to the novel's closing pages. His dress, however, has transformed from "the summer-dress of the woods" (*OO*, 178) to the customary clothing of white people. His possession of a Catholic symbol indicated some relationship to Christianity through vestiges of the French alliance framework, but the posture as a "true American" was merely a performance meant to get him close enough to his Euro-American enemies to kill them. Now some three decades later, Peter has become "a subdued, benevolent Christian" whose "very soul was love" (*OO*, 496). His phallic body offers no threat to penetrate another for assault, sexual pleasure, or reproduction; his heart is transformed from stone "to the heart of a woman" (*OO*, 506).

This transformation alone justifies, in the narrator's mind, the now-completed cruelty and violence of white settler colonialism. Accompanying colonialism, "we find civilization, the arts, moral improvement, nay Christianity itself, following the bloody train left by the conqueror's car, and good pouring in upon a nation by avenues that at first were teeming only with the approaches of seeming evils!" Admittedly, the expropriation of Indigenous land and the enslavement of Africans proved to be a crime of terrible proportions. The debt for this sin, however, can be erased by the transformative process that has remade Peter "into a civilized man and a Christian!" (*OO*, 496). Like Niagara Falls, he retains the appearance of natural, physical power but no longer inspires the same terror that accompanied even the mention of his name. The narrator sees Peter "like a striking monument of a past that was still so recent and wonderful," the appearance of virility but still transfixed by the moment of conversion. True to his nickname *le Bourdon*, Boden owns and has gotten wealthy and politically powerful off of the land on which Peter "had hunted and held savage councils" and the labor of the bees he now keeps in domesticated hives (*OO*, 502-503). Even the bees, now domesticated in human-made hives, conform to the pattern of ordered transformation to white management in the production of civilization and profit.

History as re-creation

Anishinaabe leader Andrew Jackson Blackbird was concerned first and foremost about the lies that white writers—like Cooper, de Tocqueville, and Jefferson—told about Indigenous people. In the opening passages of his 1887 book *History of the Ottawa and Chippewa Indians of Michigan*, he evokes a relation between knowledge and power. He is especially intent on correcting the errors in Euro-American writing (perhaps with Cooper's *The Oak Openings* in mind) about the Anishinaabe that distorts their values, their cultures, and their history. "I have seen a number of writings," he observes, "by different men who attempted to give an account of the Indians" who lived near the Great Lakes. Blackbird labels this knowledge production ignorant, inaccurate, or exaggerated no less than seven times on the first page alone.[38] His corrected accounts of the Anishinaabe military leader Pontiac and the structure of Odawa social and political organization are among his first examples. Pontiac had led an attack on the British at Detroit in 1763. In the negotiations with the British colonial government after the conflict, an Odawa chief named Ego-me-nay implored the British to restrain any planned retaliation against the Anishinaabe who fought with Pontiac. Acknowledging British power, he added, "Oh, my father, you are like the trees of the forest, and if one of the forest trees should be wounded with a hatchet, in a few years its wound will be entirely healed" (*History*, 7-8).

Because the speech primarily sounds conciliatory and deferential, it is easy to miss how Pontiac's failed uprising had actually disclosed Anishinaabe power. The negotiations in which Ego-me-nay participated ultimately leveraged the British 1763 prohibition on colonial expansion into Anishinaabe lands, and other Native territories west of the Appalachian Mountains, ultimately propelling the events that led to the collapse of British control of much of North America. Blackbird revisits Ego-me-nay's relation of self-healing with power later with a story of the legendary Odawa warrior Kaw-be-naw who displays a similar capacity for restoration. Blackbird deploys the Kaw-be-naw legend linked with the myth of the magic kettle to stake his claim as an authentic and skilled Odawa storyteller with proper knowledge of Anishinaabe history. Like Blackbird's account of Ego-me-nay's speech, those stories register an intentional resistance to Cooper's conversion narrative and Euro-American colonial mythologies of the frontier, inscribing the future of his restored people.

Blackbird identifies his accurate knowledge of Anishinaabe history with traditions and stories told by his ancestors. He maintains that his grandfather and great-grandfather were highly ranked Odawa leaders alive during the negotiations with the British. Blackbird's father was an Odawa *ogimaa* of the Arbor Croche or Middle Village band, which lived in the northwestern section of the main peninsula of Michigan. Blackbird traces his personal and family history to the moment of its adoption into the Odawa. His ancestors, known as the "Underground race," had been captured in a war "in the far west" and were brought back to Odawa territory. "But they were afterwards adopted as children of the Ottawas," he states, "and intermarried with the nation in which they were captives." Once they had been integrated into the village, Blackbird's ancestors rose to political and military leadership by demonstrating their skill as warriors and hunters. They proved to be an "intelligent class of people" who understood agriculture and possessed a system of government, a language, and a "national emblem," the hawk (*History*, 25-26).[39] Such details serve as an origins story, a traditional means of self-introduction within a broader historical and kinship narrative.[40] Blackbird foregrounds his people's civilizational features (language and history, political and economic institutions, family and military customs), and establishes the long-followed practice of incorporating foreign enemies into a new cultural system like family and allies. This practice of inclusion worked as a means of restoring the kinship network after the resolution of conflict. It frames the purpose of the text, establishing Anishinaabe adaptation within the U.S.[41]

Like the opening passages in Cooper's text, the Blackbird also maps the geography of Odawa territory—but with a different ideological purpose. He describes how his family lived semi-permanently in Arbor Croche but made annual winter trips south to their hunting camps on the Muskegon River via canoe on Lake Michigan. This seasonal migration pattern followed the traditional ways of Odawa life on the eastern shores of Lake Michigan. The Arbor Croche band eventually merged with other area Odawa bands. After a century-long struggle for recognition by federal agencies, those bands were incorporated as the Little Traverse Bay Bands of Odawa Indians (or the Waganakising Odawak).[42] Blackbird's traditional references to his ancestors, Anishinaabe cultural practices of adaptation, some territorial features of his people's traditional lands, and the complex socio-political formation of his people foreshadow the reemergence and restoration of Waganakising Odawak. Combined, geography, origins stories, spatial mobility, and inhabitation of an embodied people assert the ancient presence of the Anishinaabe peoples. Much of the mythology of the frontier—a discourse of elimination—depended (and still does) on a false thesis of empty land, or at best, a land inhabited by a people without a history. *History* is thus a textual claim for Anishinaabe permanence and territorial ownership.

History was published with the assistance of the Ypsilanti, Michigan Auxiliary of the Women's National Indian Association (WNIA) in 1887, the same year as the passage of the WNIA-supported Dawes Act. This law forced the fragmentation of Indigenous lands in Oklahoma under the guise of social progress and assimilation. Blackbird's autobiographical account of the Odawa is strategically aligned with a social movement that, in the name of liberal humanism, advocated "the systematic conversion of communal Indian land and cultural practices into individuated 'civilized' forms amenable to market capitalism and liberal democracy" that served this project of alienation, or a colonial genocide masked as charity.[43] On strategic alignments such as this, Malea D. Powell observes of Sarah Winnemucca Hopkins' book *Life Among the Piutes*, which appeared in print four years before Blackbird's *History*, that it should be read as a "deliberate performance of the kind of Indianness" that would appeal to whites and mobilize support for her people.[44] The same could be said of Blackbird, despite the antithetical intentions of those who financially backed his book's publication. Blackbird's adaptation of Western cultural tools to Native narrative production implicates and validates the Native origins of its possibility and, as Blackbird insists, is centered on "indigenous ways of knowing."[45]

History champions shape-shifting as part of the Anishinaabe struggle for sovereignty, cultural renaissance, social cohesion, and economic survival. Blackbird's immediate aim seems to have been to publish a book as a source of income, but his larger goal lay in a struggle against potential erasure from the dominant historical narrative (*History*, 24-25).[46] The Anishinaabe capacity for shape-shifting is indicated by the narrative's publication in English.[47] Scholar Lisa Brooks argues that "[a]s European writing entered Native space, it was transformed, both in interaction with indigenous systems of communication and in response to the needs of indigenous communities."[48] In Anishinaabewaki in the mid-1800s, "[t]he

Odawag," for example, "anticipated future treaty negotiations and wanted their children to have the skills necessary to deal directly with the agents of the federal government," as well as to handle property and other legal issues, and increasing numbers of interactions with Euro-American settlers.[49] Anishinaabe experiences with the U.S. government's habitual disregard for its treaty obligations made relevant "the usefulness of speaking, reading, and calculating in English and stressed the need for quality mainstream education."[50] Beyond this practicality, Anishinaabe adaptation of cultural practices (language, dress, religion) of their new allies and neighbors had traditionally embodied the performance of a culturally specific practice of signaling their recognition of mutual kinship obligations and alliance.

In addition, indigenous colonization of English served Anishinaabe cultural purposes as "tactical refigurings."[51] Blackbird's narrative production of Odawa legends, such as the story of Kaw-be-naw and the magic kettle, interwoven with his biography in the *History* functions as an "embodied tribalography" to "show continuance."[52] Blackbird yokes his biography to that of his people, signaling the assertion of self-determination over the form and content of his people's history, and denying that control of memory to whites. Blackbird's act of writing is a bold declaration of "intellectual sovereignty," or the right to shape and define the form and content of a body of ideas closely identified with one's own culture. Native-authored, experienced-based non-fiction is "the oldest and most robust type of modern writing that Native people in North America have produced as they sought literate means of through which to engage themselves and others in a discourse on the possibilities of a Native future."[53] This discursive (re)production of a community with a socially cohesive and legible future by definition positioned Native non-fiction as a resistant discourse to supposed settler-colonial inevitabilities. It was a deliberate strategic implementation of this mode of communication to effectively engage the political struggle against colonialism, strengthen the Odawa community, and defy colonizing discourses of "vanishing" and an "empty wilderness."

Blackbird's text appeals to Euro-American "humanitarian" laments about the "vanishing" Indian, no doubt, because of its relation to his WNIA financial backers and their enthusiasm for literary sentimentalism and Indian reforms. At the same time, this emotional rhetoric of vulnerability features Blackbird's palpable anxiety about changing Odawa cultural values, its relatively diminishing power, and shrinking land base. Indeed, the closing chapter of Blackbird's *History*, "A Lamentation," adopted much of its style, subject, and language from sentimentalism and the discourse of "vanishing." The chapter was probably first crafted in 1858, just three years after the Treaty of Washington extorted remaining Odawa land titles in a time of intense conflict with Michigan state and the federal government over the allocation and uses of promised resources. This adaption to white sentimentalist discourses prompts some to read Blackbird only "in the tragic key."[54] Blackbird's openness to adaptation to a new world can be read as "tragic" only if the Anishinaabe-specific shape-shifting "habit of mind" is denied or rendered invisible through an inscription of settler discourse disguised as sympathy. An alternative frame for reading *History*, one that registers its protest and indexes sovereignty through Anishinaabe restorative power and cultural continuance is needed.

The magic kettle and origins stories

In *History*, Blackbird relates a brief story of a magic kettle that opens with some attention to theories of Indigenous origins in North America. He dismisses Eurocentric, science-based theories as "nothing but speculation," and immediately shifts to Native oral tradition. As evidence, he describes the discovery of a "magical kettle" by the Odawa leader We-me-gen-de-bay, and dates the discovery to the 1630s. This "great copper kettle," large "enough to cook a whole deer or bear in it," was partially hidden in the ground and covered by tree roots. The finding led to the discovery of a nearby copper mine. It provided evidence for the existence of a highly developed metalworking culture ("advanced in art and civilization" generally) before the arrival of the Odawa. Blackbird writes, "[t]heir idea with regard to this kettle was that it was made by some deity." The tone here suggests some skepticism about this belief and, given his own stated Christianized beliefs, that skepticism is appropriately expressed (*History*, 95-96).

Instead, Blackbird seemingly favors a more anthropological interpretation of the discovery as indicating a highly developed Indian culture before the Odawa and before French or other Europeans. Based on the "evidence" he has enumerated in his recording of this orally transmitted and ritualistically preserved narrative, "it is evident that this country has been inhabited for many ages." The repetition of the word "evidence" and "evident" hints at an appeal to social science. His reliance on his people's oral traditions for evidence suggests his claim to his people's authority in defining and narrating a history that has nothing to do with Europeans and uses modified adaptations of the scientific method to substantiate.

To suggest further the kettle's and its accompanying narrative's distinction from European manufacture and authority, Blackbird describes the kettle as having been made with no rounded rim around its edge and no arched metallic handle (or "bail") "for hanging while in use, as kettles are usually made." It had been propped up by wooden beams on squared shoulders on its upper edges while hung over a fire. As a trained blacksmith, who worked for five years as an assistant to the federally appointed Indian blacksmith at the Old Mission at Grand Traverse, and a reasonably well-educated person, Blackbird understood the operations and uses of different types of metalworking. Further, he says that local villagers had enlisted him to alter the kettle to allow it to be used for maple sugar manufacture, which required an iron rim and a bail. This story and action identify Blackbird—*ogimaa*, metalworker, and storyteller—with the oral tradition of the magic kettle. The story, reflecting the reality of its teller and his Odawa band, is about a process of physically and culturally shape-shifting the object for contemporary Indigenous purposes (*History*, 96). Further, his acknowledgment of his appointment to the task of mending the kettle and telling its story by the community indicates that Blackbird's role as craftsperson and storyteller "derives from the collective will of the community."[55]

Blackbird's Native version of archaeology, anthropology, and historical narrative null biblically-originated assertions or contemporary scientific theories about Indigenous and Anishinaabe origins. It records how the Odawa people adopted the magic copper kettle into their social and religious system. After finding the kettle, "the Indians kept it as a sacred relic" to be used only at "great feasts" and kept it hidden away from the village. For sugar production, Blackbird notes, it was used "in common." In other words, the Odawa transformed an archaeological discovery (something produced in a different society) into a sacred object for ritual and ceremony and incorporate it as a functional object. They, then, alter the object for their own pragmatic needs and sacred uses (*History*, 96). Indeed, the kettle's communalized sugar-making power enhances its status as a "mani-tou-au-kick," or *manidoo* kettle, a device used ritualistically to transmit power from the spiritual to human realms (*History*, 96).

The story closes by returning to speculations about Native peoples' origins in the Americas. After asserting an intellectual autonomy founded in Native oral traditions, utterly distinct from European knowledge systems or historical accounts, Blackbird revisits his earlier indicated doubts about European knowledge about Indigenous origins. "[I]t is evident that this country," he concludes, "has been inhabited for many ages, but whether by descendants of the Jews or of other Eastern races there is no way for us to determine" (*History*, 96). These latter two remarks reference once-popular theories of Native peoples being the "lost tribes" of Israel and the newly emergent "scientific" theories of migrations across a fabled land bridge.[56] Blackbird's emphasis here is that white theories and "scientific" claims about Native peoples' origins remain uncertain, even beyond viable proof, unlike the evidence borne by the magic kettle, Native oral traditions, communal subsistence, and economic practices, rituals, and ceremonies.[57] Native origin stories affirm that they have "always [been] present in America, a move that establishes an unquestionable peoplehood ... which in turn works to endow that community with an inherent sovereignty demanding respect and protection."[58]

Blackbird's treatment of origins theories mirrors this Anishi-
naabe-centric method and perspective.[59]

Nearly 40 years after Blackbird's account was published,
researchers found evidence that a large, well-organized society
that live on the shores of Lake Superior had a means of extract-
ing large quantities of copper and processing the ore to make
items like knives, spear points, and basins.[60] A single archaeological site at McCargoe Cove, on an island in Lake Superior
near the borderlines of what Euro-Americans would eventually call Canada and the U.S., yielded tons of the remnants
of stone hammers used for mining. Evidence that thousands
of "cubic miles" of material had been moved in the mining
operation was unearthed. Amateur archaeologist William P.
F. Ferguson expressed a stereotypical and racist view when
he reported, "the character of the work speaks of a national
industry organization, quite beyond anything 'Indian' of
which we know." He claimed to have discovered a city where
the miners lived during their seasonal migration to the copper
mines.[61] At the time, because they refused to identify Native
societies with the technological and social organization of the
Mound Builder civilization, Euro-American academics dated
the findings to the Mound Builders, which Ferguson claims
died out before the emergence of the Anishinaabe. Blackbird's
connection of Odawa oral traditions to that mining society
counters Euro-American claims about civilizational discon-
nects between the Mound Builders and the Native inhabitants.
Instead, Native encounters with colonizing whites disrupted
a complex economic, political, and social development trajectory. The kettle story unearths and reclaims this buried history.

Blackbird's self-insertion into the textual rendering of this
oral tradition establishes his role as a community leader and
transforms the magic kettle story into a "communal historical narrative."[62] Beyond Blackbird's written text's immediacy,
the communally-constructed narrative, spatially and rela-
tionally over time, produces a "the simultaneous unity and
diversity of time, in convergence, and the concurrent mean-
ingfulness ... of all things past and present."[63] The historical
process of enhancing the magic kettle and its story of special

powers preserves the ritual and ceremony by the numbers of generations of Odawa people who use it. In this manner, the collective production of this text, in which the labor of writing is only one feature, surfaces. Blackbird, thus, produces a text in which history—his personal narrative, his family's history, the history of his "nationality"—share a relation to "the history of the Ottawas of the State of Michigan, to whom I am immediately connected in their common interests and their future destinies" (*History*, 25). Thus, the magic kettle, upon which Blackbird had worked as a blacksmith to alter its appearance and functionality, and its story are re-shaped. This story relates a process of cultural shape-shifting, establishing the historical, continuance, and restoration of the people in the new circumstances of U.S. settler colonialism. It also anticipates the end of that violence.

History positions the space of its present moment into a more extensive historical process of social change and communal historical narrative production. It recenters Anishinaabe history, space, and culture by contextualizing major social and cultural transformations driven by encounters with Euro-Americans as the most egregiously disruptive force in the past few hundred years. In his telling, Blackbird shifts the U.S. to the margins of Anishinaabe history, converting the U.S. into "an event" in a bigger frame of historical time and demotes it from an "origin or an inevitability" to another part of a much longer story that extends deep into the past and far into the future.[64] Blackbird's *History* operates within a communal knowledge system that sees "[t]he world [as] in a constant state of activity, and the telling of history operates as a force that can make sense of transformation and can empower people to be constructive participants."[65] This interaction of the past and present, personal and communal, historical and mythological, and oral and written reflects Native "natural reason,"[66] distinct from Euro-American dualistic rationalism, logic, and rules of academic or legal evidence. The centering of the Anishinaabe, the communal authorship of narrative production, and the underpinning "natural reason" that infused Blackbird's thought link it to Indigenous ways of knowing and the specific cultural history, language, and life of the Anishinaabe.

The legend of Kaw-be-naw and Anishinaabe restoration

Blackbird's approach to communal historical narrative production is also exemplified in his account of the legend of the great Odawa warrior and prophet Kaw-be-naw. A complete tale of Kaw-be-naw "would require a large book," Blackbird warns his reader. Blackbird's decision to include only a single account about the Kaw-be-naw's life suggests his confidence in the Odawa oral tradition's survivability and the necessary autonomy from his white settler audience. Nevertheless, Kaw-be-naw's feats in war and society were so numerous and extensive that he grew tired of his near-immortality and wanted to die. The last great act of his life was to defend his village from an attack by the We-ne-be-go tribe in a way that demonstrated his great power. When read in relation to the oral tradition of the magic kettle story, the legend emphasizes how tragic losses are mixed with struggles for survival, healing, and restoration.

Kaw-be-naw learns the We-ne-be-go are preparing to attack the Odawa. The We-ne-be-go leader instigated war mainly because he wants to assert his personal power in a one-on-one battle with Kaw-be-naw. As the We-ne-be-go launch their invasion, Kaw-be-naw leaves the village to meet them. He refuses to warn his people of the impending attack, pretending to go collect cedar bark. When he meets the We-ne-be-go, they do not recognize him and ask him to direct them to where Kaw-be-naw can be found. When he truthfully tells them that Kaw-be-naw is not at home, they imprison him in a large pit and leave to attack the Odawa village.

After they leave, Kaw-be-naw "magically release[s] himself" from the pit and goes to warn his people of the attack. The following day, the attack comes, and the We-ne-be-go leader fights fiercely, demanding to know where Kaw-be-naw is. Remaining in hiding until the last minute, Kaw-be-naw shows himself, meets the We-ne-be-go leader in combat, and quickly kills him (*History*, 85-89). When the We-ne-be-go see their leader has been killed, they retreat. Kaw-be-naw mocks them as they flee. He had been scratched on the nose during the battle, and as he chases the retreating enemy, he declares dramatically, "O, you have killed me," pointing to a spot of blood on his face (*History*, 87). His enemies continue to flee, fearing a trick. He finally convinces them that he is on the verge of death, and they capture him. Fearing his immortality and power, they tie him to a large rock and throw him into the lake. Forgetting that he had once already escaped them by magic, they prematurely celebrate as they continue their homeward journey.

At their camp that night, Kaw-be-naw reappears to them and taunts them. He tells them that they have to remove all the flesh from his body in small pieces to kill him. Of course, they are afraid to do this as he had already killed their most outstanding leader and used magic to survive their attempts to kill and imprison him. So, he cuts a piece of skin and muscle from his body to entice them to act. After a discussion, they decide to hack him to pieces. "That is the way you must do. What are you afraid of?" he derides their reticence. As they finally slay him, he warns that his successor will destroy them in like measure (*History*, 88-89). True to his word, his successor leads a contingent of warriors against the We-ne-be-go and defeats them soundly.

In this account of self-mutilation and death, Kaw-be-naw reveals the power he holds as a warrior and a prophet. While torture was relatively rare in Anishinaabeg military practices, brutalizing an enemy might disclose the existence of a power that the victim holds. Kaw-be-naw's practice of mocking his enemies during his mutilation signaled to experienced warriors his incredible supernatural power. His actions divulge a power beyond his physical life and abilities, blurring the supposedly distinct lines between life and death and the human and spiritual worlds. Kaw-be-naw's deeds uncover the difference between power brandished as immediate physical force and power wielded through ritual beyond the immanence of the present. The narrative extends the great leader's personal power beyond his physical body to his successor and, thus, to his village kin's next generation. In addition to divulging an Anishinaabe concept of spiritual power, this legend of Kaw-be-naw is a forward-looking narrative that, even with the death of a great leader, predicts the communal power of the people.

As noted above, Blackbird's penultimate chapter, "The Lamentation," was written many decades earlier. Its positioning near the end deceptively presents it as among Blackbird's closing ideas about the subject of this book. "The Lamentation" mourns "ruin and desolation" that resulted from the forced alliance of Anishinaabe with the U.S., which meant the sharing of land in Michigan with Euro-Americans under threat of forced removal "at the point of a bayonet" (*History*, 98). Despite its apparent relation of Anishinaabe loss and potential erasure, "The Lamentation" indexes resistance. Blackbird writes, "When the white man took every foot of my inheritance, he thought to him I would be the slave. I would sooner plunge the dagger into my beating heart and follow the footsteps of my forefathers, than be slave to the white man" and is signed with Blackbird's Odawa name (*History*, 103). Given this note of resistance in the vein of Kaw-be-naw, "The Lamentation's" physical position before a final chapter on Odawa "Grammar" suggests not simple tragedy or loss. Instead, it strikes a note of cultural preservation and continuance simply "changing shape without being completely melted."[67] Thus, "The Lamentation" may be more fruitfully read as his opening idea; the introduction to this *History* reflects a nadir in Anishinaabe-U.S. relations. With the legend of Kaw-be-naw and the story of the magic kettle at work in the book, however, the narrative shifts from tragedy to creation, from an ending to an account of restoration.

Native and African relations

As noted in the introduction to this book, U.S. economic development depended fundamentally on the expropriated labor of enslaved Africans, the transformation of their bodies into capital, and the subsequent investment into lands stolen or extorted from hundreds of Native societies. These processes created what historian Tiya Miles calls the "settler colonial slavery complex," which also mediated knotty and contradictory cultural, political, and social relations among Native peoples and Africans living in the North American territories that would be forcibly incorporated into the U.S.[68] A second reading of Cooper's *The Oak Openings* shows how it sought to represent a white supremacist-controlling mediation of those relations. Relying on white- and Native-authored documentation of Anishinaabe societies, Cooper's novelistic attempt to reproduce this controlling and colonial mediation represents dialogues, scenes, descriptions, and images of Anishinaabe characters, cultural patterns, and ways of thinking that mirror scientific, autobiographical, and historical texts about and by Indigenous people. Instead of uplifting Native aspirations for freedom and sovereignty, *The Oak Openings* transmits and projects dominant Euro-American ideological and cultural constructions of "race," racial difference, and the relations of racialized groups onto imagined literary Indians.

Within the "settler colonial slavery complex," Native statements and views of Black people create openings for inter-group solidarity. For example, in his memoirs published a few years after his death in 1856, Anishinaabe writer Peter Jones briefly describes what he calls Ojibwe views of African-descended people. His statement may be read as an expression of camaraderie among the Anishinaabe and Black people: "[Ojibwe] consider the Negroes were made inferior to the other races of the human family, and deeply commiserate their unhappy state in being bound with the iron band of slavery. They imagine the Indian comes next to the Negro in the endurance of wrongs committed by the white man; and with this idea they call them 'our fellow-suffering brethren.'" Jones adds, however, that Native peoples resist the idea of intermarriage with Black people and "boast of their freedom."[69] Jones, a leader of a Northern Ojibwe band, advocated religious conversion and traveled around North America and England, displaying his national costumes and lecturing on his people's culture, history, and language. Notably ambiguous, Jones' statement came from a position where his financial situation reliance on friendly whites shaped his choice of words.

At the same time, Jones criticizes dominant racial theory and white supremacy, directly disputing then-popular claims about human biological differences based on providentially ordained racial classifications. The accompanying passages register implicit counternarratives of race by delivering observations on the genocidal tendencies of Yankees, the nobility and cultivation of the British (the rulers of Canada to whom his band had conceded land in exchange for money, goods, and territorial recognition), and the wealth and stylishness of the French (historical allies and adopted kin of the Anishinaabe people). However, the kinship equation of Black and Ojibwe made in his statement—rather than the typical hierarchy that tended to place Indigenous people above Blacks—derives from the shared condition of African-descended and Native peoples. It elicits a rupture in the dominant consensus of white superiority. First, the relativization of white cultures—itemized as brutal Yankee, cultivated English, and stylish French—displaces European pseudo-scientific schemes and religious doctrine as bases for universalized and immutable racial categories. Instead, Jones reorients European peoples into a Native epistemological system and political theory of alliances and kinships.

Further, while Jones uses the phrase "made inferior," the context reveals it as a social constructivist claim, not a doctrinal or biological one. Slavery and colonialism manifested as genocidal behavior, subjugating and denigrating the collective conditions of Native and African people. Racist policies placed Native and Black people into similar circumstances of existence (i.e., "next to" one another), making them into kin, or "brethren." This meaning renders Jones's words into a statement of solidarity and a shared determination for liberation and endurance.

Euro-American values and power could not entirely determine the limits of the relations among Native peoples and Black people. Indeed, African-descended people echoed Jones's guarded expression of solidarity. "Perhaps more than any other space in the United States," argue Miles and Holland, "Indian Territory, broadly defined, has held out the promise of home to Black slaves and their descendants." Black people's resistance to slavery and Jim Crow racist oppression were often "inflected by the idea of migration to Native American spaces and of literal and metaphorical relationships with American Indian people."[70] African Americans sought out Native spaces in which to build Black towns. In these spaces, they remade a self-image as respectable, successful, and free where communitarian values superseded dominant Euro-American individualism. The emergent Black Town narrative is a discourse of endurance and survival where a Black self-conception is configured dialectically as part of a collective identity.[71] This move mirrors the Native struggle for perseverance against Euro-American logic of elimination.

Native peoples have often reciprocated a Black "desire for connectivity."[72] Likewise, Anishinaabe political and cultural theory has long advocated "radical inclusiveness," which applies to both established kinship relations and the practice of extending those relations beyond existing borders and beyond the present moment to those yet to be born.[73] For example, Jean DeBaptiste Pointe du Sable, who escaped enslavement in Haiti and moved to Detroit in 1760, was adopted into the extended family of the famed Odawa leader Pontiac. Similarly, Black trader and translator George Bonga played an essential role in shaping Black-Native relations for the Anishinaabe in the Great Lakes region. Histories of the Underground Railroad in Michigan reveal that Native peoples there played a role in aiding self-liberating Blacks to escape U.S. racial slavery.[74] Andrew J. Blackbird also fought for his "fellow-suffering brethren." While most of his adult life centered on protecting the cultural legacies and the material well-being of his Odawa band, his political activism saw him labeled a "Black Republican," and the cultural forms he adapted in his writing reflected much influence from African American literary sources.

Historians of slavery and settler colonialism rarely link the two peoples in positive relationships. The migration of Blacks to the west, particularly to Michigan, is typically retold as a reflection of a Euro-American settler "pioneer" ethos. Miles argues that this historical narrative elides the reality that "Black survival utterly depended either on forming alliances of kinship with Native people or putting down stakes on taken lands controlled by the U.S. nation-state or its white citizens."[75] The "pioneer" narrative mobilizes Black people exclusively as allies of white settler colonialism, even as it uplifts anti-Black ideologies and rhetoric. Ignoring the dilemma and placing all Black migrants or inhabitants into the category of pioneer or settler erases the history of those who sought alliances with Indigenous people.

International imperialist conflict and the political strategies of Indigenous nations are the conditions of possibility for the plot of *The Oak Openings*. Set on the eve of the War of 1812, the novel purports to explore the formation of Native alliances meant to halt Euro-American invasions of Anishinaabewaki. Tecumseh eventually led those alliances (in alliance with the British Empire) from 1812 to 1814. The novel invokes these events not as affirmations of Native agency or sovereignty but as terrifying events that threaten Euro-American peace and U.S. territorial and economic development. In several scenes, Cooper's narrator details the war councils Scalping Peter organizes to build the alliance, which happen to intersect with the commodity and land interests of Ben Boden, the white bee-hunter who thwarts their plans with a small hodge-podge band of white settlers and turncoat Indians. The argument of Cooper's novel, as discussed above, rests on the moral persuasion for Peter's ultimate conversion to Christianity and apparent assimilation.

Parson Amen, a comedic white religious figure who joins Boden's group, helps develop the text's racial theory and assimilationist rhetoric by advocating the once-popular idea that Native Americans descended from the ten lost tribes of Israel.[76] While the narrator gently mocks the theory, Cooper's Native characters resist the notion that Indigenous people might be the descendants of white people altered only by isolation and exposure to harsh environmental conditions. This discourse on Jewish and Native racial origins produces a fascinating racialization discourse. Although Parson Amen has difficulty accounting for anti-Semitism, Jews are still fundamentally white, a fact upon which the novel's otherwise disputatious characters agree. Natives, thus, cannot be Jews, Peter and his comrades conclude. If racial transformation resulted from only environmental and social factors (like injustice), surely Native people would be Black, Scalping Peter notes at one point. "If suffering can do *that*," he argues in response to Parson Amen's assertions about alterations in skin color, "I wonder we are not *black*. When *all* our hunting-grounds are covered with the farms of your people, I think we shall be *black"* (*OO*, 281). Like the ambiguity in Peter Jones's statement of solidarity with enslaved Blacks, Scalping Peter hints at an environmentalist theory of cultural difference, wherein white conquest equals enslavement and racialization, not unlike the experiences of African people. He may also be hinting at Native people's shape-shifting power, perhaps to become Black. While Cooper's narrator invokes a discourse of despair at being likened to Black people, disrupting potential solidarity, I suggest that Scalping Peter is proposing, in fact, a political alliance of Native and Black people in an armed uprising against their shared oppression and oppressor. It is this potential "savage terror" in conjunction with "Black Republicanism" that Cooper's *The Oak Openings* fears and denounces, but which Blackbird subtly cultivates in his *History*.

Ideological divisions

Euro-Americans treated capitalist relations, private property, and commoditized exchange values as natural phenomena that they believed Native people did not understand and that enslaved African-descended people were excluded from as they were private property themselves. "One would think that the idea of property is implanted in us by nature," Cooper's narrator opines, "since men in all conditions appear to entertain strong and distinct notions of this right" (*OO*, 341). Adopting natural rights discourse, the narrator asserts that property is a universal legal and individualist principle. As they develop toward civilization, humans *naturally* discern and exalt property, rights, and the individual as part of their *natural* existence as rational creatures (*OO*, 340–341). Thus, whites have developed these concepts as foundational for a highly productive and industrious social formation.

In contrast, Native people remain trapped in the state in which land is considered the property of the tribe or the band, while equipment and household goods are the individual's property (*OO*, 340–41). Capitalist ideology, here, is closely linked to the dominant racial discourse of whiteness and constructed distinctions as elements of hierarchical difference, locating Indigenous people at some distance from what it means to be fully human. Under this particular equation, capitalism, individualized property, productivity, and industriousness were self-evidently and racially marked as not only civilized qualities but also as specifically white (closely identified with what it means to be human). The supposed rigidity of this racial boundary is further supplemented and complicated by the novel's exploration of the claim that Native Americans descended from the ten lost tribes of Israel. Peter's understanding of U.S. racial hierarchies appears to be natural, as if Indigenous people, too, know about Black inferiority and accept this fact in a manner not unlike whites. This scene constructs a fictional Indian man who reaffirms for his readers what they likely already believe: the racial inferiority of Black people. Even more significantly, Cooper's Indian then constructs Indian racial identity as a not-Black identity worthy of white sympathy and redemption, the ultimate logic of the novel.

Cooper's narrator reminds the reader that Indigenous people differ from Blacks in one great regard: they had never been enslaved. While this assertion belies historical fact,[77] it also suggests that destiny and fate shape group experiences and group racial identity. When Blacks were enslaved, this argument goes, it was not primarily because of the greed and cruelty of white enslavers and the systemic foundation of capitalism but because of Black people's inferior condition and destiny (OO, 281). The fate of becoming Black may serve as a compelling reason to accept conversion and assimilation. It may be a fate worse than genocide or extinction. At the suggestion of becoming Black, "[s]igns of powerful disgust [became] visible among the listeners, an Indian having much of the contempt that seems to weigh so heavily on that unfortunate class, for all the color mentioned" (OO, 281). In other words, Coopers Indians are aware of American racial hierarchies, and they respond to those hierarchies, like Euro-Americans, as if they are natural and universal across culture, time, and space. In this rendering, Black inferiority is naturalized, and Indians, of course, resist the notion that they might be classed similarly. Cooper suggests that white sympathy for them could stem from the fact that, if they are not "Red" Jews, at least they are not Black (infidels or Christian) (*OO*, 281).

Real alliances

The presence or persistence of slavery, white supremacy, capitalism, and white settler colonialism have marred interactions between Native and African-descended peoples. Many historians have emphasized divisions among Native nations and African Americans, especially in the 19th century when white slaveholders hired Indians as fugitive slave hunters and deployed African Americans as soldiers in conflicts with Native nations.[78] Others point to practical, if conflicted, organizational alliances between the abolitionist and anti-removal movements.[79] Euro-American male abolitionist newspaper editors like John Greenleaf Whittier and Benjamin Lundy and white women authors such as Lydia Maria Child, Lydia Sigourney, Catharine Beecher, and Mary Peabody Mann created and maintained vital intersections among the Indigenous rights and abolitionist movements. They also shepherded the publication of fiction, subaltern personal narratives, and Native histories in the mid-19th century.[80] Likewise, progressive education movements such as the Hampton Institute deployed education to promote assimilation for both groups with, at best, mixed results and, at worst, attempts at cultural genocide.[81] By the late 19th century, however, the abolition coalition had succumbed to the restorationist rhetoric, policies, and failures of post-Reconstruction politics. Some of the religious and activist elements from those earlier radical movements converged in founding the Women's National Indian Association, which financially backed the publication of Blackbird's *History*.[82]

Before the Civil War, within the territory that became Michigan, abolitionist sentiments among Native American communities had been reportedly strong. According to a letter to the American Missionary Association (AMA), which organized and funded missionary efforts aligned with the federal government's "civilizing projects" in Michigan, including the Old Wing Mission located just south of the Grand River, the Odawa supported the anti-slavery cause. Rev. George N. Smith told his AMA superiors in Washington, D.C. that "[t]he Indians have a high appreciation of liberty—to them the thought is extremely abhorrent that a human being, even if black, should be bought and sold." Smith's inclusion of the phrase "even if black" reveals how Euro-Americans constructed "Indian" views of African Americans through their own racial lenses. His perspective was similar to Cooper's, holding that Blackness is universally recognized as the least desirable racial identity. Smith worried that if they discovered the truth about white Christians, the Odawa would be angered by the fact that many of their white neighbors were implicated in both the brutality and lucrative profits of the slave system. This observer cited Native views on the slavery question for why most eligible Anishinaabe voted Republican enthusiastically in the crucial elections leading up to the Civil War.[83] The AMA was closely aligned with the anti-slavery movement, and Smith's remarks suggest that he propagandized among the Anishinaabe on behalf of ending the peculiar institution. Thus, a potential organizational link existed between Blackbird and the anti-slavery cause. Smith likely shared anti-slavery literature with community members and included abolitionist themes in his sermons.[84]

In addition to political agitation, Black and Native alliances extended to anti-colonial guerilla warfare and slave insurrections. Numerous publications about the U.S. war with the Seminole nation in Florida appeared in the mid-1830s highlighting the role of African-descended Indians, fugitive slaves, and other Black "renegades." Black and Native warriors decimated U.S. military invaders, provoked numerous slave insurrections and escapes from nearby plantations, and inspired conspiracies to kill whites and destroy their non-human property.[85] The prospects of a Native and African alliance on a large scale prompted former President John Quincy Adams to warn his Southern neighbors that foreign powers would use such a group as a "natural fifth column."[86] These fears recalled the Anishinaabe uprising led by Pontiac in 1761, wherein they sought to leverage the alliance with France to pressure the British recognition of Anishinaabe territorial sovereignty.

Such interracial interactions extended to the realm of culture as well. The influence of Indigenous oral traditions on African-originated folklore tales has been documented. Colonial and U.S. laws forced Native and enslaved and freed African-descended people to occupy similar social spaces in the southeastern states. U.S. laws enforced the elimination of Native identities and sovereign territories and the imposition of a "colored" identity on African- and Native-descended peoples. Forced composites of identities occasioned shared social spaces that proved to be a fertile ground for cultural diffusions among some Native nations and enslaved Africans.[87] Cultural and political interactions such as these are likely foundational for Blackbird's seeming connection to African American issues, to the presence of a rhetorical-discursive (if not a practical or organizational) alliance.

For his part, Blackbird does not explicitly discuss any direct relationships with African American people. However, he does note that in 1856, he earned the ire of the Democratically appointed Indian agent Henry Gilbert for voting for the "Black Republican" ticket. Gilbert was widely known for using his control over federal annuity payments and other treaty-sanctioned resources to force eligible Indians to vote Democratic.[88] At that time, Michigan ballots were cast publicly. The Democratic activist "was so furiously enraged" at Blackbird and his Indigenous "companion," who were seen placing their ballots in the Republican ballot box. Gilbert attempted to force Blackbird's friend to vote Democratic, but he, too, refused. Later, when Blackbird visited Gilbert to seek financial support for his education, which had been guaranteed for Native youth by the 1855 Treaty of Washington, Gilbert reminded Blackbird of his vote in the election and denied his request. Blackbird writes that Gilbert "bluffed me off by saying that he was sorry I had voted the 'black republican ticket' at the general election, which took place that fall of 1856" (*History*, 65).[89]

That year was a decisive presidential election campaign around which the issue of slavery and its future fate served as the single defining and unifying issue of the newly formed Republican Party.[90] Michigan voters who openly cast ballots for John C. Fremont, the Republican presidential candidate, did so with public recognition for their support for Black Republicanism. Democratic Party activists used the term "Black Republican" to denounce the Republican Party's anti-slavery platform and derogatorily identify Republican voters, activists, and elected officials as supporters of racial equality with African Americans. The term invoked fears of Black revolt and violence against white rule, particularly linking present-day abolitionists to the Black Jacobins that ousted the French regime from Haiti and caused so much fear and anxiety in the U.S.[91] For example, South Carolina's pro-slavery Congressman Preston Brooks used the phrase to characterize Radical Republican Senator Charles Sumner's position on slavery after viciously beating the latter more than 30 times with a heavy cane on the floor of the U.S. Senate.[92] The author of a pamphlet purportedly from an "Old Clay Whig" characterized "Black Republicanism" as "repugnant to decency and propriety" in its advocacy of slave rebellion, perhaps even more so when urged by white race traitors.[93] Deep partisan passions (and occasional violence) against siding with the Black Republicans manifested as a direct threat to his livelihood. This made Blackbird's support for the Republican ticket a profound choice that closely identified him with the well-being of African Americans.

Blackbird's political alignment with African Americans may have also been reflected in his literary alignment with them. A conspicuous feature of *History* is its physical and generic resemblance to the slave narratives published a generation or two earlier.[94] While an over-simplification of either Blackbird's *History* or the corpus of slave narrative for easy comparison would be an exaggeration, some basic similarities between the two suggest Blackbird drew on this literary tradition to write, revise, and organize his *History*. Obvious physical resemblances to the published slave narratives include the reiterated claim of self-authorship often in the title, preface materials, and in the sentimental style of addressing the reader familiarly. A signed preface authored by a white patron or editor attesting to the authenticity of the author's identity, their high moral character, and the worth of the narrative suggests an additional similarity. Most slave narratives and Blackbird's

History were made in close collaboration with a white editor who also served as a source of access to the publishing industry. The relation to the slave narrative tradition emphasizes Blackbird's perceived conscious construction of an alliance of Native American people and interests to those of African descended people within the context of the settler colonial system and white supremacy.

Blackbird's one reference to slavery occurs in the closing chapter titled "The Lamentation of the Overflowing Heart of the Red Man of the Forest," which, according to his biographer, he had written several decades earlier, approximately the same time he had gone on a lecture circuit speaking about Indian-related issues.[95] Blackbird writes: "When the white man took every foot of my inheritance, he thought to him I should be the slave. Ah, never, never! I would sooner plunge the dagger into my beating heart, and follow the footsteps of my forefathers, than be slave to the white man" (*History*, 102). The slavery trope equates settler colonialism to racialized slavery. Unlike Cooper's Indians, Blackbird refuses to use the slavery issues to position Native peoples as racially distinct from Black people. In an era of "Bleeding Kansas" and John Brown's raid on Harper's Ferry to launch a war against slavery, Blackbird's use of this trope opens the horizon of possible political alliance, closely linking the struggle of Native Americans to retain their land, their identity, and their sovereignty to the struggle for the liberation of enslaved Blacks. If anything, Blackbird's likening of white settler colonialism to slavery places Native and African-descended peoples in close social proximity, connecting each to the tradition of rebellion. It recognizes the potentiality of overlap between Native autobiographical writing with the slave narrative tradition by logical extension.

During the Civil War, Blackbird's fierce anti-slavery sentiment extended to his efforts to prevent anti-war Democrats from stirring up such sentiments among the Odawa. Blackbird writes, "During the Rebellion I was loyal to the Government, and opposed the bad white men who were then living in the Indian country, who tried to mislead my people as to the question of the war, to cause them to be disloyal" (*History*, 70). The signed authors of the *History*'s preface provide more detail. Blackbird sided with the Union cause during the war, "for which he met much opposition by designing white people, who had full sway among the Indians, and he broke up one or two rebellious councils amongst his people" (*History*, 3). The "bad white men" mentioned here were called "copperheads" for spreading the poison of white supremacy to call for the maintenance of slavery as a resolution for the war. Copperheads exploited fears of empowered African Americans as equal citizens to convince whites that Lincoln's war aims were ill-advised.[96] Blackbird fights these arguments and insists that his people retain the correct opinions about "the question of the war." In other words, Blackbird's political commitments to the anti-slavery coalition tied him in concrete ways to the struggle for African American liberation.[97] This intersection suggests that Blackbird understands how the origins and development of the U.S. relied explicitly on the genocidal and expropriative policies toward Indigenous nations and the super-exploitation of African labor. Indeed, the expansion of the slavery-based capitalist system, a necessary fact for its survival, depended directly on how rapidly Native peoples and lands could be subdued and expropriated, surveyed and plotted, and resold or redistributed to white owners of capital (bankers, agribusiness, railroad builders, mining corporations, lumber companies, etc.). A more careful analysis of Blackbird's views might have led his white allies to believe he sought the dissolution of the settler-colonial regime.

Another point of intersection at which Native American autobiographers and slave narrative authors meet is the unique point of subjectivity produced by the creators of this genre. As Houston Baker argues, the slave narrative genre emphasizes the author's isolated existence, anxiety, and emergence as a subject within a totality of suppressed humanity through violence, brutality, and the arbitrariness of abusive power.[98] While the conversion of experience (the horizon of the social context) into discourse alters the power relation of the subaltern to the social relation under discussion (slavery or settler colonialism), the subaltern autobiographer has a special problem of creating a liberated Self that can exist without reflecting an existing literary landscape or identity. Still, writing and publishing re-configures how knowledge of this social relation becomes possible only through the subaltern's perspective and voice, substantiating a specific kind of authority and knowledge production that white writers lack.[99] Though Baker's focus is on the literary concerns of the slave narrative authors, similar problems of subjective relation to audience, authority, social reality, and the production of a comprehensible collection of signs entail the conundrum of Native autobiography writers. Writing in English and deploying sentimentalist rhetoric allowed the Native autobiographer to become familiar with "the reader" and claim a particular subjectivity and authority assigned to the authenticated subaltern writer. Familiarity, the utterance of Native names, the production of a legible Native culture and history beyond *and* within the spatiotemporal geopolitics of the U.S. "actualizes their presence." It makes discursive spaces for a contestable future that they will participate in making.[100]

In contrast to the Euro-American Self, produced in white-authored autobiography, the racially and nationally oppressed Self constructs and projects itself in and against a language and literary culture that is not of its own making or origins. The author of the slave narrative and the Native autobiography "had to seize the word. His being had to erupt from nothingness." This assertion is relational and metaphorical as the subaltern writer speaks from a cultural tradition that is not simply erased through movement and enslavement as the colonizer-enslaver would like to pretend. The writers of slave narratives necessarily bend the literary tradition and language they have adopted to the specific experiences of the enslaved and the colonized. The slave narrative author deploys a public language to become a public figure and adapts a social system of signs to construct a textual self in relation to others and within a political context of struggle. In claiming this "public language," the author of the slave narrative relies on relating to a system of "political, civic, and moral virtues and codes" held by the dominant audience that otherwise views the subaltern's being with contempt.[101] This epistemological and ontological experience of literary self-production works for both the slave narrative author and the Native author.

Such connections are recognizable in specific details slave narrative authors provide about their encounters with Native Americans. In her study of several African American-authored slave narratives, Maria Diedrich documents how writers such as Henry Bibb, Josiah Henson, Solomon Northrup, and Austin Steward seemed to downplay negative aspects of their interactions with Native Americans (such as their encounter with Native participation in slavery and their role in "slave catching"). Instead of simply denouncing perpetrators, they promote a complex social analysis of systemic dimensions of white racism, the dominance of whites in the construction and maintenance of slavery, and even the white origins of widely held stereotypes of Indian "savagery." These writers consistently blamed anti-Native and anti-Black racism on white people and institutions. Slave narrative authors insisted that Native cultural systems authentically advocated hospitality and generosity toward African American fugitives rather than oppression. While slave narrative authors were knowledgeable of anti-Indian stereotypes and idioms, they typically manipulated that idiom to emphasize a critique of white racism, in which those stereotypes and their institutional expression originated.[102]

Writers of slave narratives and Native autobiography both express a tension between deploying and resisting sentimentalism, tropes of conversion and the "success story" to propel their narratives. Sentimentalist literature aimed to forge a bond of sympathy between the reader and the perceived subjects of the writing. As indicated above, the absence of a literary tradition in English required slave narrative authors and Native autobiographers to strategically adapt dominant writing styles. The pervasiveness of sentimentalist expectations certainly played a significant role in shaping generic choices. But, sentimentalism's alignment of the reader's emotional responses to the subjects' physical and emotional conditions proved attractive, especially given the tendency for much of the white majority to withhold sympathy and denigrate Native and African people as a whole. Blackbird's *History* emphasizes personal, emotional, and physical conditions that could produce this sympathy in his audiences. In his account of his childhood, for example, Blackbird foregrounds nostalgic happiness and plenitude, innocent Indian spirituality, romantic affiliations of Indigenous people with Nature, and the broadly democratic life of his people. These features tapped into modes of thought and expression that touched the sympathetic nerve-endings of a potential readership conditioned by and habituated in sentimental tropes.

Slave narratives also reproduced a progressive story that celebrated the possibilities of upward economic mobility. The autobiographical Self moves through increasingly complex and freer stages of thought and development, replicating the popular nineteenth-century success story (discussed further in the next chapter). Such narratives of progress followed a model of stages of development of the Self that roughly correspond to social status, cultural capital, educational attainment, or levels of civic engagement. In other words, a progression from an anxious, ill-defined existence to a stable, educated, Christian identity, engaged effectively with public life.[103] This progression necessarily deployed Christian tropes and often a conversion narrative that closely linked the fugitive Self to the national body politic as an assimilable subject. For some slave narratives, this progression also aimed to mirror dominant Euro-American cultural values—individualism and heteronormative patriarchy—and index differences between the writer and the adherents of traditional African culture.[104]

Conversion to Christianity, both as a collective and individuated process, anchors the progress of Blackbird's *History* and strategically forms the cultural basis of social cohesion and sovereignty. In *History*, the conversion narrative produces an opportunity to emphasize Native agency rather than subjugation to settler-colonial supremacy. Blackbird provides two conversion accounts: one to Catholicism in the 1820s and a personal one to Protestantism as an adult. In the first, Blackbird discloses that the collective conversion to Christianity resulted from Odawa initiatives and discussion. Claiming, once again, control of the narrative on behalf of his people, he debunks the notion that "some white people and missionary societies brought the Christian religion" to his band (*History*, 47). Blackbird's reclamation of the strategic function of the religious conversion narrative prominent in sentimentalist narrative corresponds with the adaptation framework that the Anishinaabe had until the early 19th century pursued. The failure of nativist and non-accommodationist strategies leading to Anishinaabe involvement in the War of 1812 suggested their overall weakened relation to the spiritual world, accompanied by the loss of powerful allies.[105] In these passages on conversion, Blackbird alludes to internal consultations on the need to alter and adapt new cultural practices. This tension between conversion and traditional spiritual values differs from the slave narrative form in that it does not index progress by the movement away from tradition.

As Blackbird indicates, Odawa leaders chose to combine new spiritual practices with substantially altered social practices generally, including the land tenure system and agricultural practices of whites, acceptance of various forms of Christianity (Catholicism, Methodism, Presbyterianism, Baptism), acquisition of new spiritual blessings to strengthen the community, and to empower it through the formation of new alliances with intruding whites.[106] Conversion accompanied the end of annual southern migration, the adoption of permanent homes, and the more systematic pursuit of white forms of education (*History*, 47). Instead of simply a surrender to whites, however, the Arbor Croche band fought for control over the mission's location, the appointment of Odawa leaders to federal agencies, and management of the rhythms and schedules of religious and secular instruction (*History*, 47–48).

Despite significant and rapid changes in everyday life, Blackbird insists, "my people were very happy in those days." Happiness resulted less from deeper spiritual fulfillment and more from the fact that "they were all by themselves and possessed a wide spread of land, and no one to quarrel with them as to where they should make their gardens, or take timber, or make sugar" (*History*, 50). Conversion to Christianity provided some stable autonomy as it temporarily satisfied Euro-American "civilizing" demands. While conversion served as a collective response to changing global circumstances, it remained a choice at the individual level. Blackbird notes that missionaries provided baptism to "all those Indians who felt disposed to receive the religion" (*History*, 46). Indeed, sovereignty in their collective social formation and autonomous relations within the community served as touchstones of what counted as "happiness," reflecting adherence to long-held cultural values.

Thus, the conversion narrative reveals another point of connection with the slave narrative genre. Like the slave narrative generally, the conversion narrative in Blackbird emphasizes agency and sovereignty, positioning the Odawa people not as completely subjugated and submissive victims of white American society but instead as a people capable of defining themselves, asserting a cultural agenda, and linking it to economic and social aspects of their community life. In comparison, Mary Helen Washington's introduction to an edition of *The Narrative of Sojourner Truth* emphasizes that Truth's conversion was deeply rooted in her relation to "traditions of Africanity and Christianity alike."[107] In other words, Blackbird's account of religious conversion reveals a people modifying their social formation through discussion and debate, but, in the end, claiming a shared control over what they define as their collective possession. By its logic and message, it is a statement of Anishinaabe endurance and persistence as a people. It is a rejection of the Euro-American mythology of the frontier.

Notes

1. Wayne Franklin, *James Fenimore Cooper: The Late Years*, (New Haven: Yale University Press, 2017), 431-433.
2. James Fenimore Cooper, *The Oak Openings: Or, the Bee-Hunter*, (New York: The Co-operative Publication Society, 1900 [1848]), 7. Hereafter cited as *OO* in the text.
3. Historian Michael Witgen uses this Anishinaabe term to name "the land of the Aninishnaabeg." The term Anishinaabeg is a collective noun identifying both the "infinity of nations" which occupied Anishinaabewaki and the modern peoples of the region comprised of the Ojibwe, Odawa, and Bodéwadmi. Anishinaabemowin refers to the language system generally shared across the region. Michael Witgen, *An Infinity of Nations: How the Native World Shaped Early North America*, (Philadelphia: University of Pennsylvania Press, 2012), 1, 14.
4. Susan Fenimore Cooper, "Introduction to *Oak Openings*," in *Pages and Pictures from the Writings of James Fenimore Cooper*, (New York: 1861), 380-382.

5. S. Cooper, 380-382.
6. Rob Hardy, "Bee Line: How the Honey Bee Defined the American Frontier," *Readings*, Vol. 2, no. 1 (2016): 2-4.
7. Cooper had used beavers, another well-organized animal species as tropes for cultural differences and white supremacy. Beavers served a similar objective in his most famous novel, *The Last of the Mohicans*. James Fenimore Cooper, *The Last of the Mohicans*, (New York: E.P. Dutton and Company, 1951 [1826]), 284ff.
8. Isaac Watts, *Divine Songs: Attempted in the Easy Language of Children*, 1761, www.gutenberg.org/ebooks/13439. Accessed 25 Mar. 2019.
9. Carol Devens, *Countering Colonization: Native American Women and Great Lakes Missions, 1630-1900*, (Berkeley: University of California Press, 1992), 24.
10. Devens, 24; Carey Miller, *Ogimaag: Anishinaabeg Leadership, 1760-1845*, (Lincoln: University of Nebraska Press, 2010), 64-112.
11. Peter Edwards, *One Dead Indian: The Premier, the Police, and the Ipperwash Crisis*, (Toronto: McClelland and Stewart, 2003), 38-39. In 1827, the *ogimaa* Joshua Wawanosh, the leader of a band of several hundred Ojibwe people Ontario, Canada, signed the Treaty of Amherstburg along with several other Ojibwe *ogimaag*. Altogether they were forced to cede more than two million acres to the British government in exchange for annual gifts of money and goods. Wawanosh signed with a pictograph of a bird in flight, indicating the *doodem* of his hereditary leadership as *ogimaa* and his family connection to the manidoo represented by that image. The name and the doodem linked him by kin to the flow of power between the spirit world and the human world. Cooper's use of a historical Native name also suggests Native origins and inspirations for this story, as Scalping Peter/Onoah/Wawanosh may have borne this same kinship relation. *Ogimaa* is the Anishinaabe term for a political leader; ogimaag is the plural form. On Anishinaabe rituals related to *manidoo* and *doodem* see Miller, 113; Charles E. Cleland, *Rites of Conquest: The History and Culture of Michigan's Native Americans*, (Ann Arbor: University of Michigan Press, 1992), 66-70.
12. Lisa Brooks, "Turning the Looking Glass on King Philip's War: Locating American Literature in Native Space." *American Literary History*, Vol. 25, no. 4 (2013): 720.
13. Michael Witgen, *An Infinity of Nations: How the Native World Shaped Early North America.* (Philadelphia: University of Pennsylvania Press, 2012), 15.
14. Robert Warrior, *People and the Word: Reading Native Nonfiction*, (Minneapolis: University of Minnesota Press, 2005), xv.
15. *Manidoo* refers to the ancestral entity that inhabits all things through which power flows. It connects creatures, humans, and a specific territory in a common struggle to survive. See Miller, 22-25. The Anishinaabe men likely saw Boden's interaction with the bees in this light.
16. Miller, 27-28.
17. Richard White, *The Middle Ground: Indians, Empires, and Republics in the Great Lakes Region, 1650–1815*, (Cambridge: Cambridge University Press, 1992).
18. It seems likely that Cooper's concerns about Indigenous military self-defense resonated with the Euro-American memory of Anishinaabe involvement in Tecumseh's and Pontiac's wars in 1814 and 1761 respectively, among myriad other Indigenous operations, insurrections, and insurgency aiming to halt Euro-American atrocities.
19. Hedges, 31.
20. Bohaker, 50-51. This resilience should never be used as a mitigation of European and Euro-American atrocities.

21. Miller, 79-80.
22. Beth H. Piatote, *Domestic Subjects: Gender, Citizenship, and Law in Native American Literature*, (New Haven: Yale University Press, 2013), 124-125.
23. Meghan C. L. Howey, "Colonial Encounters, European Kettles, and the Magic of Mimesis in the Late Sixteenth and Early Seventeenth-Century Indigenous Northeast and Great Lakes," *International Journal of Historical Anthropology*, Vol. 15, no. 2 (2011): 329-332, 352.
24. Miller, 24.
25. Carey Miller, "Thomas King: Shifting Shapes to Tell Another Story," in *The Native American Renaissance: Literary Imagination and Achievement*, eds. Alan R. Velie and A. Robert Lee, (Tulsa: University of Oklahoma Press, 2013), 166.
26. C. H. Chapman, H. R. Schoolcraft, and W. Johnston, "The Historic Johnston Family of Sault Ste. Marie, Michigan," (Iron Mountain, Michigan, Mid-Peninsula Library Cooperative, 1982), 14-17.
27. Witgen, 74-76.
28. Witgen, 76.
29. Witgen, 80.
30. Noodin, 21-22.
31. Heidi Kiiwetinepinisiik Stark, "Transforming the Trickster: Federal Indian Law Encounters Anishinaabe Diplomacy," in *Centering Anishinaabe Studies: Understanding the World through Stories*, eds. Jill Doerfler, Niigaanwewidam James Sinclair, and Heidi Kiiwetinepinisiik Stark, (East Lansing: Michigan State University, 2013), 262.
32. Philosopher Lewis R. Gordon describes guilt of this sort as "a condition of aggression turned inward." Gordon, *Fear of Black Consciousness*, (New York: Farrar, Straus and Giroux, 2021), 103.
33. See Michael A. McDonnell, *Masters of Empire: Great Lakes Indians and the Making of America*, (New York: Hill and Wang, 2015), 154; Gregory Evans Dowd, *A Spirited Resistance: The North American Indian Struggle for Unity, 1745-1815*, (Baltimore: John Hopkins University Press, 1992), 14-16; Andrew J. Blackbird, *History of the Ottawa and Chippewa Indians of Michigan: A Grammar of Their Language, and the Personal History of the Author*, (Ypsilanti, Mich.: Ypsilantian Job Printing House, 1887), 85-86.
34. See Miller, 131; McDonnell, 137; Blackbird, 88; Dowd, 162–165; Michelle Cassidy, *"Both the Honor and the Profit": Anishinaabe Warriors, Soldiers, and Veterans from Pontiac's War through the Civil War*. University of Michigan, PhD dissertation, 2016, 47–49.
35. James A. Clifton, George I. Cornell, and James M. McClurken, *People of The Three Fires: The Ottawa, Potawatomi, and Ojibway of Michigan*, (Grand Rapids: The Grand Rapids Inter-Tribal Council, 1986), 50.
36. The economic collapse of 1837 and again in 1847 saw Euro-American settlement in West Michigan and subsequent capitalist development there slow to a trickle until after the Civil War. Many reported being dependent on Indigenous neighbors for subsistence.
37. Margery is Boden's "love interest." They marry and aid the novel's ideological closures.
38. Andrew J. Blackbird, *History of the Ottawa and Chippewa Indians of Michigan: A Grammar of Their Language, and the Personal History of the Author*, (Ypsilanti: Ypsilantian Job Printing House, 1887), 7. Hereafter cited in the text as *History*. When quoting Blackbird, I use the anachronistic spelling Ottawa; otherwise, I use the contemporary spelling Odawa.

39. Disputes between Anishinaabe bands and the Dakota (Oceti Sakowin) occa-
    sionally resulted in military actions. The relations between the two powerful
    social formations of Anishinaabe and Oceti Sakowin can best be viewed as an
    alliance. Negotiated settlements often resulted in the exchange of kin as restitu-
    tion for killing or wounding enemies. See Witgen 162-167; 209-210. Blackbird's
    account of the adoption of the "underground race" substantiates a discourse of
    kinship.
40. Miller, 108-109.
41. Witgen, 74-76, 79-80. One important example of this adaption in Blackbird's *His-
    tory* is the conversion to Christianity. Briefly put, many Anishinaabe practitioners
    of Christianity (unlike Cooper's depiction of Peter) "tried to maintain social and
    political autonomy" and "attempted to make sense of Christianity from an indig-
    enous perspective." Choices about which denominations to adhere to rested on
    "reasons connected to kinship, resources, worship styles, and faith." See Cassidy
    91-94. A collectively authored history of the Little Traverse Bay Bands of Odawa
    Indians indicates that Christian beliefs were often "incorporate[d]" into existing
    spiritual systems. Little Traverse Bay Bands of Odawa Indians, "Our Land and
    Culture: A 200 Year History of Our Land Use," 2005, 16. http://www.ltbbodawa
    -nsn.gov/Arch/Our%20Land%20and%20Culture%20for%20web.pdf. Accessed
    7 June 2019.
42. Little Traverse Bay Bands of Odawa Indians, "Our Land and Culture."
43. Piatote, 2.
44. Malea D. Powell, "Rhetorics of Survivance: How American Indians Use Writ-
    ing." *College Composition and Communication*, Vol. 53, no. 3 (2002): 403-404; Powell,
    "Sarah Winnemucca Hopkins: Her Wrongs and Claims," in *American Indian Rhet-
    orics of Survivance: Word Medicine, Word Magic*, ed. Ernest Stromberg, (Pittsburgh:
    University of Pittsburgh, 2006), 69-70.
45. Margaret Noodin, *Bawajimo: A Dialect of Dreams in Anishinaabe Language and Litera-
    ture*, (East Lansing: Michigan State University Press, 2014), 19. For a discussion of
    History's origins, see Theodore J. Karamanski, *Blackbird's Song: Andrew J. Blackbird
    and the Odawa People*. (Lansing: Michigan State University Press, 2012), 227-228.
46. Karamanski, xiii, 222.
47. Womack argues that Native use of English might be understood as how
    "Indians ... colonized English rather than the other way around." Craig Womack,
    "Alexander Posey's Nature Journals: A Further Argument for Tribally-Specific
    Aesthetics," *Studies in American Indian Literatures*, Vol. 13, no. 2&3 (2000): 50. This
    appropriation began with Native adoption of "trade languages" during encoun-
    ters with other tribal nations and European traders. Embracing English for trade
    purposes saw "no concomitant reduction in their cultural viability." Sean Kicum-
    mah Teuton, *Red Land, Red Power: Grounding Knowledge in the American Indian
    Novel*, (Durham: Duke University Press, 2008), 28. See also, Jace Weaver, "Turning
    West: Cosmopolitanism and American Indian Literary Nationalism," in *Native
    American Renaissance: Literary Imagination and Achievement*, eds. by Alan R. Velie
    and A. Robert Lee. (Tulsa: University of Oklahoma Press, 2013), 30.
48. Lisa Brooks, *The Common Pot: The Recovery of Native Space in the Northeast*, (Minne-
    apolis: University of Minnesota Press, 2008), 220.
49. Cassidy, 99.
50. Benjamin Ramirez-Shkwegnaabi, "The Dynamics of American Indian Diplomacy
    in the Great Lakes Region," *American Indian Culture and Research Journal*, Vol. 27,
    no. 4 (2003): 67.
51. Powell, "Rhetorics," 405

52. Leanne Howe, "Embodied Tribalography: Mound Building, Ball Games, and Native Endurance in the Southeast," *Studies in American Indian Literatures*, Vol. 26, no. 2 (2014): 77.
53. Warrior, xx.
54. Karamanski, 221 ix.
55. Heidi Kiiwetinepinisiik Stark and Kekek Jason Stark, "Nenabozho Goes Fishing: A Sovereignty Story," *Daedalus*, Vol. 147, no. 2 (2018): 22.
56. Meghan C. Howey, "'The question which has puzzled, and still puzzles': How American Indian Authors Challenged Dominant Discourse about Native American Origins in the Nineteenth Century," *American Indian Quarterly*, Vol. 34, no. 4 (2010): 439.
57. See Jack D. Forbes, *The American Discovery of Europe*, (Champaign: University of Illinois Press, 2010). Forbes's scholarship on the Native discovery of Europe enlists this uncertainty. Anishinaabe culture documents large quantities of origins stories "without ever mentioning migration from the area of the Bering Strait," deepening the layers of doubt about the veracity of the migration hypothesis. See Noodin, 2.
58. Howey, "The question," 446.
59. Blackbird's origins story contrasts significantly with Jefferson's *Notes* (see the introduction) and Cooper's *The Oak Openings* (discussed in this chapter below). Those accounts reflect the colonial obsession with discounting Indigenous cultural identities, humanity, and history by insisting they must have originated elsewhere. Euro-American obsessions with Asian civilizations (see footnote 28 in chapter 4) are also highlighted in these origin stories.
60. William P. F. Ferguson, "Michigan's Most Ancient Industry: The Pre-historical Mines and Miners of Isle Royale," *Michigan History Magazine*, Vol. 7, no. 25 (1923): 153-162.
61. Ferguson, 158-160.
62. Brooks, *Common Pot*, 241.
63. Joseph Bauerkemper, "Narrating Nationhood: Indian Time and Ideologies of Progress," *Studies in American Indian Literature*, Vol. 19, no. 4 (2007): 41.
64. Maureen Konkle, *Writing Indian Nations: Native Intellectuals and the Politics of Historiography, 1827-1863*, (Chapel Hill: North Carolina University Press, 2004), 12.
65. Brooks, *Common Pot*, 243.
66. Gerald Vizenor, *Native Liberty: Natural Reason and Cultural Survivance*, (Lincoln: University of Nebraska Press, 2009).
67. Noodin, 22.
68. Tiya Miles, "Beyond a Boundary: Black Lives and the Settler–Native Divide," *The William and Mary Quarterly*, Vol. 76, no. 3 (2019): 420.
69. Peter Jones, *History of the Ojebway Indians; with especial reference to their conversion to Christianity*, (London: A. W. Bennett, 1861), 219.
70. Tiya Miles and Sharon P. Holland, "Introduction," in *Crossing Waters, Crossing Worlds: The African Diaspora in Indian Country*, eds. Miles and Holland, (Durham, NC: Duke University Press, 2006), 4, 9.
71. Karla Slocum, *Black Towns, Black Futures: The Enduring Allure of a Black Place in the American West*, (Chapel Hill: University of North Carolina Press, 2020), 43.
72. Miles and Holland, 9-11.
73. Lisa Brooks, "The Constitution of the White Earth Nation: A New Innovation in a Longstanding Indigenous Literary Tradition," *Studies in American Indian Literatures*, Vol. 23, no. 4 (2011): 61.
74. Max Grivno, "'Black Frenchmen' and 'White Settlers': Race, Slavery, and the Creation of African-American Identities Along the Northwest Frontier, 1790–1840,"

Slavery and Abolition, Vol. 21, no. 3 (2000): 75–93; Sharon-Elizabeth Sexton, "The Red and Black Connection," *Michigan Citizen*, 2 May 1998; Blanche Coggan, "The Underground Railroad in Michigan," *Negro History Bulletin*, Vol. 27, no. 5 (1964): 122–26.

75. Miles, 417, 419.

76. Howey, "The question," 441-442.

77. Gerald Horne, *The Apocalypse of Settler Colonialism: The Roots of Slavery, White Supremacy, and Capitalism in Seventeenth-Century North America and the Caribbean*, (New York: Monthly Review Press, 2018).

78. Weaver, 127.

79. Mary Hershberger, "Mobilizing Women, Anticipating Abolition: The Struggle against Indian Removal in the 1830s," *Journal of American History*, Vol. 86, no. 1 (1999): 15–40.

80. Linda Kerber, "The Abolitionist Perception of the Indian," *Journal of American History*, Vol. 62, no. 2 (1975): 271–95.

81. Jacqueline Emery, "Writing against Erasure: Native American Students at Hampton Institute and the Periodical Press," *American Periodicals*, Vol. 22, no. 2 (2012): 178–98.

82. Blackbird, 6.

83. Smith's words are quoted in Kerber, 284-285.

84. Cassidy, 171-172.

85. John Porter, "John Caesar: Seminole Negro Partisan," *The Journal of Negro History*, Vol. 31, no. 2 (1946): 191–196. Porter cites three such incidents from the 1830s alone. See also, Kerber, 275–76; Gerald Horne, *Negro Comrades of the Crown: African Americans and the British Empire Fight the U.S. Before Emancipation*, (New York University Press, 2014), 81-82.

86. Quoted in Kerber, 281.

87. Jay Hansford C. Vest, "From Bobtail to Brer Rabbit: Native American Influences on Uncle Remus," *American Indian Quarterly*, Vol. 24, no. 1 (2000): 28-29.

88. Karamanski, 156. Michigan had enfranchised some Native people in 1850.

89. See Richard White, *The Burt Lake Band: An Ethnohistorical Report on the Trust Lands of Indian Village*, (East Lansing: Michigan State University Press, 1980), 61-64.

90. Eric Foner, *Fiery Trial: Abraham Lincoln and American Slavery*, (New York: W. W. Norton and Company, 2010), 79.

91. Gerald Horne, *Confronting Black Jacobins: The United States, the Haitian Revolution, and the Origins of the Dominican Republic*, (New York: Monthly Review Press, 2015), 246.

92. Stephen Berry and James Hill Wellborn, "The Cane of His Existence: Depression, Damage, and the Brooks–Sumner Affair," *Southern Cultures*, Vol. 20, no. 4 (2104): 15.

93. Old Clay Whig, *Reflections and Suggestions on the Present State of Parties*, (Nashville, Tennessee: G. C. Torbett and Co., 1856), 7-8.

94. A. LaVonne Brown Ruoff, "Three Nineteenth-Century American Indian Autobiographers," in *Redefining American Literary History*, eds. Ruoff and Jerry W. Ward Jr., (New York: Modern Language Association of America, 1990), 252. Ruoff attributes the similarity between the two bodies of literature to a semi-conscious "[incorporation of] aspects of the slave narratives" in Indigenous autobiographical writings. Since this argument, few passing references to similarities between Indigenous autobiography and slave narratives have been made. See Heidi M. Hanrahan, "'[W]orthy the imitation of the whites': Sarah Winnemucca and Mary Peabody Mann's Collaboration," *MELUS*, Vol. 38, no. 1 (2013): 122; H. David Brumble, *American Indian Autobiography*, (Lincoln: University of Nebraska Press, 2008), 61; Powell, 69-94.

95. Karamanski 221. Giving talks about his experiences, Blackbird may have toured the eastern cities with educator Samuel Bissell, founder of the Twinsburg Institute, Blackbird's alma mater. In a letter to Bissell a few years before, Blackbird expresses similar emotions of despair as articulated "The Lamentation." Samuel Bissell and Andrew J. Blackbird, "Letter to the Editor," *New York Observer and Chronicle*, 1 May 1847, 18, 25.

96. Copperhead arguments about the slavery debate and racial equality rested on the same logic and evidence James Fenimore Cooper gave in his defense of slavery. See footnote 3 in chapter 2.

97. Blackbird shared this view with many Anishinaabe people who participated in large numbers in the Union Army. U.S. Army "Company K" from Northern Michigan was overwhelmingly comprised of Anishinaabe men. See Michelle Cassidy, *"Both the Honor and the Profit": Anishinaabe Warriors, Soldiers, and Veterans from Pontiac's War through the Civil War*. University of Michigan, PhD dissertation, 2016.

98. Houston A. Baker, "Autobiographical Acts and the Voice of the Southern Slave," in *The Slave's Narrative*, eds. Charles T. Davis and Henry Louis Gates, Jr., (New York: Oxford University Press), 246.

99. Baker, 245-247.

100. Fabrice Le Corguille, "Writing Against Vanishing: Native American Autobiography and the Trope of an Ever-Pending Vanishment," *Revue Electronique D'études Sur le Monde Anglophone*, Vol. 15, no. 1 (2017): 3-4.

101. Baker 245, 251, 252.

102. Maria Diedrich, "The Characterization of Native Americans in the Antebellum Slave Narrative," *CLA Journal*, Vol. 31, no. 4 (1988): 414, 418–19, 434.

103. Baker, 250.

104. Christopher S. Lewis, "Conjure Women, Root Men, and Normative Visions of Freedom in Antebellum Slave Narratives," *Arizona Quarterly* 74, no. 2 (2018): 113, 117. Blackbird's *History* reverses the developmental progress of the "success genre." It emphasizes an original happiness altered by the harshness of Euro-American relations, deepening its anti-colonial message.

105. Catherine Murton Stoehr, "Nativism's Bastard: Neolin, Tentskwatawa, and the Anishinabeg Methodist Movement," in *Lines Drawn Upon the Water: First Nations and the Great Lakes Borders and Borderlands*, ed. K. S. Hele, (Waterloo: Wilfred Laurier University Press, 2008), 175–90.

106. Stoehr, 187–88.

107. Mary Helen Washington, "Introduction: The Enduring Legacy of Sojourner Truth," in *The Narrative of Sojourner Truth*, ed. Washington, (New York: Vintage Books, 1993), xxxvi.

Chapter 4

Self-made men

I must be understood as protesting as the representative of the independent Philippine Republic that the United States has no jurisdiction, natural or acquired, through any of its agencies to adjudicate in any manner upon the rights of my country and people. –D. Felipe Agoncillo to U.S. Secretary of State and U.S. Senate, 30 January 1899.

I want no prisoners. I wish you to kill and burn. The more you kill and burn the better you will please me.... I want all persons killed who are capable of bearing arms in actual hostilities against the United States.... The interior of Samar must be made a howling wilderness. ... Kill everyone over ten. –Gen. Jacob H. Smith to Maj. Littleton W.T. Waller, October 1901.

The killing-spree did not end there, as the U.S. continued to enforce a "scorched-earth policy" until 1902, which meant the total destruction of the Balangiga and its people.... Filipino historians believed that around 50,000 Filipinos were killed in the genocide. –Jhemmylrut Teng, journalist, 13 February 2021.

General Jacob H. Smith was a self-made man. He was one of many in an era of empire and power. Theodore Roosevelt. P.T. Barnum. Henry Ford. Andrew Carnegie. Davy Crockett. And the fictional ones: Fitzgerald's Jay Gatsby. Horatio Alger's Walter Conrad. Stephen Crane's Thomas G. Somebody. Sinclair Lewis's George Babbitt. All self-made men. To be self-made, a (cisgender, able-bodied, American citizen, white) man must be able to claim an affiliation with "a race of sturdy stock," immigrant and pioneering roots (if not actual deeds), and a preference for the "strenuous life." The "self-made man's" markers of masculinity and racial superiority—violence, racism, xeno-phobia, physicality—are often emphasized in contrast with the effeminate and sensitive college-educated intellectual or "elite." In a body of literature produced about work, business, or politics, the exceedingly individualistic "self-made man" is ready and willing to exploit, colonize, destroy nature, kill other humans, and celebrate this life in the service of civilization and white supremacy.[1] While being "self-made" suggests innovation and originality with each new being, the "self-made man" was, in reality, an attempt to reproduce copies of embodied white, masculine power.[2] Of course, the last three on my list of examples above are imaginary, and there is much satire embedded in the self-made-ness of those.

Self-serving autobiographical accounts of success and social mobility are closely affiliated with a genre of political writing designed to boost the author's fortunes, to craft a subjectivity of whiteness, masculinity, power, and leadership. Being self-made, then, was closely linked to producing a narrative in the "success" genre, such as a political pamphlet, an autobiography, a university's alumni magazine, promotional materials for a corporation, and that sort of thing. It also formed the plots of many popular novels and stories, the most famous of which were authored by Horatio Alger.[3] The self-made man mythology in the U.S. context is an ideological self-delusion. It is adopted to hide, even embrace, the reality of social contradictions that constitute the social system.[4] This mythological context forms a substantial sub-genre of U.S. hegemonic cultural production. From Emerson, Crockett, and Lincoln to stories of relatively unimportant "pioneers on the frontier," self-made man mythology, from its early days, justified, spurred on, and assuaged guilt over capitalist forms of accumulation, racial slavery, settler colonialism, and heteronormative patriarchy. By the end of the 19th century, it served as a justification for U.S. imperialism beyond what became the continental U.S. To put the point slightly otherwise, capitalism, imperialism, settler-colonialism, racial slavery, and patriarchy served as the "conditions of possibility"[5] for the self-made man and his ideological self-delusion.

Born in 1840 and raised on the Ohio and Kentucky border, Jacob H. Smith attended a military academy in Kentucky. He joined a contingent of U.S. Army troops headed for action in the Civil War from that border state. He rose in the ranks during the war despite his questionable record. He was implicated in an embezzlement scheme to steal bounty money to enlist Black soldiers in the Union Army. Commanders repeatedly accused him of insolence and exposed him for lying in his written reports. After the war, he was sued several times for failure to pay debts, had a long record of being away from his military assignments in the Plains territories, and was accused of using enlisted men as house servants. One historian's account of Smith's record describes it as an indication of a terrible promotion system in the Army rather than excellent leadership skills. His final promotion to Brigadier General may have been done to encourage his retirement. However, the war with Spain and subsequent war during which the U.S. destroyed the Republic of the Philippines prolonged it.[6]

His otherwise ordinary and unremarkable service record was further marred by his orders to hold an estimated 50,000 residents of the province of Samar, Philippines, in concentration camps and to destroy crops, buildings, and any other signs of life, including anyone over the age of 10 who refused to be herded into the concentration camps. Estimates range from 15,000 to 50,000 people killed due to his orders.[7] Smith's actions were part of a larger war that Filipino scholars believe killed 1.4 million of the country's residents.[8] Some historians claim that Americans were "shocked" to learn about Smith's orders and the actions of his subordinates in the mass killings. The truth is that many U.S. people supported Smith and cared little about the deaths of Filipino people. More may have been shocked at the Philippine insurgency's initial successes against superior U.S. firepower. The insurgency lasted until 1913. As it stands, thousands came to honor Smith with a hometown parade after his return in 1902. When Roosevelt ordered his early retirement without criminal punishment, he praised Smith publicly for a "distinguished" career.[9] Charges at Smith's court-martial centered on undermining "discipline" and "military order," not the commission of atrocities.[10] Military analysts praised and endorsed Smith's orders. Many of Smith's most vocal supporters were angrier at Roosevelt for hypocrisy than at Smith for mass murder. During his welcome-home parade, Smith elaborated a concise history of the country of "self-made men":

> We have fought to make this a united country; to wrest the great West from the hordes of Indian savages and to protect the frontiersman and his wife and children in their homes; to bring the blessings of liberty and good government to our neighboring and distant isles of the sea; to avenge the massacres in the harbor of Havana, to compel obedience to our authority in the Philippine Islands and to pacify and subdue the most savage tribes of the earth.[11]

Above all, it was "the politics of the moment," not any "shock" at what Smith had done that had the biggest impact on his dismissal from service, despite the occasional characterization of the Samar genocide as "criminal."[12] Balancing the country's public image with imperialist aggression was foremost in Theodore Roosevelt's mind. Even today, most U.S.-based sources on the events in Samar downplay those atrocities and the imperialist nature of the war on the Philippines.[13] They typically elevate the danger into which U.S. policy placed its troops, tacitly justifying Smith's genocidal response. In other words, historical work on those events does more to reflect the moods of the adoring crowds than to denounce the U.S. military's actions.

Making more than a self

1902 also saw the return of Yung Wing (Rong Hong),[14] a Yale-educated, would-be leader of the republican revolutionary movement in China, to the United States. Both Smith and Yung returned to the U.S. from dangerous overseas involvements to tenuous status in the U.S. Smith's trials and tribulations led to his retirement and fading into obscurity. Yung, who had acquired U.S. citizenship in 1852, had to steal his way back into the country disguised as a European man. His citizenship had been revoked without a hearing by the State Department in 1898 based on a retroactive application of the 1870 Naturalization Act.[15] Yung lived the final decade of his life with a price on his head, attending to events in China from a distance, and writing his autobiography, *My Life in China and America* (1909).[16] As the republican revolution swept the Qing dynasty from power in 1912, Sun Yixian (Sun Yat-sen), the republic's founder, wrote to Yung, asking him to return to help lead the country into a new era.[17] Failing health prevented his return. Yung died within months of seeing his life-long dream come to fruition.

Yung Wing was born in Guangdong, near the island of Macao, to poor parents of peasant backgrounds. His parents sent him to a missionary school on the island, believing fortuitously, as Yung suggests, in the value of education and that Western education would open doors for his future (*MLCA*, 2). He attended a British-run school in Macao. His autobiography tells little of his time there, except for an early attempt to flee the island in a boat with other children, indicating dissatisfaction with his parents' decision (*MLCA*, 4). In his early teens, he entered the Morrison School, a second British-funded but American-operated missionary school. The British-instigated Opium War, which was fought to force the Chinese government to accept British opium, resulted in the forced cession of Hong Kong. The war compelled the school's relocation from Macao to Hong Kong and Yung with it. After completing the courses, school officials brought Yung and several other students to the U.S. They attended Monson Academy for three years before entering Yale University. During his time at Yale, Yung excelled at athletics and English composition and acquired U.S. citizenship (before the era of Chinese exclusion).[18]

Yung graduated as the first Chinese person from Yale University in 1854. He returned to China intending to establish himself in business and government work as a basis for creating a study abroad program for Chinese students. His primary life mission was to launch a project to "work out an Orientalist civilization on an Occidental basis," founded foremost on an educational program (*MLCA*, 106). Upon his arrival, he admits he had to relearn Chinese because he had forgotten so much of it. He interacted sympathetically with leaders of the Taiping rebellion but refused the temptation to join the revolt. He believed that the Taiping uprising showed potential for overthrowing the "imperialist" Qing government (*MLCA*, 100), which he described as weak, backward, and unable to defend the people against British (and other European) imperialism. He writes, "I thought then that the Taiping rebels had ample grounds to justify their attempts to overthrow the Manchu regime." Ultimately, however, Yung chose to stay focused on his educational project (*MLCA*, 57-58). He saw Western education as a way for China to encourage the influence of Western ideas, political systems, and economic forms to spur the country's development. After a series of failures, the program was launched in the 1870s as the Chinese Education Mission. While heading the mission, Yung married a white American woman with whom he had two children. He also served as an official Chinese ambassador to the U.S. In that capacity, he appealed to the Grant and Hayes administrations on behalf of U.S.-based Chinese people who faced racist violence from their white neighbors (a fact that he leaves out of the autobiography).[19]

The Qing imperial court ended the mission in 1881, and Yung returned to China. There, at least initially, he attempted to work within the existing system to promote modernization and reform. He purchased a railroad concession from the Chinese government based on being a U.S. citizen, but with the primary intention of raising Chinese capital for internal development and trade (*MLCA*, 142-143). When his claim was contested by German interests who wanted the rights to the railroad, he appealed to the U.S. embassy for their support for his rights as a U.S. citizen. His appeal for protection as a citizen appears to be less an attempt to claim a strong affiliation with U.S. imperialism and more of a strategic safeguard for mobilizing capital investment for Chinese development.[20] Despite presenting legal documentation of his 1852 naturalization, the U.S. State Department retracted his citizenship. Contradicting its claims to liberal protection of citizenship rights, the racial capitalist U.S. state could not extend that protection to Yung and maintain its white supremacist internal logic of the "alien" Chinese. It preferred to surrender some imperialist control over Chinese territory to deny a Chinese-born person the ability to claim to be a citizen.

Yung ultimately adopted the role of republican revolutionary, supporting the failed 100 Days reforms in 1898. After the palace coup that ended the reforms, Yung became a wanted man. He fled to Shanghai's foreign settlement, where he established a republican think-tank called the Deliberative Association of China. Fear for his safety forced him to escape to the British-controlled island of Hong Kong in 1899. While living in Hong Kong, Yung visited Taiwan briefly, which included a harrowing encounter with Japanese colonial authorities who controlled the island since wresting it from China during the 1894 war (*MLCA*, 145).[21] In 1902, Yung returned illegally to the U.S. and lived out his remaining years in Connecticut.

A large body of Chinese-language scholarship celebrates Yung's historical role in Chinese modernization, patriotism, and innovative approaches to education and technological development during the revolutionary period leading up to the republic.[22] Yung's autobiography aids this move to claim him for modern Chinese national identity. He repeatedly emphasized his patriotism for China and his "undying love for China."[23] In some sense, his detour through U.S. cultural and institutional racism served as a sacrifice to aid his fundamental ambition. "I was determined," he writes, "that the rising generation of China should enjoy the same educational advantages that I had enjoyed." Western education would provide new technical and cultural expertise with which "China might be regenerated, become enlightened, and restored to its former power in the world system." Driven by this idea and its practical implementation, Yung focused "all my mental resources and energy" (*MLCA*, 42). Yung here expresses his immersion in the Chinese republican philosophy of "Chinese learning as body, and Western learning for use" [中体西用, *zhongti xiyong*] commonly associated with his patron and mentor, Zeng Guofan.[24]

U.S.-based scholars emphasize Yung's "Americanness," though almost always as an unstable and contested identity. Some scholars present Yung as a person undergoing an identity "metamorphosis" while in the U.S. They point to Yung's criticism of what he called the Chinese government's narrow-minded refusal to adapt to modern modes of learning, technology, and economic organization as an indication of a massive cultural and civilizational shift in his frame of mind from Chinese to American.[25] Yung's adoption of Christianity, Western education, and a preference for U.S. technology, economic activity, and political systems are marshaled to support this thesis. More recently, another scholar became concerned about the cultural "authenticity" of Yung's autobiography as a Chinese-American or Asian-American text. Authenticity in this argument is framed as a measure of how well a text reflects on specific conditions of life for people of Asian descent in the U.S.[26] Other scholars might regard the apparent "cultural hybridity" as the accumulation and adaptation of multiple cultural reference points to shape a narrative of identity, ironically as quintessentially American.[27] The emphasis on Americanness for these scholars is clearly at odds with Chinese-language scholars who claim Yung for their own.[28]

I do not intend to wade into that discussion but rather to observe it as part of a larger geopolitical context of competition for control over knowledge production that mirrors some of the specific problems Yung Wing observed in the relations between China and the West. Since it began to imagine itself as an imperial power, the U.S. has been interested in accessing, controlling, and subjugating China.[29] Controlling knowledge production about China and the Chinese people is part of that process. In her book, *The Intimacies of Four Continents*, cultural historian Lisa Lowe shows how imperialism, the European slave trade, and settler colonialism constituted the conditions of political and cultural formations deemed as natural or normal, such as liberal democracy, civilization, and wage labor. Obscured in the naturalness of these systems lay the problematic of racial difference that defined European-descended people not simply as superior but as human. That distinction positions the non-Western, the colonized, and the enslaved as non-human. As shown in the previous chapters of this book, imperialism, slavery, and settler-colonialism were premised on the non-humanness of the subject peoples and the delusion that they lacked a capacity for reason, civilization, capitalism, and rational social organization. Like their subsequent neocolonial and neoliberal regimes, the shift from enslavement to "innovative" models of imperial rule signaled merely a change in forms, not in the structure of domination.

Lowe decisively argues that imperialism, white supremacy, settler-colonialism, and capitalism are dependent on and constitute the structure of human-non-human, exploiter-exploited, colonizer-colonized. The political philosophies, cultural systems, and civil societies dominated by the former are management systems for the structure, not vehicles for remedying or reforming that structure.[30] Thus, a U.S.-centric reading only distorts the main purpose of Yung's anti-imperialist, republican intentions. I advocate for a shift in reading Yung's text from a U.S.-centered frame to one that includes and even emphasizes a Chinese-centered perspective. Such an approach would more accurately and thoroughly establish Yung's attempt to craft a republican subjectivity that neither resides nor functions entirely in the dominant culture of Chinese officialdom or the hegemonic U.S. formation. In contrast to playful hybridity and exilic subjectivity, Yung's ideas are rooted in Chinese patriotism bolstered by a deep political commitment to a futuristic conceptualization of an emergent, republican China as a global power.

Simply put, *My Life in China and America* adopts postures, forms, strategic inclusions and exclusions that may appeal to currents in Asian American literary criticism. Yung's text, however, should not be regarded primarily as an "authentic" Asian American text rooted in resistance to hegemonic U.S. values and systems. Nor should we read it as mainly located in a tradition whose primary purpose is to craft a political subjectivity apart from mainstream U.S. cultural identities, or even via an "exilic positioning."[31] Each of these currents emphasizes and centers on the U.S. In Yung's lifetime, however, the U.S. had not yet become the dominant world power that has conditioned the possibility of much of Asian American literary criticism in the late 20th century and beyond. Instead, his mind was on China and its past and future.

Yung's life journey comprises locations-in-motion. He is a global traveler, an American citizen, and a Chinese patriot who makes extended international trips to propel Chinese political reforms. His text emphasizes China and its free development. He primarily identifies with reform and revolutionary movements in China. The authorship of his autobiography in English reveals a life fundamentally conditioned by U.S./European imperialism and the struggle to build resistance to that system. His book, which deploys the "success" genre's ideological formula for the "self-made man," strategically crafts a subjectivity of resistance through a projected appeal for an alliance with U.S. readers. A global partnership might lead the world system away from European-led interventions in East Asia and against growing Japanese domination of the region. Above all, it could open space for an insurgent Chinese republic utilizing Western political models, adapted cultural habits, and advanced technological and scientific infrastructure. Yung elevates China's potential independence and power by calling for these steps. By juxtaposing his role in the republican revolutionary movement in the latter decades of the 19th century with his overt appropriations of U.S. cultural signposts, Yung reveals a complex, strategic project that some scholars, referring to other contexts in the 19th century, call "republican internationalism."

I contend that republican internationalism is a political philosophy rooted in global alliances and the radical political transformation of social formations from feudalism to bourgeois democracy. It is a historically specific political subjectivity that, for Yung, originates in what Chih-ming Wang calls "transnational patriotism."[32] Despite adopting some Western cultural practices, Yung's primary loyalties lay with a vision of modernizing China. Republican internationalism is also based on bourgeois notions of liberal democracy as the optimal or highest stage of human development. In the 19th century, the Latin American bourgeoisie resisted European imperialism and control on a republican basis. Simon Bolivar is one famous example of a republican internationalist who led several Latin American territories to independence from Spain and into nationhood. He continues to be claimed by revolutionary movements in Venezuela and nationalist movements in many parts of the continent.[33] Before Bolivar, Toussaint Louverture and the forces that gathered to him or were inspired by the Haitian revolution may be regarded as republican internationalists.[34] Martin Delaney and Ida B. Wells, and, as I argue below, Booker T. Washington were African Americans who espoused republican internationalism.[35]

The concept cannot be regarded as universally progressive. Adopted as an ideological cover for international aggressions and a vigorous defense of its enslavement of Africans, U.S. imperialism used the rhetoric of republican internationalism to denounce European imperialism as a vehicle for gaining a foothold in the scramble for the world. The Monroe Doctrine is the earliest statement from those quarters. Republican internationalism fueled demands for successful conquests of portions of Mexico, and it nearly pushed the U.S. into aggressive acquisitions in the Caribbean and Brazil.[36] By the mid-19th century, the concept gave U.S. imperialism an entry point into exploiting China and acquiring its trade and territory. A generation later, U.S. imperialism used the idea in conjunction with its racial development theory explaining the incapacity of non-white people for self-government. It became an excuse to insist that glaringly aggressive and criminal actions in the Caribbean and South Pacific were motivated by the highest humanitarian ideals.[37] From the late nineteenth-century perspective, an affinity with the stated aims of U.S. actions on the ideological basis of republicanism (subtracting its racist, imperialist conditions of possibility) may have appealed to Yung. Shared rhetoric of this nature enabled his access to U.S.-made technology and weapons that played a big part in the modernization he envisioned for China.[38] And modernization, Yung believed, was also the foundation for eliminating the monarchy and creating republican political systems.

The following section of *My Life in China and America* illustrates how Yung's text maps China's physical and social landscape and establishes its capacity for national self-development, self-sustainable economic activity, and political modernity.

On the 15th of March, I left Hangchau to ascend the Tsien-tang River, at a station called Kang Kow, or mouth of the river, about two miles east of the city, where boats were waiting for us. Several hundreds of these boats of a peculiar and unique type were riding near the estuary of the river. These boats are called Urh Woo, named after the district where they were built. ... These boats ply between Hangchau and Sheong Shan and do all the interior transportation by water between these entrepots in Chehkiang and Kiangsi. The distance between the two entrepots is about fifty lis, or about sixteen English miles, connected by one of the finest macadamized roads in China. The road is about thirty feet wide, paved with slabs of granite and flanked with greenish-colored cobbles. A fine stone arch which was erected as a landmark of the boundary line separating Cheh-kiang and Kiangsi provinces, spans the whole width of the road. On both sides of the key-stone of the arch are carved four fine Chinese characters, painted in bright blue, viz., Leang Hsing Tung Chu:

両省通衢[39]

This is one of the most notable arch-ways through which the inter-provincial trade has been carried on for ages past. At the time when I crossed from Sheong Shan to Yuh-Shan, the river ports of Hankau, Kiukiang, Wuhu and Chinkiang were not opened to foreign trade and steamboats had not come in to play their part in the carrying trade of the interior of China. This magnificent thoroughfare was crowded with thousands of porters bearing merchandise of all kinds to and fro—exports and imports for distribution. It certainly presented an interesting sight to the traveler, as well as a profound topic of contemplation to a Chinese patriot.

The opening of the Yangtze River, which is navigable as far as Kaingchau, on the borders of Szechwan province, commanding the trade of at least six or seven provinces along its whole course of nearly three thousand miles to the ocean, presents a spectacle of unbounded possibilities for the amelioration of nearly a third of the human race, if only the grasping ambition of the West will let the territorial integrity and the independent sovereignty of China remain intact. Give the people of China a fair chance to work out the problems of their own salvation, as for instance the solution of the labor question, which has been radically disorganized and broken up by steam, electricity and machinery. This has virtually taken the breath and bread away from nine-tenths of the people of China, and therefore this immovable mass of population should be given ample time to recover from its de-moralization (*MLCA* 83-85).

In this narrative, Yung enunciates a massive historical shift. He contrasts a world from before Western imperialist interventions with the conditions in China at the time of writing—the era of Western exploitation. Just after entering the archway that marks the road between the two provinces (the point Yung records the Chinese phrase), he evokes an image of a pre-imperialist past, bustling tradespersons, river transportation technology, and well-designed highways. Like the passage between two provinces, Yung's text here is a passage into memory to envision a possible future. It serves as an imaginative bridge between memories of China before imperialist intervention and a restored future independent of foreign domination and internal oppression. The memory suggests that an ancient and modernizing society before "the grasping ambition" of European exploitation drove diverse, enriching economic activities toward producing goods and wealth solely for export, pushing the mass of Chinese people to poverty and the verge of starvation. These images inspired Yung. Like Blackbird, who worked on transforming the magic kettle, Yung is a witness to and a participant in China before the imperialist world system "has virtually taken the bread and breath" of the people away. His life mission is to restore the once-great path, but with adaptations of Western education, science, and technology as tools for that restoration.

This deliberately anti-imperialist text subtends the autobiography, conditions its essential meanings, and should register in scholarly readings of this text. Yung projects his republican, anti-imperialist politics into the past. He had witnessed a time when China's interior spaces "were not opened to foreign trade and steamboats had not come in to play their part in the carrying trade of the interior of China" (*MLCA* 85). Thus, Western imperialism, greed, and violence—and his desire to be in the struggle to end these through a radical transformation of Chinese social structures—are the conditions of possibility for this text. This point puts into new light scholarly concerns about identity formation and his affiliation with an authentic Asian American identity or the play of signifiers in the formation of U.S.-centric cultural hybridity.

For the republican internationalist, making a vigorous, transnational autobiographical Self was a tool to achieve this goal. Writing (especially in English) had always been something at which Yung excelled. He had hoped to study medicine or agricultural chemistry at Yale, but his best grades were in English composition. In the missionary school he attended in China, Yung wrote an essay, which he had titled "An Imaginary Voyage to New York and up the Hudson." Reflecting on that essay later, Yung muses "that sometimes our imagination foreshadows what lies uppermost in our minds and brings possibilities within the sphere of realities" (*MLCA*, 24). The relations and interplay of these three moments—dreams, writing, and actions toward realization—function dialectically. Thus, producing an anti-imperialist autobiography speaks to a similar relation between desire, narrative, and republican revolution in China.

Yung's book deploys clear "success" genre signals. The "self-made man" narrative plots a life journey through educational success and personal wealth accumulation. Daring adventures and heroic, if sometimes violent, confrontations with personal enemies mark the stages of the life story toward eventual success.[40] Aside from the satirical dimensions that serve as oblique critiques of the ideological function of the "self-made man" (as in Crane, Lewis, and Fitzgerald), the role of this myth is ideological. It aims to resolve the contradiction between the experiences of the individual and structural and institutional limits on or assistance with social mobility, the formation of a coherent and positive social identity, and the accumulation (or lack) of social power. The claim that the "self-made man" overcomes personal shortcomings or obstacles in the rise to greatness obscures how the children of wealthy families inherit social power. Thus, the myth serves as an example to other white men that individual striving is the key to success. It also operates to define their roles, by the end of the 19th century, in aiding U.S. imperialism. The "self-made man" myth is about modeling a specific type of powerful white American man.

So why would Yung Wing enable and adapt this gendered, individualistic mythology in his autobiographical narrative? To answer that, we have to explore how he uses the concept and read how he intends his English-speaking, American audience to link that mythology to his life story. The text uses the term "self-made man" precisely three times in its 275 pages to characterize three different men who influenced Yung's life considerably. The first usage occurs in a description of Rev. S. R. Brown, the Yale-educated leader of the Morrison School in Hong Kong.[41] This usage identifies Brown as "[showing] evidences of a self-made man" in contrast with assistant teacher William Macy.

Between the two men, "there was a marked difference" (*MLCA*, 17). The textual evidence suggests Macy's presence in the narrative serves little more than to make this contrast, for he seems to deliver hardly any other impression on Yung's life. So, what precisely is the contrast between the two men? Both are Yale-educated, religiously oriented teachers. Both have an affinity for China and appear courageously willing to undertake the rigors of global travel in the early 19th century. Brown is "cool in temperament, versatile in the adaptation of means to ends, gentlemanly and agreeable, and somewhat optimistic" (*MLCA*, 17). While indeed features of the mythical self-made man, these virtues do not provide a complete picture. The contrast with Lacey is not a parallel one. Lacey is not intemperate or disagreeable. Instead, the critical distinction between the two men lies in that Lacey has little experience in the profession "and was a man of sensitive nature, and of fine moral sensibilities—a soul full of earnestness and lofty ideals" (*MLCA*, 17). The contrast between earnest, sensitive idealism and versatility in adapting a means to an end suggests the distinction between an emotional, mental person and a person who acts first and then reflects on the consequences later. Yung admires Brown's approach to life more as he named his oldest child after him.

In the second instance in which Yung uses the term "self-made man," he describes Charles Hammond, the principal of the preparatory school Yung attended before entering Yale, as "in every sense a self-made man" (*MLCA* 28). This definitive ascription contrasts somewhat with his description of Brown, who showed "evidences." Also, a graduate of Yale, Hammond's self-made-ness lay in his "character and experience." "[F]ond of the classics and an admirer of English literature" (especially Shakespeare), Hammond held "liberal views and broad sympathies." While these qualities are not closely associated with "self-made manhood," Hammond's modeling of "temperance and New England virtues" (self-sacrifice and self-reliance) signals the myth. A well-liked teacher and writer, Hammond taught his students to appreciate a well-crafted sentence rather than the rules of grammar (*MLCA*, 28, 31-32). Through Hammond's facilitation, Yung may have learned much about the craft of writing in English, a vehicle for translating imagination into reality through action.

The third usage of the term "self-made man" breaks the racial-civilizational mold of the myth. Zeng Guofan [曾国藩][42], a viceroy who led an independent army in alliance with the Qing emperor's forces to finally suppress the Taiping rebellion in 1864, is the third example.[43] Yung qualifies his description of Zeng. "As a military general," he notes, "he might be called a self-made man" (*MLCA*, 147). Does this sentence reference Zeng's military capabilities, his repression of an insurgency that threatened the rule of the Qing emperor through brutal force? If so, Yung may see him much like he may have understood how Americans saw Jacob H. Smith. Further, the qualification of the description with the phrase "might be called" suggests something unstable about the claim or perhaps the myth itself. Hammond was "in every sense" a self-made man. Brown showed "evidences" of this quality. Zeng "might be called a self-made man." Zeng's rise followed an interesting trajectory. Like the self-made man myth, Zeng had moved from legal scholarship to military leadership, and a mere 10 years later had succeeded in suppressing the Taiping revolt (*MLCA*, 148). The move from the life of the mind to a life of action, more than an increase in power, fame, and wealth, registers the meaning of the myth in Yung's mind.

Because the American ideology of self-making may not apply to a Chinese man regardless of his accomplishments, the usage of the myth reveals Yung's encounter with its discursive limits and white supremacy's vision of who counts as "man." He confronts the barrier of who can "make" themselves within the terms and conditions of the mythology. As we saw in the previous chapters, Yung writes in a time and place that has elevated a scientific discourse on race and civilization that denies non-white peoples, colonized subjects, and non-capitalist social formations the possibility of a philosophy, a history, and a capacity for modern development. It has relegated them to non-human status. U.S. politicians, writers, activists, labor union leaders, and capitalists are almost unanimous in talking about the inferiority of the people in Yung's country of origin and neighboring geographies. Like Jacob H. Smith, they have waged war on peoples they regard as "savages" and incapable of ruling themselves.

Yung personally confronted this reality of U.S. racism (his loss of citizenship) and professionally in his protests to U.S. officials about racist violence targeting Chinese people (*MLCA*, 209). Aside from directly naming the multi-class expressions of anti-Chinese racism sweeping U.S. society, his commitment to battling U.S. racism also registers the limits of the text's adaptation of the "self-made man" discourse. By contrast, in establishing the possibility of Zeng's self-making, especially within an anti-imperialist text that uplifts the necessity and possibilities of republican internationalism and revolution, Yung simultaneously critiques U.S. racism and elevates the republican components of the self-made mythology.[44] His portrait of Zeng also aims to make the heroic republican figure intelligible to his U.S. readership paralyzed by stereotypes of Celestials, "yellow perils," and "coolies." Indeed, Yung's use of "self-made men" in this book functions to create models of republican internationalism, which Yung uses to frame and enact his worldview.

It is significant, however, that after this description of Zeng, i.e., the second half of the book, Yung never uses the term "self-made man" again. If "self-made man" rhetoric "rests on the need to dramatize the ambivalent desires and conflicting goals that are part and parcel of individual and social growth," what are those desires and conflicts in this text? Why does Yung drop an urge to dramatize them after recalling his initial meeting with Zeng? Mythology always fails to provide material resolutions for conflict or social contradictions. It can, however, "provide a specific representation of psychological and social conflict" that gives a person a framework through which, despite the contradictions, they may "establish their rightful place."[45] Put another way, the myth functions to justify events, actions, and relationships within a social order that provide avenues of privilege for some or deny such for those without a rightful place in that order. If a social order, such as the U.S., operates through the denial of the humanity of people like Yung and Zeng, if its conditions of possibility lie in the facts of racial slavery, settler colonialism, white supremacy, and bloody imperialism, no mythology that pretends a Chinese man can be self-made can be met with credulity. Thus, dropping the self-made man myth signals a massive turning point in the text that does not work on the same rhetorical registers as the book's first half.

Further, the latter half of Yung's text explores and demystifies class struggle in late-imperial China. By framing the first half in the mythic ideology of the "self-made man," Yung produces an expectation that such an abstract universal (from the perspective of the Euro-American) can be framed to identify similar abstract, individualized processes in other historical-cultural contexts. This expectation is sharply contradicted by the reality of competing forces—never reduced to individual personalities in the text—that block or aid the collective republican revolutionary process. Yung's narrated subjectivity is centered within this network of social conflict in ways that symbolize material social forces at the level of the mode of production. The primary focus, as noted, in this half of the book is on Yung's role as a Chinese official in the U.S. and China. His account of these interactions reveals a ruling class formed as an alliance between the imperial regime, the bureaucracy, and the emergent Chinese capitalist class with the most substantial ties to foreign trade dominated by European powers. He typically characterizes bureaucrats and capitalists loyal to this regime as lazy, corrupt, and appointed based on connections to the court rather than clever and innovative ideas. Above all, they try to undermine modernizing efforts.

One such official is his co-commissioner of the Chinese Education Mission, Wu Zedong (Woo Tsze Tung), who ultimately provides multiple reports that distort Yung's leadership, causing the Mission's closure (*MLCA*, 201-202). A second example was Xing Sunwei (Shing Sun Whei), a capitalist who scuttled Yung's plan for a Chinese national bank and embezzled the 10,000,000 taels state investment for the proposed bank into his private enterprise (*MLCA*, 234-236). These men are depicted as scheming, self-interested, grasping men who dominate a corrupted economic and political system that cannot transform into a progressive republican system. While the "self-made man" myth tries to resolve the contradiction, the disappointment of this anticipated process in the second half of the text works to demystify class struggle, even as Yung is ill-equipped to utilize overt Marxian categories for that purpose.

The project of Chinese modernization and its revolutionary transformation was not an individualistic enterprise that could be wedged into U.S. ideological discourse. Instead, the latter half of the book is devoted to discussing the Chinese Educational Mission, Yung's work to secure modern technology for the Chinese government, his investigation and disruption of the "coolie trade" in Peru, his personal life, his involvement with the republican struggle in China, and his flight from China via Taiwan and Hong Kong to retirement in New England. At the level of his republican internationalism, Yung's text sublimates an explicit confrontation with U.S. racism (which the record shows he actively fought) to an ideal type of republican alliance that can move China into a progressive standpoint in relation to European imperialism.

Though Yung offers no explicit acknowledgment that U.S. imperialism provides a progressive alternative to European imperialism, his larger project of weakening Europe (to U.S. advantage) and removing the internal barriers to China's rapid modernization might have (optimistically) nulled concerns about the U.S. simply replacing Europe as global hegemon. While his contemporaries and later generations of his readers may have scoffed at his optimism, these events have transpired over the long 20th century. China's revolutionary transition to a republic might be the twentieth-century version of a world-historical moment not unlike 1776, given its similar rapid economic and social development and its rise in power on the global stage. Like his high school essay on traveling to New York, Yung's book attempts to translate a dream into the actual course of human events.

Dialectics of self

1902 also saw the return of James N. Calloway from a year-long stay in the West African country of Togo, at that time a German colony. He had spent more than a year there leading a German Empire-financed expedition. His job was to establish an agricultural education program similar to the model farms at Tuskegee Institute by Booker T. Washington. According to historian Angela Zimmerman, Calloway's expedition came about from negotiations between Washington and a German envoy tasked with studying the U.S. cotton-production system to learn how to recreate it in Germany's African colonies. Calloway led a handful of other Tuskegee instructors, students, and family members. Early deaths and illnesses caused the expedition to fail, as most participants returned to the U.S. by 1904. Still, John W. Robinson married and settled in Togo, establishing a model farm where German officials forced Togolese people to learn how to reorganize local agricultural systems, cultural values, and productivity. The German goal was to cause a shift in diversified agricultural commodity production to a monoculture of raw cotton for export to German and other European textile mills. German authorities created an extractive structure that set the stage for

Togolese underdevelopment and dependence on raw exports to Europe.[46]

The urge to support German interests likely derived from Washington's sympathy with a Pan-Africanist version of republican internationalism, at least early in his career. As Zimmerman documents, two years before the Togo expedition and the publication of his famous autobiography, Washington publicly praised Louverture, consorted with Haitian intellectuals on at least one trip to Europe, and endorsed the first Pan-African conference.[47] Like many of his contemporaries, this Pan-Africanism rested on a belief that Black Americans represented the most "advanced" section of the world's Black people. It was their duty to help uplift African peoples. In Washington's version of this thesis, an uncritical alliance with imperialism was a vehicle for modernizing African societies on Western terms. It is also well-known that Washington's private support for legal cases that battled segregation contradicted his domestic accommodationist public stances and political agenda.[48]

Beyond his back door political maneuvering, Washington had attempted to hire Du Bois and succeeded in bringing in George Washington Carver.[49] Each of these men was imbued with important political implications. Carver's role was "to assist in transforming the lives of African Americans" by developing alternative agricultural products that would create a "material challenge to the cotton economy."[50] Cotton monoculture was the backbone of debt peonage for tenant farmers and sharecroppers who comprised the large majority of African American farming households in the South. The introduction of other agricultural products seemed like a good way to create new markets, sources of income, and economic opportunities for Black farmers and emergent industries. Zimmerman identifies the Togo expedition as a turning point in Washington's thought and already quietist political orientation to open-throated advocacy for African workers to be subjugated as the primary labor force for imperialism's colonial project.[51] I argue that there is less of a turning point and more continuity between the political activist Washington and the accommodationist Washington. A reading of his autobiographical work reveals a consistent pattern of thought rooted in an ideological affirmation of capitalist development as the final stage of history.

Like Yung's text, Booker T. Washington's autobiography *Up from Slavery* (1901) uses the success genre, emphasizing upward mobility through educational experience, hard work, sacrifice, and the complicated process of making oneself through narrative production. Here, I contrast *Up from Slavery* with *My Life in China and America* by examining how Washington's use of the "self-made man" myth differed from Yung's and how Washington's republican internationalism reinforced U.S.-European imperialisms by attempting to forge an alliance of the U.S. ruling class with African Americans. This comparison emerges by exploring what Washington repeatedly calls "impressions" on his memory and character from his experiences. Additionally, contextualizing the book's self-making with omissions from the text related to his "secret life"[52] enables the discovery that this text undermines the anti-imperialist republican aspirations of people outside of a Black-white binary within the U.S. social formation.

Washington's prominent utilization of the success genre and notions of racial uplift has generated reams of criticism of his program, his ideological stances, and his political role from scholars since W. E. B. Du Bois first broke with his leadership in 1903. *Up from Slavery* adopts multiple features of the gendered genre: the rise from squalor to prominence, the role of education in shaping the consciousness and virtues of the man, the cultivation of talents that become decisive features of the successful man's character, frequent dismissal of institutional barriers to generalizable forms of success, and the emphasis on overcoming individualized barriers (such as poverty, racism, or other setbacks to the forward line of personal achievement). Further, Washington denigrates what he regards as "abstract" in favor of practical usefulness and experience over what is found in "text-books"[53] (*UFS*, 66-67). He related an account of his literal and figurative journey from the total darkness, danger, and poverty of a West Virginia coal mine to the brightness, beauty, and benevolence of Hampton Institute, which he calls "a new world" (*UFS*, 58) and "the promised land" (*UFS*, 51).[54]

Washington's humble attitude to producing his life story is typical of his self-effacing public posture. His preface portrays the writing of the book as something of an accident. He contends it was a response to demand from his supporters and nothing more than the result of work in his scarce spare time—on trains, waiting for trains, or in late hours after long days of administering and fund-raising on behalf of Tuskegee Institute. Despite his claims of serendipity, the book serves the project of self-making, the core mission of his thought and action. In an aside on learning public speaking at Hampton, Washington decries "abstract public speaking" for the sake of hearing oneself talk. Instead, he writes, "from my early childhood I have had a desire to make the world better, and then to be able to speak to the world about that thing" (*UFS*, 67). *Up from Slavery* is the written form of this desire to speak; it was a necessary feature of Washington's philosophy.

Like others involved in engineering the "self-made man," Washington understood the process as closely linked to narrative production. Thus, the writing of an autobiography is a narrative about the practical activity of making his life. What sets Washington apart from the mythologies of self-made men described above is his attempt to establish a clear relation between himself and the African American people rather than separate from them. On its surface, Washington's narrative is not a treatise on pure individualism or the ideological attempt to deny absolutely the reality of social systems, institutions, or relationships with other people (even if he diminishes their negative impacts). In fundamental ways, Washington's narrative places it directly within the working-class "self-made man" mythology discussed in footnote number one of this chapter.

Washington establishes his "typicality" from the opening pages. He was "a slave among slaves," the first chapter's title states. He repeatedly asserts that he is nothing extraordinary and that his eagerness for education was learned from and mirrored that of most Black people. "My case will illustrate that of hundreds of thousands of black people in every part of the country," he writes assuredly (*UFS*, 36). This construction of typicality places his Self, his acts of self-making, and the narrative of self-making near the mass of African American people. His unwavering ideal for all human activity is the necessity of service to others, especially the downtrodden and socially excluded. He writes that one of many enduring impressions of his time at Hampton Institute "was the unselfishness of the teachers" (*UFS*, 66). Happiness as an effect of success reaches a pinnacle if the individual exhibits this virtue of selflessness as a habit. Working for others might negate the individualistic self in the dominant idealized "self-made man" mythology, the hapless, isolated self, entombed in the dark coal mine. Through this process of self-making in relation to others, the lonely self is sublated into a happy self "doing most for others." Narrative, or the discursive act of saying something about what has been done, is the creation of consciousness of this process. The self is transformed into a "typical" version of a collective self, the possibility of collective success or empowerment.

This idealization of self and others, however, is arrested and produces a "false totality." As Barbara Foley argues, a "false totality" is an ideological assertion of an idealist oversimplification of human relations abstracted from historically specific social relations of production.[55] Washington asserts freedom of self-making that functions primarily as a matter of will, as a universal principle, despite white supremacy, capitalist social relations of production, and imperialism. Some people (like himself) internalize positive willfulness naturally. For others, it has to be modeled and taught through the action of narrative (like an autobiography). But it is individual will or its lack, not poverty, racist violence, law, resource allocation, or other structural matters, that is the primary cause of the internal motion of this system.[56] Those systems are mere obstacles, like the need for a coat (*UFS*, 63), the loss of found money (*UFS*, 63), or the need to pay for books (*UFS*, 59, 64-65, 75). Barriers exist as accidents (real and universal, to be sure) to be overcome through will and individual practical problem-solving. Washington denigrates the importance of collective resource-sharing and political struggles, especially those directed by working-class-led organizations. Radical social transformation based on careful inventories of specific social relationships that produce poverty, child labor in coal mines, a generalized lack of books or coats, and so on, are unnecessary and more harmful than beneficial. For all of Washington's talk of the preference for practical activity, his thought remains dependent on the abstraction of idealized individual will. Disinterested in a *struggle* for collective power for radical social transformation, the text's false totality idealizes internal resources and intrinsic motivations that return the collective self into the individualized, isolated self.

This mystification of concrete dialectical social relations into an idealized, isolated self mimics capitalist "free market" ideologies in which each is at war with all.[57] At best, Washington offers a politics of representation that serves as a substitute for justice or revolutionary systemic transformation.[58] The element of work in service to others merely highlights the philanthropic capitalism on which Washington's financial model for Tuskegee was founded. A key pillar of "uplift" theory is the philanthropic role of white, capitalist savior discourse.

Instead of a productive sublation into a demystified social reality, Washington's discourse of "self" is aided by the production of an aestheticization of social conflict and class struggle: poverty (*UFS*, 33, 63), work, racism, pain, exposure, violence, houselessness, self-sacrifice (*UFS*, 64-65), child labor (*UFS*, 26, 30), social death, abandonment, goodwill, and optimism (*UFS*, 16, 65), and other outcomes of systemic oppression and exploitation as simply the "obstacles" that need to be overcome in the abstract and universalized project of social mobility (*UFS*, 37). Even service to others as the primary objective of useful work denies a dialectics of typicality that could propel revolutionary collective action. Instead, we are treated with an object lesson, a model for virtuous behavior that substitutes for transformative political action. Harmonious with the demands of the success genre, Washington's choice of a politics of aesthetics also indexes personal virtues of integrity, will, honesty, leadership, responsibility, and commitment to manual or physical labor as the primary function of learning for African Americans (*UFS*, 37, 41, 82). The performance of these virtues is more important than Black power and a reordering of social relations. A politics of aesthetics exemplifies

Social Darwinist language of the evolution of racial groups (*UFS*, 17), Black people as children (*UFS*, 21, 83), and descriptions of collective ignorance that even seep into the urge and demand for liberal education. Washington places oppression as "an advantage" (*UFS*, 39-40), for "merit" is always "recognized and rewarded" (*UFS*, 41).

The formalistic demands of the success genre, to which Washington is ideologically and materially committed, necessitate such inversions of social reality and reification of naturalized racial hierarchies combined with exploitative class processes. It overlooks or obscures how capitalist development and white supremacy "[depended] on conceptions of African Americans as devoid of will." Such ideological inversions of social realities justify a logic of African American service, not just to others but to whites and capitalism. According to scholar Grace Kyungwon Hong in *Ruptures of American Capital*, this contradiction is reproduced in the form and content of *Up from Slavery*, wherein "Washington's narrative must paradoxically articulate his lifestory as a triumph of the will and a submission of the African American will to white power."[59]

Sidebars on history

Both Yung and Washington include a chapter in their books that comments on a larger social dynamic distinguished from their primary autobiographical purposes. To observe further the relation of each text to its conditions of possibility, I explore here a brief comparative and reflexive reading of the chapters titled "Reflections on the Taiping Rebellion" in *My Life in China and America* and the "The Reconstruction Period" in *Up from Slavery*.[60] Each chapter diverts from the personal narrative, examines globally important, potentially epoch-shifting historical events, and establishes conditions of possibility and intelligibility for each text within the motion of social forces in each country. The choice of inclusion of each chapter intentionally positions the author and their political commitments in a dialectical relation to innovative, disruptive moments in and around the historical development of capitalism. For Yung, that affiliation is with the cutting edge, vanguard social force attempting to lead a stadial shift from feudalism to bourgeois-dominated society, inflecting his life and narrative with a radical and even revolutionary motion. By contrast, Washington textually aids in reifying a structurally subordinated relation of Black labor within technologically dynamic industrial capitalism that coincides with the U.S. shift to self-conscious imperialism. It, thus, produces conservative rhetoric positioned within the logic of racial capitalist accumulation as it transitions onto the global stage of the imperialist world system, forcing readjustments and new contradictions in that overtly white supremacist system.

A comparative reading reveals the historical specificity of each text and the formal contradictions produced within their choice to use the "self-made man" mythology and success genre of narrative production. Yung's adaptation of that form is attenuated and disrupted, while the literary form of *Up from Slavery* serves to solidify the relation of narrative to society. For example, Washington's text, via the success genre, links the serving, virtuous Black person to a structurally perpetuated subordinate status in the capitalist class formation and reifies the role of loyal protector of the imperialist order.[61] This model of service is cultivated within the self-made mythology, even as that revised mythology stretches the racial boundaries implied in the dominant cultural frame. In addition to local space-bound social relations, both chapters locate each author and social formation within a world system.

Notable similarities between the two authors emerge as a result of this reading. First, returning to these chapters highlights how each author was tempted to play some role or join the leading, progressive forces in the respective movements. Yung was sympathetic to the Taipings, met with them several times, and even submitted a proposal for potential social reforms to Hong Xiuquan,[62] their leader, for consideration (*MLCA*, 118-119). After returning to his hometown from Hampton Institute to claim a teaching post, Washington was also tempted to run for elected office as a Republican among a growing number of African American political activists during Reconstruction. Ultimately, both say they chose to pursue the larger altruistic path of building an educational program rather than entering political life.

In his chapter commenting on the Taiping rebellion, Yung adopts the stance of an observer of events rather than the participant expected in an autobiographical text. This narratorial stance lends objectivity to the commentary, altering the tone and form of the reading experience. His account opens by establishing 2,000 years of Chinese history as marked by many "revolutions and rebellions," but without fundamental alteration in forms of power and material social relations. Instead, the "history of China" and its development "bears the national impress of a monotone dead level—jejune in character, wanting in versatility of genius, and almost devoid of historic inspiration" (*MLCA*, 114).[63] This characterization nearly echoes Western denigration of non-Western societies as lacking philosophy and history. It is dissonant with the image of the pre-imperial life of the country Yung recreated at the moment of crossing the "two-provinces gateway" discussed above. The contradiction present with this dissonance reveals that Yung believed stagnation of modern development did not result from biology or a state of savagery. Rather, creativity and vitality are always potential and imminent, always on the verge of being unleashed in China. Stagnation, thus, was a function of a political system that controlled and suppressed the people's natural vitality and innovative genius. The imperial Qing government created the fetters that denied China its chances at modern development. This condition shaped the conditions of the possibility of the Taiping rebellion.

Indeed, the rebellion began as little more than a weird religious cult, launched by a deviant reading of Christianity, which Yung calls a "foreign product" (*MLCA*, 115). Notably, the American missionary, Issachar Roberts, who influenced Hong's knowledge of Christianity, was known as an intemperate and violent man and was forced to flee the movement due to accusations that he brutally murdered a child.[64] Nevertheless, Hong's use of some Christian elements to create a utopian religious community shows a foreign influence. Still, it was initially rooted in a desire for a new form of social organization within indigenous Chinese conditions. Indeed, as Hong's cult attracted more people to its comprehensive attempt to reinvent spiritual and material life collectively, the Qing imperial government grew deeply concerned. By Yung's account, the reaction to the Taipings and the effort to repress the movement transformed it into a political rebellion. This dialectical transformation of a religious movement into a political revolt threatened to destroy the imperial government.

Yung's account lends intellectual support to the logic of his social program. Based on foreign education, Chinese people would modernize their economic, political, and cultural systems. Such steps would revolutionize the country, meet the people's needs, and protect the country's future from Western conquest and domination. If we regard these two movements in parallel, the "foreign product" that sparks each also depends on everyday Chinese people's internal desires and longings. The cause of the Taipings' failure lay in their lapse into corruption and reliance on traditional forms of culture and power in the end. They refused to implement Yung's technical and political modernization proposals (see *MLCA*, 110). Their sizeable geographical spread, military success, ability to inspire the people, an initial impulse for innovative social organization, and the exposure of the contradictions arising from the existing political order served as a model of revolutionary transformation in Yung's mind. Yung was a devoted Christian and dismissive of the Taiping spiritual distortion of that faith, "but still they were truths of great power, potential enough to turn simple men and religiously-minded women into heroes and heroines who face danger and death with the utmost indifference, as was seen subsequently, when the government had decided to take the bull by the horns and resorted to persecution as the final means to break this religious fanatical community" (*MLCA*, 118-119).

Two things are at work in this long-winded sentence. First, Yung expresses great admiration for the courage of the men and women of the rebellion. This gender inclusivity defies the masculinity of the "self-made man" and points to the capacity for revolutionary agency of all the people in moments when liberatory social forms appear as real possibilities to them. Second, it subordinates individualist mythologies to the social forces of history. The Taipings' threat to the hegemonic leadership of the imperial government necessitated a harsh reaction under the specific political conditions through which it maintained its control of the Chinese state. This attempt to negate the utopian religious movement was met with resistance and an expansion of the contradiction with Qing rule. Moreover, the contradiction and initial failures to negate the uprising sublated the religious characteristics into a political rebellion that exposed the incapacities of the imperial court to control its territory, to ensure the carrying out of its will, and its deepening failure to protect the people and meet their needs. Had events pursued another course, Hong's cult "would have remained peaceably in the heart of China and developed a religious community" (*MLCA*, 119). This motion of social forces influenced the course of action Yung pursued and shaped his theory of Chinese history and social development. Despite his intentions to appropriate an American genre and discourse rooted in ideological myths, Yung's account slips from these tenuous moorings and shifts to a partisan anti-imperialist text.[65]

In contrast, Washington sledgehammers historical analysis into the "self-made man" mythology by developing a commentary on Reconstruction that distorts the historical record. From historical analysis, his commentary reverts to autobiographical "success story" mode. The generic conflict present in this chapter reveals a contradiction in Washington's thought between the factual history of Reconstruction, the formative period of his life from the age of 9 until his exit from Hampton Institute in 1876, and the pressing need for racial accommodation as a professional mechanism for financing Tuskegee Institute after 1890. Washington reductively presents Reconstruction as a monolithic formation—instead of a contested site of class struggle pushed into motion by what Du Bois later called "abolition democracy."[66] In his commentary, Washington characterizes the period as a distortion of a natural evolutionary development process. He enlists Social Darwinist racialism to identify stages of African American development from "darkest heathenism" in Africa to generations of enslavement in the U.S., to a new world of freedom after 1865 (*UFS*, 80). Unfortunately, the radicals in Congress tried to skip stages of development. Like Yung, Washington favors a developmental model of a group's social, cultural, and political action. Yung locates this development in the nation; Washington identifies it with racial groups.

Contradictions emerge in Washington's account. He criticizes the urge among some Black people after freedom to seek a liberal education as an individualized path to personal success, which he decries as superficial, as an effort to avoid work. He chastises African Americans who want to become teachers and ministers, generalizing these professions that served as a significant source of Black community leadership as solely motivated by greed and ignorance. Ironically, these were the first professions he had chosen for himself. After leaving Hampton, he returned to his hometown and worked as a teacher for two years before entering Wayland Seminary in Washington, D.C. He ties this path to leadership as a false path, linking what he suggests are distortions in Black community development to the obstacles posed by Reconstruction (i.e., Black political enfranchisement, not white racism). In those years after the war, the central government "[forced] the Negro into positions over the heads of the Southern whites" (*UFS*, 84).[67] "Reconstruction policy," he insists, laid a "false foundation" and "was artificial and forced." Without documenting the fact of Reconstruction's complexity and diverse implementation, Washington enables the common stereotype of it as a "punishment" of the South, a motive he repeatedly denounces as antithetical to the necessary virtues for success.

Further, Washington's narrative emphasizes white leadership of the abolitionist movement, the conduct of the war itself, and the revolutionary content of much of Reconstruction policy. In these events, aside from a handful of individuals, Black people played few intelligible roles, Washington avers. This version of events complies with his view of Black people as figurative children born into a new world after emancipation and thwarted by the false start of Reconstruction. In sum, not only was it unnatural for Black people to be leaders of the U.S. political system, Reconstruction defied the success story by creating a situation where the influential classes in the North attempted to simply hand power to Black people without requiring them to move through the stages of the success story as a community. This "artificial" form of development mirrored the social distinctions he saw at Wayland Seminary, where wealthy Black families simply paid for their children to attend university and fostered a lack of "self-dependence" (*UFS*, 87).

This model of racial-historical development operates as a reflexive metaphor for personal development. Washington actualizes it in his personal narrative of rising from nothing, from the squalor and darkness at the moment of freedom, to the levels of accomplishment and success through will and determination. This pairing of historical and individual accounts renders an aestheticization of history mobilized into the success genre. Yung's exploration of history translated into a dialectical theory of history that forces the closure of the success genre. Yung is "an overt partisan narrator" of a life story that makes explicit the relations of his experiences, social reality, and the narrative of his life.[68] While Washington's thought encourages a foreclosure of "ideological dissonance"[69] through adherence to mythological norms, he cannot enforce the full completion of his "false totality."[70] He must admit that Black people are intelligent and capable. He acknowledges that racism is a structural system of unfairness outside the individualized will of the Self, and that Black collective agency is a necessary feature of social development. In other words, despite crafting a polished ideological system via the genre of self-making and success, Washington's thought cannot fully encircle and repress the impulses and foundational elements of a political program for collective liberation and revolutionary social agency. Indeed, he must allow those elements room to operate and reinforce ideological dissonance, the awareness, and consciousness of the contradictions between lived experience and mythology. This particular contradiction is rooted in Washington's insistence that Black people are self-determining human beings—a point of view that remains insubordinate to white supremacy's self-delusional position that they are not. In contrast to Yung, Washington's narration of social realities is sublimated by the success genre, and like the effects of his "secret life," the contradictions are meant to persist, if only behind closed doors.

Returning east

1902 saw at least one more "return" worth noting here. After openly criticizing the Qing government's handling of the Boxer Rebellion, diplomat Wu Tingfang was that year recalled to China. The London-trained legal scholar turned outspoken diplomat gave speeches on U.S. conditions which may seem unusual for a foreign emissary. His criticism of racist violence and segregation in the U.S., lynching, the Chinese exclusion law, and European delusions of racial supremacy were palatable enough for whites to earn their recurring praise but sufficiently potent to be lauded by radical African Americans who rejected Washington's accommodationist path. Wu continued Yung's practice of delivering Chinese government protests to the U.S. State Department about hostility toward Chinese Americans. Additionally, his opposition to Qing policy and the imperial system, and his ultimate support for the republican revolution in 1911, aligned him closely with Yung's political philosophy. Further, Wu's belief in the value of Western education, and specifically in the promise of U.S. political organization—despite its profound flaws—places him squarely within the republican internationalist tradition. It is possible that he saw claims about liberal U.S. values combined with its anti-Chinese hostility as little more than an inconsistency rather than a contradiction that constituted the socio-cultural superstructure of U.S. capitalism.[71]

Wu imagined Chinese national identity differently than he imagined U.S. culture. In its editorial section in 1909, the venerable *Journal of Education* quoted Wu's book on American culture thus:

> In the hundreds of my countrymen who went, and are going through the college halls of this country, there exists a bond of union between China and America mightier than treaties and alliances. Our American education young men constitute a bridge across the broad expanse of the Pacific ocean [sic], on which American learning American ideals, American institutions, American inventions, American products, and manufactures are conveyed in China.

They will be able to insure a peace and trade in the far East that treaties and military forces cannot insure. In one word, these students will be the most effective instruments through and with American civilization, or American university education, can exert its wonderful influence on the new China."[72]

In these comments, Wu's optimistic view of U.S.-China relations contrasts with his criticisms of U.S. racial violence and political shortcomings. Further, they differ significantly from his published views on why Chinese people in China dislike "foreigners" so much. In an address to the American Academy of Political and Social Science in 1900, Wu gave some impressions of the Boxer Rebellion. This peasant uprising initially blamed the Qing imperial court for surrendering Chinese territory to European imperialists. Fearing an overthrow, the government courted peasant leaders and helped form an alliance that generally targeted foreigners and deflected peasant anger. In sharing his impressions of the uprising, Wu noted that he likely would be "stirring up a hornet's nest" with an honest take.[73]

A naive reading of Wu's speech might shape it as an early model of intercultural competence or cultural relativity, giving it prescient status in today's diversity discourse or the multiculturalism of the 1990s. For example, the tendency of Europeans to make "sweeping denunciations of other people's ways serve only to stir up ill-feeling and antagonism, and do not carry conviction with them" ("Causes," 13). Europeans often treated all Chinese people "as inferior to them in intellect or education and unworthy of their society" ("Causes," 14). Instead of creating "bad impressions" and displaying a lack of "politeness," Europeans should "not judge us according to their own standards" ("Causes," 13-14). European actions to forcibly exploit Chinese labor, abuse Chinese people (often with physical violence), and condemn Chinese ways of living as racially backward created irreparable rifts that led to retaliation. In contrast, Wu praised those few Europeans who learned to assimilate Chinese cultural values, respect Chinese religious beliefs, and confine their interventions to building educational and medical institutions.

In contrast to Washington's focus on collectively blaming Black people for their shortcomings, Wu most directly placed blame for Chinese hostility during the Boxer Rebellion and in everyday interactions at the feet of European antagonists. He shared Yung's fervent belief in Western education's role in promoting the collective technical and material development of Chinese society. Contrary to Washington, Wu and Yung regarded internal group flaws as problems but not decisive features of conditions in China or its relation to the European-dominated imperialist world system. There is no evolutionary model for social development in their scheme that confined Chinese people to "backwardness." Instead, the needs of Chinese society and its proper development had outgrown the fetters and constraints imposed by the imperial political system and its cultural institutions. In addition to their improper cultural interactions, European interventions served as an outside catalyst for sparking the contradiction between the need for development and a feudal political system. Wu and Yung believed the republican era would synthesize that contradiction in motion.

Notes

1. One version of this myth in the "success genre" targets the working class for ideological confusion. In this version, the hero resists corporate power through the leadership of a collective struggle. The hero, however, eventually rises out of the masses to become the benevolent leader of the organization or company. In this version, "[r]esolving the tensions between individual identity and union solidarity regularly leads to pseudo-heroic self-sacrifice or sentimental visions of individualism." See James V. Catano, "The Rhetoric of Masculinity: Origins, Institutions, and the Myth of the Self-made Man," *College English*, Vol. 52, no. 4 (1990): 425. Self-denial and sacrifice persist in the rhetoric and ideologies of unorganized and isolated workers in the present, opening them to right-wing ideological appeals. See Jennifer M. Silva, *We're Still Here: Pain and Politics in the Heart of America* (New York: Oxford University Press, 2019).
2. The attempt to make oneself into the likeness of white male power is discussed in detail in Jeffrey Louis Decker, "Gatsby's Pristine Dream: The Diminishment of the Self-Made Man in the Tribal Twenties," *Novel: A Forum on Fiction*, Vol. 28, no. 1 (1994), 52-71.
3. Knowledge of Horatio Alger's role as a perpetrator of child sexual abuse has not diminished the close association of his name with this mythology. Ironically, despite valorizing being "self-made," Alger needed the protection of his well-connected father to avoid punishment.

4. Self-delusion as a cornerstone of ideology was first articulated by Lewis R. Gordon in his book *Bad Faith and Anti-Black Racism*. A condensed discussion can be found in Gordon, *Fear of Black Consciousness*, (New York: Farrar, Strauss and Giroux, 2021), 58-62. White supremacy constituted the philosophy, practice, and systems of liberal democracy, especially within the U.S. Republican ideas in the U.S., as I have shown, are rooted in white supremacy. The U.S. state could not have come into existence without racial supremacist justifications for the expropriation of Indigenous lands through genocide and the protection of the system of enslaving Africans as among its foundational building blocks. See Gerald Horne, *The Counter-Revolution of 1776: Slave Resistance and the Origins of the United States of America*, (New York: New York University Press, 2014); Lisa Lowe, *The Intimacies of Four Continents*, (Durham: Duke University Press, 2015). Foley explores the complexity of ideology conditioned by capitalist material conditions. Capitalist realities and logics create "the proliferation of inadequate, indeed false, explanatory paradigms" that function as ideology. But her analysis does not account for willful self-delusion. See Foley, *Marxist Literary Criticism Today*, (London: Pluto Press, 2019), 62. Gordon, however, helps us recognize how we often choose to adhere to delusions that provide psychological pleasure or resolution emergent from powerlessness. Indeed, delusion appears to become a form of power and may or may not comport with dominant economic models. Occasionally, they resist them though universal liberation is not the main aim.

5. Lowe, 6. Lowe uses the term to describe how settler-colonial processes, imperialism, enslavement, and white supremacy contexts make ideologies, political systems, or cultural formations possible. Aijaz Ahmad, with reference specifically to literary works, calls these "conditions of intelligibility" or "conditions of production" of those symbolic and practical systems. Aijaz Ahmad, *In Theory: Classes, Nations, Literatures*, (New York: Verso, 200), 12, 16. The concept of "self-made man" and the literature it spawns makes little sense outside of these larger historical material conditions.

6. David L. Fritz, "Before the 'Howling Wilderness': The Military Career of Jacob Hurd Smith, 1862-1902," *Military Affairs*, Vol. 43, no. 4 (1979): 186–90.

7. Jhemmylrut Teng, "Filipino Holocaust in the Hands of the Americans: Molestation, Revenge, Deprivation, Massacre, and Genocide," History of Yesterday, 13 February 2021. https://historyofyesterday.com/filipino-holocaust-in-the-hands-of-the-americans-6457a9647d2e. Retrieved 22 March 2022; Thomas A. Bruno, "The Violent End of Insurgency on Samar 1901–1902," *Army History*, no. 79 (2011): 39-40.

8. E. San Juan Jr., "Literary Studies in the Age of Empire's Collapse," *Danyag: Journal of Humanities and Social Sciences*, Vol. 14, no. 1 (2009): 9.

9. Fritz, 186-187.

10. Bruno, 43.

11. Quoted in Andrew Feight, "General Jacob H. Smith and the Philippine War's Samar Campaign," Scioto Historical, accessed March 21, 2022, https://sciotohistorical.org/items/show/109.

12. Bruno, 44; Feight, "General Jacob H. Smith & the Philippine War's Samar Campaign."

13. A scholar delivered a paper on this subject at the 1998 American Studies annual conference in Seattle in which they accused today's critics of these events of "presentism," or refusing to suspend present day ethical judgments about actions from the past.

14. The Chinese characters that signify Yung Wing's name, 容闳, in pinyin would be written as Rong Hong. Because pinyin was introduced in the 1950s, and the Wade-Giles system was not systematized until the 1860s, Yung's romanized name fits neither. This chapter uses Yung Wing's name as the author used it in his English-language writings.

15. Edmund H. Worthy, Jr., "Yung Wing in America," *Pacific Historical Review*, Vol. 34, no. 3 (1965): 283-284.

16. *My Life in China and America* was published as 西学东渐记 (*Xixue dongjianji*), or *Western Learning in the East*, in Shanghai in 1915. The history of the Chinese translation of the text is traced in Chih-ming Wang, "*My Life in China and America* and Transpacific Translations," in David Der-Wei Wang, ed., *A New Literary History of China*, (Cambridge: Harvard University Press, 2017), 85-90.

17. Lian Xi, "Returning to the Middle Kingdom: Yung Wing and the Recalled Students of the Chinese Educational Mission to the United States," *Modern Asian Studies*, Vol. 49, no. 1 (2015): 154.

18. While the 1790 Naturalization Act authorized naturalization exclusively for white people, a half-century later, some states offered citizenship to Indigenous people like Blackbird and Chinese people like Yung. This uneven liberalizing trend was disrupted in 1870 with the passage of the Naturalization Act by the Radical Republicans. That law explicitly named people defined as white and people of African descent as acceptable for naturalization. It expressly forbade Chinese naturalization. It was followed by mass violence and killings of Chinese immigrants in several Western states, passage of other laws that punished Chinese immigrants, and ultimately the exclusion acts.

19. Floyd Cheung documents Yung's role in these efforts. Floyd Cheung, "Early Chinese American Autobiography: Reconsidering the Works of Yan Phou Lee and Yung Wing," *Auto/Biography Studies*, Vol. 18, no. 1 (2003): 55.

20. In republican internationalist terms, Yung exploits differences among the imperialists, the Chinese imperial state, and the U.S. to achieve capitalist development on a republican and self-determination basis.

21. In his account of his time in Taiwan, Yung suggests that Japanese authorities attempted to recruit him as an anti-Qing agent working on their behalf (*MLCA*, 145-147).

22. Some recent examples include Pan Minfang, "On the Politics of Memory in Yung Wing's Autobiography [论容闳自传中的记忆政治]," *Literatures in Chinese*, No. 3 (2015):45-50; Zhang Xingjie and An Ge, "An Analysis of Doubts and Mistakes in My Life in China and America [《西学东渐记》疑误辨析]," *Ludong University Journal* (Philosophy and Social Sciences Edition) Vol. 37, no. 5 (2020): 44-47; Yunbo Zhao and Haowei Ji, "Rong Hong and the Concept of 'Artificial Instruments' in the Late Qing Dynasty [容闳与晚清"制器之器"理念]," *Science and Culture*, Vol. 17, no. 1 (2020): 73-87.

23. Yung Wing, *My Life in China and America*, (New York: Henry Holt and Co., 1909), iv.   https://www.gutenberg.org/files/54635/54635-h/54635-h.htm#page_013. Hereafter cited by page in the text.

24. For this insight, I am indebted to pre-modern China scholar Yilin Wendland-Liu. Yung used an early formulation of this idea "work out an Orientalist civilization on an Occidental basis" (*MLCA*, 106). Also, see a discussion of this idea in its modern context in Cheng Enfu, *China's Economic Dialectic: The Original Aspiration of Reform*, (New York: International Publishers, 2021), 21-22. Yung's education theory differed significantly with dominant U.S. theories of that social institution's

role. While the latter emphasize individual social mobility, Yung saw education as a vehicle for national technical development.

25. Worthy, 274. Other scholars emphasize Yung's American ideas as the origin and basis of his subsequent identity formation and political outlook. See Paul W. Harris, "A Checkered Life: Yung Wing's American Education," *American Journal of Chinese Studies*, Vol. 2, no. 1 (1994): 87-107.

26. Cheung, 52-56.

27. David Leiwei Li, "On Ascriptive and Acquisitional Americanness: The Accidental Asian and the Illogic of Assimilation," *Contemporary Literature*, Vol. 45, no. 1 (2004): 106 (n 1), 107.

28. That the "self-made man" mythology also had ties to Confucianism adds further complexity to national claims on Yung's autobiography. China-based American Studies scholar Tao Zhang argues that doctrines of self-reliance advocated by the likes of Jefferson and Emerson were influenced by their respective interests in Confucian philosophy. In particular, "Confucius was an inspiration on how an individual could simultaneously develop himself and advance the larger society." Tao Zhang, "The Confucian Strategy in African Americans' Racial Equality Discourse," *Dao*, Vol. 20 (2021): 310. https://doi.org/10.1007/s11712-021-09778-9.

29. Edlie L. Wong, *Racial Reconstruction: Black Inclusion, Chinese Exclusion, and the Fictions of Citizenship Account*, (New York: New York University Press, 2015), 15. In the late 19th century, "U.S. industrialists began focusing on China as an outlet for surplus overproduction and its teeming populace as future consumers of American manufactures." A Euro-American desire for interaction with China and its subordinate inclusion contradicted the dominant urge to define U.S. white supremacy through Chinese exclusion. This condition was (and is) not simply a logical inconsistency but a contradiction that constitutes the structure and motion of the totality of the U.S. social formation.

30. Lowe, 14-16.

31. For a discussion of each current, see Zhou Xiaojing, "Introduction: Critical Theories and Methodologies in Asian American Literary Studies," in eds. Zhou Xiaojing and Samina Najmi, *Form and Transformation in Asian American Literature*, (Seattle: University of Washington Press, 2005), 3-29.

32. Chih-ming Wang, 90.

33. Tom Long and Carsten-Andreas Schulz, "Republican Internationalism: The Nineteenth-century Roots of Latin American Contributions to International Order," *Cambridge Review of International Affairs*, (May 2021). https://doi.org/10.1080/09557571.2021.1944983.

34. See Gerald Horne, *Confronting Black Jacobins: The United States the Haitian Revolution, and the Origins of the Dominican Republic*, (New York: Monthly Review, 2015).

35. See Andrew Zimmerman, *Alabama in Africa: Booker T. Washington, the German Empire, and the Globalization of the New South*, (Princeton: Princeton University Press, 2010), 12-13; Carolyn L. Karcher, "Ida B. Wells and her Allies Against Lynching: A Transnational Perspective," *Comparative American Studies*, Vol. 3, no.2 (2005): 131-151. https://doi.org/10.1177/1477570005052526. My adaptation of the "republican internationalist" concept is heavily indebted to the "Horne Thesis." A running thread of Horne's work shows how African-descended people in the Americas sought international alliances to improve their conditions of life. See Erik. S. McDuffie, "Black and Red: Black Liberation, the Cold War, and the Horne Thesis," *Journal of African American History*, Vol. 96, no. 2 (2011): 236-254. Pan-Africanism (a politically diverse and complex ideology) cannot be subsumed

under "republican internationalist," a more historically specific ideological formation.

36. See Gerald Horne, *The Deepest South: The United States, Brazil, and the African Slave Trade,* (New York: New York University Press, 2007).

37. A vital distinction emerges here. Yung's republican internationalism signals an emergent political commitment to transforming China's system from a corrupt retrograde imperial bureaucracy sustained by a conservative but emergent capitalist class into a democratic republic. The republican internationalist model deployed simultaneously in the U.S. signaled a transition of abolition democracy to the "highest stage of capitalism," imperialism, following a similar trend among the Western European great powers. Zimmerman, 10-11.

38. See Yung, *MLCA,* 93-95. Yung visited the U.S. in 1863 to buy machinery. His mission was temporarily side-tracked by his impulse to join the Union cause in the Civil War, offering to serve as a courier for political and military messages. His offer was turned down. See Worthy, 275, 276; Xi, 169.

39. Pinyin: *liangxing tongqu.* Translation: Two provinces passageway.

40. The "self-made man" mythology originates in the republican self-reliance rhetoric famously deployed by Benjamin Franklin before the U.S. revolution, Jefferson's *Notes on the State of Virginia,* and Ralph Waldo Emerson's lectures and sermons. See James V. Catano, "The Rhetoric of Masculinity: Origins, Institutions, and the Myth of the Self-made Man," *College English,* Vol. 52, no. 4 (1990), 423, 428.

41. Yung Wing named one of his children Morrison Brown Yung presumably after Brown and Morrison (*MLCA,* 137). The school was named Morrison after Robert Morrison, a British missionary in Macau who had worked for the East India Company and had played an enormous role in British operations in East Asia.

42. Yung Wing writes Zeng's name thus: Tsang Kwoh Fan (*MLCA,* 138).

43. As noted, Yung had been sympathetic to the Taiping rebellion seeing the potential for a radical transformation of Chinese society, including possible leaps into modernity via a disruption of the imperial system. The rebels, however, clung to religious fundamentalism as their primary motive and refused to develop plans for advanced educational systems or adapt to Western technology. See Lian Xi, 157-158.

44. A view of Yung's textual approach as "strategic accommodation" or "resistant appropriation" may well fit these contradictions in the ideology of republican internationalism. See Floyd Cheung, "Political Resistance, Cultural Appropriation, and the Performance of Manhood in Yung Wing's *My Life in China and America,"* in Zhou Xiaojing and Samina Najmi, eds., *Form and Transformation in Asian American Literature,* (Seattle: University of Washington Press, 2005), 79, 83.

45. Catano, 422-423.

46. Zimmerman, 5-19. Angela Zimmerman's work was originally published under the name Andrew Zimmerman.

47. Zimmerman, 61-62.

48. See Louis Harlan, "The Secret Life of Booker T. Washington," *Journal of Southern History,* Vol. 37, no. 3 (1971): 393-416.

49. Like Du Bois, Carver may have retained an internationalist perspective. Du Bois famously traveled to the Soviet Union several times, including 1926. Carver, in 1930, turned down a leading role in a Soviet-backed Tuskegee-originated expedition to the USSR for a similar educational purpose as the Togo-bound group. Describing the project as "a fine thing," Carver begged off due to advanced age.

See Joy Gleason Carew, *Blacks, Reds, and Russians: Sojourners in Search of the Soviet Promise*, (New Brunswick, New Jersey: Rutgers University Press, 2008), 94.

50. Zimmerman, 56, 60. Zimmerman describes Washington's attempts to hire Du Bois as an effort to bring "emancipatory sociology" to the famous institute.

51. Zimmerman, 10, 56-57.

52. See note 48.

53. Booker T. Washington, *Up from Slavery: An Autobiography*, (Garden City, New York: Doubleday and Company, 1901), 66-67. Hereafter cited in the text as *UFS*.

54. Washington's use of terms like "new world" and "the promised land" resonate intentionally with discourses on the "discovery" of the Americas, Manifest Destiny, "pioneering" settler colonialism, and Biblical stories of Israel, Christian narratives such as *Pilgrim's Progress*, and philosophical texts like Plato's Allegory of the Cave. His recollection of his childhood work in a dark mine resonates with Sojourner Truth's recollection of her family's residence in their enslaver's dark and disease-ridden cellar (chapter 2). Those memories contrast with Blackbird's happier childhood (chapter 3).

55. Foley, 13.

56. The only social system to which Washington attributes such power is slavery (*UFS*, 16).

57. This mystified form of isolation registers as alienation, the reification of self.

58. Marx asserted that the capitalist class relishes its individual experiences of alienation because it recognizes those experiences as the effect of the socialization of "its own power." Foley, 51. The false totality of self and collectivity in Washington's model of politics articulates a denial of social revolution in favor of representations of Black leadership sprinkled throughout dominant institutions. For Washington, this model is the concrete embodiment of Black power and its limits.

59. Grace Kyungwon Hong, *Ruptures of American Capital: Women of Color Feminism and the Culture of Immigrant Labor*, (Minneapolis: University of Minnesota Press, 2006), 7.

60. E. San Juan, Jr. uses the term "reflexive reading" to describe a process of re-reading a literary text after analytical conclusions are articulated. This method generates a "politically-conscious reading" that situates historically the "psychological impact and the political and ethical resonance that the form generates, and the total experience induced in the critical reader." San Juan, Jr. "Literary Studies," 11.

61. Scholar David S. Roh shows how in the rapidly technologizing era of industrial capitalism, "[t]he mechanization of the worker in conjunction with the larger colonial or capitalist project determines the space a racialized body may occupy." See Roh, *Minor Transpacific: Triangulating American, Japanese, and Korean Fictions*, (Stanford: Stanford University Press, 2021), 40. The logic of technologically advanced industrialization created racially proscribed spaces of work and social existence for Black and Asian workers. Washington's text accommodates this system of racial segmentation. Yung seeks a re-ordering of the world system to improve the position of Chinese workers in both geographical spaces.

62. Yung renders Hong's name thus: Hung Siu Chune (*MLCA*, 116)

63. Note that Yung had used the adjective "versatile" to describe the "self-made" qualities of one his former mentors (see above). That he again uses the term to describe China suggests a radical shift from individualism to collectivism in his thought.

64. John A. Rapp, "Clashing Dilemmas: Hong Rengan, Issachar Roberts, and a Taiping 'Murder' Mystery," *Journal of Historical Biography*, Vol. 4 (2008): 27-58. Yung

states that during his visit to the Taiping-controlled provinces in the 1850s, he met Roberts and remembered him from his stay at an English school in Macao in his youth. Oddly, Yung refers to him as Ichabod Roberts, which calls to mind the school teacher Ichabod Crane in the Washington Irving story, "The Legend of Sleepy-Hollow." Perhaps this is merely a misremembrance of the man's name, a reference to childhood nicknames for a brutal former teacher obsessed with the strange and paranormal.

65. Significantly, this text opens the possibility that Yung is also rebelling against a Confucian concept of self-reliance. As noted in footnote 28 above, the Confucian influence on the American concept, though largely forgotten, was formative. Yung's conclusion of this text could be read as a rejection of dominant ideological systems in both China and the U.S. in favor of a revolutionary leap into a radical, anti-imperialist future that centers on a new China.

66. W.E.B. Du Bois, *Black Reconstruction in America, 1860-1880*, (New York: Touchstone Books, 1992 [1935]), 83.

67. Du Bois showed that even in states where Black people were in the majority, they never sought total power in the Republican Party or any government institution. Instead, Black political leaders worked for strategic alliances with white people who would help create a base for common development through education improvements, access to land, and the protection of political participation. Washington denies this reality to accommodate the dominant view of Southern white political classes and potential donors who regarded Reconstruction through a lens of victimization. See Du Bois, *Black Reconstruction*, 404, 441, 488, 529.

68. E. San Juan Jr., "Literary Studies," 10.

69. I am indebted to a graduate student, Amy Phillips, for discussions of the terminology and dialectical process that prompted me to think through this concept.

70. See note 54.

71. Discussions of Wu Tingfang's career and writings can be found in Zhen Sun, "Challenging the Dominant Stories of the Boxer Rebellion: Chinese Minister Wu Ting-fang's Narrative," *Chinese Journal of Communication*, Vol. 1, no. 2 (2008): 196-212; Julia H. Lee, "Estrangement on a Train: Race and Narratives of American Identity," *ELH*, Vol. 75, no. 2 (2008): 345-365.

72. "Editorials: Wu Ting Fang," *Journal of Education*, 70, no. 2 (1909): 43. Wu's speeches were widely reported in the U.S. press. Wu, *America, Through the Spectacles of an Oriental Diplomat*, (New York, Frederick A. Stokes Co., 1914). https://catalog.hathitrust.org/Record/000315991. Zhang, 320.

73. Wu Tingfang, "The Causes of the Unpopularity of the Foreigner in China," *Annals of the American Academy of Political and Social Science*, (January 1910): 1. Hereafter cited in the text as "Causes."

Conclusions: Exits

"What have you produced?"

This book has explored a sample of U.S. literature from the 1790s through the early 1910s, the long 19th century. It is a period of transition from a slaveholders' republic to a white supremacist empire, both conditioned by and constitutive of capitalist social relations of production and heteronormative patriarchy. Literature recorded and participated in ideological struggles that reference four recurring mythological themes: a culture of victimization, beliefs in capitalist-based social progress, frontier mythology, and the "self-made man." While Jefferson, Franklin, Tyler, Cooper, Washington, and Hurd produced thought that upheld those cultural themes and even helped to determine their contours, figures such as Wheatley, Equiano, Apess, Wilson, Truth, Yung, and Wu fostered an ideological class struggle that resisted through (at least in part) demystification of those cultural mythologies. Instead of white supremacy's fragile power, they upheld the possibility of an alternative, even utopian space rooted in the physical and political struggle.

By way of closing my discussion of this transitional period, I briefly explore the thought of Anna Julia Cooper and apply what philosopher Lewis R. Gordon calls her theory of value to a reading of W.E.B. Du Bois's first novel, *The Quest of the Silver Fleece* (1911). Cooper and Du Bois share a similar biographical timeline. The former was born in North Carolina in 1858, an enslaved person. The latter was born in 1868 in Great Barrington, Massachusetts. Cooper died in Washington one year after Du Bois's passing in Ghana in 1963. Cooper earned a Ph.D. at the age of 67 but first appeared in American letters in 1892 with the publication of her book *A Voice from the South*.

She was a "staunch ally" of Du Bois and shared the organizing responsibilities for the first Pan-African conference staged
in London in 1901. Du Bois is typically regarded as a "profeminist," aligning himself politically and intellectually with
Cooper as well as numerous other Black women leaders such
as Pauline E. Hopkins, Mary Church Terrell, and Ida B. Wells
in the 1890s and early 1900s.[1] Both Cooper and Du Bois resisted
Booker T. Washington's effort to corral African American
activism toward an accommodationist politics of representation and submission to the capitalist logic of accumulation,
racialized labor segmentation, and imperialism. Cooper paid
the price for her defiance after a Washington-controlled newspaper spread false rumors about her personal life and caused
her to be fired. Du Bois turned down a job offer at Tuskegee
and garnered fame with his collection of essays, *Souls of Black
Folk*, which included a scathing critique of Washington's
thought. The difference in the experiences and outcomes of
Cooper's professional and political choices undoubtedly can
be traced to her identity as a Black woman organizer, social
critic, teacher, writer, and defiant leader.

Philosopher Lewis R. Gordon argues that Cooper's theory
of value, which is rooted in but not confined to a labor theory
of value, is a fundamental pillar of Africana philosophy.[2] Both
Gordon and Gaines[3] explicitly link Cooper to the field of twentieth-century politics. For purposes of this book, however, I regard
her thought as a framework for reading Du Bois's novel, which
I consider one of the final nineteenth-century novels.[4] Gordon
synthesizes Cooper's philosophy of value as the socialization of
"worth," which "was a function of what an individual produced
in relation to that which was invested in him or her."[5] Cooper
inquires, "What have you produced, what consumed? What
is your real value in the world's economy? What do you give
to the world over and above what you have cost? What would
be missed had you never lived? What are you worth?" (*VFS*,
123). Building on the implications of these questions, Cooper
adds, "[a]re we a positive and additive quantity or a negative
factor in the world's elements?" Her argument, delivered as a
series of philosophical, stock-taking questions, drives toward
an estimate of this ratio as the basis of individual and group

worth (*VFS*, 124). Worth is a measurable ratio of the aggregate creation of social and cultural goods produced by individuals, as members of groups, to the goods with which they started in a given time and spatial frame. While the terms "individual" and "you" are used, the context in which Cooper deploys those terms shows that she means them in forms of generalizable typicality and collectivity.[6]

African Americans produced a measurable quantity of economic, social, and cultural value as enslaved people into whom little capital was invested for their technical and cultural development, not to mention their general reproduction as a laboring class. Despite this disadvantageous, super-exploitative relation, large quantities of U.S. society, capitalist development, cultural identities, and values came from the physical and mental labor of Black people, before and after Emancipation. Indeed, much of the contents of this book and its possibility for existence derive from that labor. After emancipation, the racist basis for withholding investments in education, economic development, and cultural enhancements for African Americans changed little. Therefore, by measuring this ratio of the starting point to vast and resulting ponderous contributions, the value of Black people, in Cooper's calculus, can be established as far higher than a relative value measured by the ratio of investment of input and the actual outputs produced by Euro-Americans (even given a substantially larger population). Such a theory of value can be assessed for different types of collectivities: classes, intersectional subject positions (e.g., Black women, etc.), and regions (e.g., the Southern Euro-American enslavers before the Civil War) (*VFS*, 127).

Gordon's focus on the philosophical parts of Cooper's ideas does not deny the interdisciplinary nature of her thought. Cooper, a skilled mathematics teacher who took a Ph.D. in French literature and spent most of her career teaching various high school subjects, proposes a political economy of racial capitalism. As noted, her theory of value is rooted in labor, the value added to an object (or cultural product, an idea, a person) via human physical or mental labor power. This positions the creation of value, the worth of value, primarily within the domain of the working class—as the pre-established wealth and power of capitalists preclude them from a high net worth in Cooper's calculation. In addition, the bodies of workers are a fundamental site of value creation.

Every human body is a historically constructed body and conditioned by the social relations into which it has been born. Cooper states, "These bodies of ours often come to us mort-gaged to their full value by the extravagance, self-indulgence, sensuality of some ancestor" (*VFS*, 125). In addition, "[t]he materials that go to make the man, the probabilities of his character and activities, the conditions and circumstances of his growth, and his quantum of resistance and mastery are the resultant of forces which have been accumulating and gath-ering momentum for generations" (*VFS*, 125). Cooper thus echoes Truth's sentiments (see chapter 2). She affirms value added via human labor in social production and reproduction, the site of which is mediated by the historically constructed human body.

Social systems construct the potentialities and the limits, the openings and the boundaries that define the material conditions in which bodies function. Indeed, the "slavehold-er's republic" constitutes such a system that uses skin color to determine its laws, values, margins, exclusions, and the limits of citizenship. Even with dominant systems of racism, exploitative class processes, patriarchal gender relations, and other structured forms of social marginalization, the concur-rent reality of collective forms of disruption and autonomous power-building (political struggle, counter-hegemonic edu-cational work, labor organizing, and cooperative economic activities) can turn the tables. Cooper argues that this latter element lies at the heart of African American progress since its enslavement in the Americas. Black-created and -defined forms of power, wealth, culture, land, and history arose from so few inputs, so much squalor—think of the dank, dark cel-lar in which Sojourner Truth's family lived or the pitch-black coal mine Booker Washington worked in. The creation of so much from so little defined the true (unpaid) value of African-descended people in the U.S.

The relationship between Cooper's theory of value and African American power-building can be detected in three signal events that either shaped post-Civil War life or signaled transitions in forms of struggle. First, the Civil War-era "General Strike," the mass movement of thousands of enslaved people out of the plantation and into the historical struggle for freedom, fundamentally altered the political aims of the Civil War and made the U.S. victory in that war possible.[7] W.E.B. Du Bois's discovery and amplification of the import of this particular historical moment shaped fundamentally by Black people's actions, decisions, and aspirations sometimes overshadow in our memory the second major event: the struggle, as he writes, "to establish agrarian democracy in the South."[8] This activity took many forms, but the establishment of Black-owned and -controlled settlements throughout the South and Midwest stands out not just because of its "separatist" composition. Settlements like Promiseland, South Carolina drew directly on the "General Strike" tradition and the philosophy of collective development that is expressed in Sojourner Truth's thought and Cooper's philosophy. Promiseland, located near Abbeville, South Carolina, was a settlement of Black landowners and tenant farmers. In 1870 South Carolina's Reconstruction government created a land commission mandated to expropriate Confederate-owned land and sell it at low cost and low interest to Black farmers. This is how Promiseland was born.[9]

Over the next few decades, Promiseland's Black farmers never formally created a municipal government, preferring to manage the community's needs through its social institutions: the school, the churches, and the marketplace. As the state's white planters and capitalists restored racist white power, Promiseland leaders knew that a formal government structure would have opened the people to outside control. In addition to this approach to government, the people organized a self-defense committee that, according to historian Elizbeth Rauh Bethel's book *Promiseland*, more than once thwarted white attempts to attack the settlement. Promiseland farmers also resisted the monoculture cotton market because white plantation owners continued to dominate it. Instead, Black farmers produced a variety of crops for the market and subsistence. For example, they grew sorghum and built processing facilities to make molasses. As Reconstruction ended, racist restrictions on new land purchases stunted the growth and development of the settlement. Within just two generations, as the families grew, the plots of land shrank. By the 1920s, the crash of cotton prices generally devastated the regional economy, which forced many small farmers to sell more and more bits of land to survive. Instead of making a living on their family farms, many of the younger generations migrated to Southern and Northern urban areas to secure industrial work.

A third event that exemplifies a theory of value rooted in the valorization of human bodies and labor is the 1881 Atlanta washerwomen's strike. As Tera W. Hunter shows in her book *To 'joy my freedom: Southern Black Women's Lives and Labors after the Civil War*, the struggle in Atlanta was a feature of longer and more widespread battle by Black women domestic workers and laundry workers to win rights, better wages, and power across the South. Laundry workers in that city had organized a "protective association" several years leading up to the strike, often under police surveillance and threats of violence. These labor union activities coincided with the city's resurgent Black political activism, protests against racist abuses and lynching, attempts to gain control of the Republican Party, and competitive participation in the city council elections. In the summer of 1881, Black laundry workers met, created the "Washing Society," and mobilized broad public support through Black churches in the city for their demands for increased pay and union recognition. Thousands of Black women and their supporters fought a white-dominated city government and its ruling class for control over their labor, human dignity, rights as workers, and rights to civic participation.[10] These events help establish tangible links between the philosophy and action of African Americans as the 19th century drew to a close.

When she published her first book, *A Voice from the South* (1892), Cooper disclosed a high ratio of Black value relative to the little created by the most powerful Euro-Americans who had been born with so much. Cooper's negation of the inward-turned, individualized self through collective action turns Washington's thought on its head. Further, Cooper's theory of value had clear implications for the four mythological frameworks explored in this book. It disturbs and illuminates the psychological fragility nestled within imperialist and white supremacist aggressions mystified by the culture of victimization, the frontier mythology, and ideological assertions of being "self-made." By linking social progress to the culture and activity of the working class, Cooper further disrupts the dominant mythology of capitalist progress. This is the framework in which Du Bois's *The Quest of the Silver Fleece* can be read fruitfully in that historical transition.

Struggle in the swamp

Literary critics today describe W.E.B. Du Bois's first novel, *The Quest of the Silver Fleece*, variously as "utopian" fiction, sociological fiction, an "economic study," and a feminist-informed realist novel.[11] This generic conflict stems from Du Bois's imaginative dramatization of the emergence of monopoly capitalism, its reliance on white supremacy and heteronormative patriarchy for labor management and social control, and its discourses on philanthropy and academic knowledge production as tools of social control. The novel also centers on a Black working-class woman as the source and site of class struggle to build a united, African American-led working-class community against systems of exploitation and oppression and the intellectual fountainhead of an alternative world.

These qualities of Du Bois's novel place him in close relation to the ideological struggle that shapes the content of *Mythologies*. *The Quest of the Silver Fleece* adds to this inheritance and critical exposé of monopoly capitalism, dominated by finance capital.[12] An exploration of the novel's opening pages reveals a partial geography of monopoly capitalism in the advancing years of the 19th century. Bles Alwyn, the African American male protagonist, arrives late in the night in Tooms County, Alabama, to attend Mrs. Smith's school for Black youth. He has become lost in a swamp, where among other things, he meets Zora, the African American female protagonist. While sharing a meal with her, he asks her for directions. Those directions place the symbolic significance of the swamp at the center of the novel's geography, at least from their now-shared perspective. Pointing to the north of their location, Bles asks Zora what is in that direction. She replies, "Cresswell's big house." Pointing west, she indicates the school that Bles and she will ultimately attend. Toward the swamp, presumably farther south or east or southeast of their location, we discover the swamp to be a place of "dreams," magic, mystery, unoppressed sexuality, liberty, and so on.[13]

The significance of this geography and its relation to social power is amplified some pages later when Bles begins at the school. Part of his tuition is worked off by helping to plant, cultivate, and harvest the cotton crop, which the school sells to the nearby Cresswell plantation. This relation to the Cresswell plantation both provides some financial support for the school and serves as the material basis for the manual labor curriculum of the school. As Bles works in a field of partially grown cotton, cutting the weaker stems, he meets Miss Mary Taylor, a white teacher at the school. During a brief conversation, Mary Taylor discovers that Bles is well-acquainted with cotton production, putting her inadequate knowledge of the subject to shame. (Ironically, Bles's knowledge of cotton belies the dominant white perception that Black youth need to be taught farming techniques.) Their horticulture discussion winds up as Bles glances up the hill toward the Cresswell mansion to see two white men watching his interaction with Mary Taylor. He quickly returns to work, aware of the social power inflicted by their gaze. Mary Taylor moves on, oblivious but suddenly engrossed by the idea that during the conversation, "the fact of the boy's color had quite escaped her" (QSF, 31-32). She had forgotten Bles was Black and regarded him as her equal. In this spatial positioning, we see the Cresswells on the hill to the North, the precariously positioned school funded by philanthropic whites to the west, and the "red" swamp full of magic and freedom and dreams to the southeast.

The Cresswell patriarch and his son dominate the political economy of the region. They own 50,000 acres of primarily cotton-producing land on which hundreds of small tenant farmers, mostly Black, work in conditions of debt peonage to cultivate and harvest the crop for markets in the North and Europe. The work conditions differ little from slavery except perhaps in freedom of movement out of the plantation scheme. Since the Civil War, the dominant position of the planter class, represented by the Cresswells, has shifted. Now a murkier power dominates cotton. Mary Taylor's brother, John Taylor, works for a Wall Street finance firm symbolically named Grey and Easterly. Taylor, a middling employee, wants to make his fortune in the manner of the "self-made man." So, he concocts a scheme for the Grey and Easterly firm to mobilize its finance capital, political control of the U.S. Senate, and philanthropic resources to pull the Cresswells and its alliance of planters into a Cotton Trust. Thus, the text ties the "self-made man" mythology to the middle-class aspiration for power in partnership with the capitalist class.

Taylor's idea is to control the labor and raw materials of cotton production as a starting point to build a monopoly on cotton and textile manufacturing. He envisions an educational scheme via donations to Mrs. Smith's school to better manage Black workers than the old plantation model of coerced exploitation.[14] By organizing the largest planters into an association that Taylor's firm controlled through loans and debt, the Northern capitalists could manipulate the supply and prices of the raw cotton. With control over large amounts of finance capital—money, credit, bond sales, insurance policies, and so on—they would also lure the manufacturers, the shippers, and the distributors into the trust. This cotton monopoly would be carefully supported and protected by the firm's pawns in Congress with sympathetic legislation on tariffs, labor issues, and bank regulation. Much of the novel's attention to spaces dominated by Euro-Americans centers on forging these inter-capitalist class alliances foundational to monopoly capitalism reinforced by the cultivation and manipulation of white supremacy and the control of Black people.

In this hegemonic social formation lie the dreams and aspirations, and struggles of Bles and Zora. The two discover an empty field of "virgin" land (QFS, 78) in the swamp that they clear, drain, and plow in preparation to plant their own cotton (QSF, 76-78). In the geography of social relations, the swamp, a "field of dreams," symbolizes a historical refuge from white supremacy, enslavement, and settler colonialism. It holds a mixture of magic that might identify it as an Indigenous space. Indeed, it has harbored runaway slaves of maroon heritage.[15] Black maroon societies in the mid-19th century had formed independent communities with autonomous trajectories of social development in the hinterlands of the North American colonies and subsequent U.S. states and territories. Often in alliance with Indigenous nations, as discussed in chapter 3 of this book and as Gerald Horne has shown in *Negro Comrades of the Crown*, they formed some of the fiercest resistance to settler colonialism, re-enslavement, and U.S. integration into and positioning within the imperialist world system.[16] At the same time, the swamp is a site of magical, profane, and pagan resistance to Euro-American power. It also serves as a place in which utopian dreams of the modern development of autonomous political and economic power in the tradition of the maroons. In addition, its position to the south and east locates it in contradistinction to the western orientations of dominant frontier mythology.

Cooper's theory of value is evident in this text. Zora, variously characterized as troublesome, a "heathen," and immoral, overtly rejects property rights as a basis of ownership and use. In two closely positioned scenes, she steals a gold pin from Mary Taylor and borrows a mule from the Cresswell barn to help clear and plow the swamp in preparation for cotton planting. When confronted by an angry Mary Taylor for stealing the pin, Zora denies that simple possession of a thing does not constitute ownership. "Did you make that pin?" Zora inquires. "Why is it yours?" Pushing the logic further, Zora notes, "folks ain't got no right to things they don't need" (*QSF*, 79). The incident with the pin and the mule foreshadows Zora and Bles's reclamation of the swamp and the ultimate utopian project of transforming the school and the area into a site of Black power and economic development. The novel's plot trajectory sees Zora move from a "wild" individualism to strategic collectivism oriented toward Black liberation. While Easterly, Taylor, and the Cresswells control vast amounts of finance capital, the law, land, and force, their negative relation to value creation subverts the ethical basis for their ownership of this power.

Instead, Black people, poor whites, and their allies in the middle class hold ethical primacy in Du Bois's socialist imaginary through creative labor and need. It portends and stakes out an agricultural- and land-based multi-racial utopia built on shared ownership and cooperative social relations.[17] While even with these cursory notes on *The Quest of the Silver Fleece*, it is possible to connect this early novel to the later Harlem Renaissance and the subsequent proletarian literature movement, I argue that *The Quest* is best fitted as a bookend to the long 19th century of U.S. literature and criticism. Its social vision would no longer be recognizable a generation later. The exit from this agricultural world was clearly marked as industrialization, migration from rural to urban locations, and the centering of the industrial labor movement as a critical site of class struggle shifted the locus of the search for power.

Final notes

In my book *The Collectivity of Life*, I argued that contradictions between the ideological and mythological constructs that justify the "natural" order of social relations and lived experiences shape working-class culture, values, and acts of resistance to dominant ideologies, and even its complicity with the ruling class in its subjugation.[18] In this study of the long 19th century of U.S. literature (in its multiple forms, genres, and styles), *Mythologies* illuminates the sources and effects of those contradictions. Even authors who closely aligned their thought with the dominant hegemonic ideologies could not fully contain society's contradictions within their texts. The struggle for human liberation has coincided with the retrograde ideas and forces that attempted to ensure the subjugation or enslavement of vast swathes of humanity. Indeed, the existence of the ideas of liberty, democracy, and equality that supposedly informed the political and economic system of the U.S. from its founding through the close of this long 19th century (and beyond) were conditioned and over-determined by enslavement, expropriation of land, white supremacy, and exploitative class processes that structure capitalism and its highest stage in imperialism.

While much of the literature produced within the U.S. justified, mystified, or ignored the reality of these conditions and contrived imaginary worlds that approved of them on racial and civilization grounds or glorified their extension through violence and war, key literary texts contested those values, relations, and realities. They imagined alternative ethical futures that negated dominant power constructs and elevated the oppressed and exploited as the human material basis of a new world. While not all of us share identical cultural, racial, or ethnic affiliations (or all of the historical contexts those positionalities embody) of Blackbird, Truth, Anna J. Cooper, and Yung in this literary history, their work remains our true intellectual and creative inheritance. We must make peace with it, embrace it, and let it inspire our future collective and united struggles for this country's working-class power and social leadership.

Notes

1.   Barbara McCaskill, "Anna Julia Cooper, Pauline Elizabeth Hopkins, and the African American Feminization of Du Bois's Discourse," in *Souls of Black Folk 100 Years Later*, ed. Dolan Hubbard, (Columbia: University of Missouri Press, 2003), 71; Joy James, "The Profeminist Politics of W. E. B. Du Bois with Respects to Anna Julia Cooper and Ida B. Wells-Barnett," in *W.E.B. Du Bois on Race and Culture*, eds. Bernard W. Bell, Emily R. Grosholz, James B. Stewart, (New York: Routledge, 1996), 141-160.

2.   Lewis R. Gordon, *An Introduction to Africana Philosophy*, (Cambridge: Cambridge University Press, 2008), 69-73.

3.   See a discussion of "woman and the labor question" in Kevin K. Gaines, *Uplifting the Race: Black Leadership, Politics, and Culture in the 20th Century*, (Chapel Hill: University of North Carolina Press, 1996), 128-151.

4.   Its southern orientation and rural focus on agricultural labor date it to a pre-Great Migration spatiality. The mass movement of close to half of the African American population out of the rural South and into urban, industrial settings dramatically altered the class composition and political dynamics of that community and the country generally. That event has to be regarded, along with the Russian and Mexican revolutions, the first World War, and the founding of the Chinese Republic, as the opening shots of the 20th century.

5.   Gordon, 71; Anna Julia Cooper, *A Voice from the South, By a Black Woman of the South*, digital edition, (Chapel Hill: University of the North Carolina, 2017), 123-124. Hereafter cited in the text as *V.F.S.*

6.   Cooper's theory of value also challenges mainstream economic measurements of productivity that use similar terms, but solely in relation to commodified labor and goods to help capitalists measure capital utilization rates. Instead of value

deriving from human bodies put into motion through labor-power (as in Cooper's theory), productivity is used to measure necessary increases in exploitation (surplus-value extraction) to manage the rate of profit, predict economic crisis, and solicit new investments in new technologies.

7. W.E.B. Du Bois, *Black Reconstruction in America*, 1860-1880, (New York: Touchstone Books, 1992 [1935]), 55-83.

8. Du Bois, *Black Reconstruction*, 67.

9. Elizabeth Rauh Bethel, *Promiseland: A Century of Life in a Negro Community*, (Columbia: University of South Carolina Press, 1981), 18, 115.

10. Tera W. Hunter, *To 'joy my freedom: Southern Black Women's Lives and Labors after the Civil War*, (Cambridge: Harvard University Press, 1997), 74-97. I am indebted to Erica Smiley and Sarita Gupta for drawing my attention to some of these events in their book *The Future We Need: Organizing for a Better Democracy in the Twenty-first Century*, (Ithaca: I.L.R. Press, 2021), 29-30.

11. Such differences caused one scholar to regard it as a "generic mess." Christine A. Wooley, "Haunted Economics: Race, Retribution, and Money in Pauline Hopkins's *Of One Blood* and W.E.B. Du Bois's *The Quest of the Silver Fleece*," in *Haunting Realities: Naturalist Gothic and American Realism*, eds. Monika Elbert and Wendy Ryden, (University of Alabama Press, 2017), 132. Wooley identifies *Quest* with realist traditions. For its sociological content, see Rashad L. James, "Du Bois' *The Quest of the Silver Fleece*: Sociology Through Fiction," *Sociation Today*, Vol. 10, no. 2 (2012). http://www.ncsociology.org/sociationtoday/v102/fleece.htm; and Charisse Burden-Stelly and Gerald Horne, *W.E.B. Du Bois: A Life in American History*, (Santa Barbara, Calif.: ABC-CLIO, 2019), 70-71. For its utopian elements, see Verena Adamik, *In Search of the Utopian States of America*, (New York: Palgrave Macmillan), 197-226. For a reading of its "economic" elements, see Brett Clark and John Bellamy Foster, "Land, the Color Line, and *The Quest of the Silver Fleece*," *Organization and Environment*, Vol. 16, no. 4 (2003): 459-469.

12. Readings of Du Bois's most significant work, *Black Reconstruction in America*, rarely explore or elevate his analysis of monopoly capital's role in drawing Reconstruction to a close as a capitalist class strategy for managing the social order and sustaining capitalism during the 1870s depressions. The germination of that analysis can be found in *Quest*.

13. W.E.B. Du Bois, *The Quest of the Silver Fleece*, (New York: Negro Universities Press, 1969 [1911]), 18-19. Hereafter cited in the text as *Q.S.F.*

14. Clearly, Du Bois intended this particular relation to expose the Tuskegee Machine's purpose for existence.

15. Adamik, 209.

16. Gerald Horne, *Negro Comrades of the Crown*, (New York: New York University Press, 2014), 81. However, the critical relationship between Black and Indigenous forces remains undisclosed and is one of the least developed elements of *The Quest*.

17. Adamik, 223.

18. Joel Wendland, *The Collectivity of Life: Spaces of Social Mobility and the Individualism Myth*, (Lanham, Maryland: Lexington Books, 2016), 105.

Bibliography

Alarcón, Ricardo. "Opening Speech at the International Conference: 'The Work of Karl Marx in the 21st Century.'" *Nature, Society, and Thought* 19, no. 1, 2006, 17–27.

Ahmad, Aijaz. *In Theory: Classes, Nations, Literatures.* New York: Verso, 2000.

Amin, Samir. *Eurocentrism,* translated by Russell Moore. New York: Monthly Review Press, 1989.

Apess, William. "The Indians: The Ten Lost Tribes." In *On Our Own Ground: The Complete Writings of William Apess, a Pequot,* edited by Barry O'Connell. Amherst: University of Massachusetts Press, 1992 [1833].

Aptheker, Herbert. *Early Years of the Republic and the Constitution, 1783–1793.* New York: International Publishers, 1990.

———. *American Negro Slave Revolts.* New York: International Publishers, 1993.

Baker, Houston A. "Autobiographical Acts and the Voice of the Southern Slave." In *The Slave's Narrative,* edited by Charles T. Davis and Henry Louis Gates, Jr., 242–61. Oxford: Oxford University Press, 1985.

Baptist, Edward. *The Half Has Never Been Told: Slavery and the Making of American Capitalism.* New York: Basic Books, 2014.

Bassard, Katherine Clay. "'Beyond Mortal Vision': Harriet E. Wilson's *Our Nig* and the American Racial Dream-Text." In *Female Subjects in Black and White: Race, Psychoanalysis, Feminism,* edited by Elizabeth Abel, Barbara Christian, and Helene Moglen, 187-200. Berkeley: University of California Press, 1997.

Bauerkemper, Joseph. "Narrating Nationhood: Indian Time and Ideologies of Progress." *Studies in American Indian Literature* 19, no. 4, 2007, 27-53.

Berry, Daina Raimey. *The Price for Their Pound of Flesh: The Value of the Enslaved from Womb to Grave in the Building of a Nation.* Boston: Beacon Press, 2018.

Bethel, Elizabeth Rauh. *Promiseland: A Century of Life in a Negro Community.* Columbia: University of South Carolina Press, 1981.

Black, Jason Edward. *American Indians and the Rhetoric of Removal and Allotment.* Jackson: University Press of Mississippi, 2015.

Blackbird, Andrew J. *History of the Ottawa and Chippewa Indians of Michigan: A Grammar of Their Language, and the Personal History of the Author.* Ypsilanti: Ypsilantian Job Printing House, 1887.

Bloodsworth-Lugo, Mary K., and Carmen R. Lugo-Lugo. *Containing (Un)American Bodies: Race, Sexuality, and Post-9/11 Constructions of Citizenship.* (Amsterdam: Brill/Rodopi, 2010.

Bohaker, Heidi. "*Nindoodemag*: The Significance of Algonquian Kinship Networks in the Eastern Great Lakes Region, 1600-1701." *William and Mary Quarterly* 63, no. 1, 2006, 23-52.

Brooks, Jennifer. "'John Chinaman' in Alabama: Immigration, Race, and Empire in the New South, 1870-1920." *Journal of American Ethnic History* 37, no. 2, 2018, 5-36.

Brooks, Lisa. *The Common Pot: The Recovery of Native Space in the Northeast*. Minneapolis: University of Minnesota Press, 2008.

——. "The Constitution of the White Earth Nation: A New Innovation in a Longstanding Indigenous Literary Tradition." *Studies in American Indian Literatures* 23, no. 4, 2011, 48-76.

——. "Turning the Looking Glass on King Philip's War: Locating American Literature in Native Space." *American Literary History* 25, no. 4, 2013, 718-750.

Brown, Kathleen. *Good Wives, Nasty Wenches, and Anxious Patriarchs: Gender, Race, and Power in Colonial Virginia*. Chapel Hill: University of North Carolina Press, 1996.

Burden-Stelly, Charisse, and Gerald Horne. *W.E.B. Du Bois: A Life in American History*. Santa Barbara: ABC-CLIO, 2019.

Carby, Hazel V. *Reconstructing Womanhood: The Emergence of the Afro-American Woman Novelist*. New York: Oxford University Press, 1987.

Cassidy, Michelle. *"Both the Honor and the Profit": Anishinaabe Warriors, Soldiers, and Veterans from Pontiac's War through the Civil War*. 2016. University of Michigan, Ph.D. dissertation.

Chang, Kornel. *Pacific Connections: The Making of the U.S. Canadian Borderlands*. Berkeley: University of California Press, 2012.

Cheung, Floyd. "Political Resistance, Cultural Appropriation, and the Performance of Manhood in Yung Wing's *My Life in China and America*." In *Form and Transformation in Asian American Literature*, edited by Zhou Xiaojing and Samina Najmi, 77-100. Seattle: University of Washington Press, 2011.

——. "Early Chinese American Autobiography: Reconsidering the Works of Yan Phou Lee and Yung Wing." *Auto/Biography Studies* 18, no. 1, 2003, 45-61.

Cooper, Anna Julia. *A Voice from the South, By a Black Woman of the South*. Digital edition. Chapel Hill: University of North Carolina Press, 2017 [1892].

Cooper, James Fenimore. *The Pioneers*. New York: Lancer Books, 1968 [1823].

——. *The Oak Openings: Or, the Bee-Hunter*. New York: The Co-operative Publication Society, 1900 [1848].

Cox, Oliver Cromwell. *The Foundations of Capitalism*. New York: Philosophical Library, Inc., 1959.

Davidson, Cathy. *Revolution and the Word: The Rise of the Novel in America*. New York: Oxford University Press, 1985.

Delgado, Grace. *Making the Chinese Mexican: Global Migration, Localism, and Exclusion in the U.S. Mexico Borderlands*. Stanford: Stanford University Press, 2012.

Deloria, Philip J. *Playing Indian*. New Haven: Yale University Press, 1998.

Devens, Carol. *Countering Colonization: Native American Women and Great Lakes Missions, 1630-1900*. Berkeley: University of California Press, 1992.

Du Bois, W. E. B. *Black Reconstruction in America, 1860-1880*. New York: Touchstone, 1992 [1935].

——. *The Quest of the Silver Fleece*. New York: Negro Universities Press, 1969 [1911].

——. *The Suppression of the African Slave Trade*. In *Du Bois: Writings*, edited by Nathan Huggins, 1–356. New York: Library of America, 1986 [1895].

Equiano, Olaudah. *The Interesting Narrative of the Life of Olaudah Equiano*. New York: St. Martin's Press, 1995 [1791].

Foley, Barbara. *Marxist Literary Criticism Today*. London: Pluto Press, 2019.

——. *Radical Representations: Politics and Form in U.S. Proletarian Fiction, 1929-1941*. Durham: Duke University Press, 1993.

Foner, Philip S. *Women and the American Labor Movement: From Colonial Times to the Eve of World War I*. New York: Free Press, 1979.

——. *Organized Labor and the Black Worker, 1619-1973*. New York: Praeger, 1974.

Foner, Eric. *Fiery Trial: Abraham Lincoln and American Slavery*. New York: W. W. Norton and Company, 2010.

Forbes, Jack D. *The American Discovery of Europe*. Champaign: University of Illinois Press, 2010.

Gaines, Kevin K. *Uplifting the Race: Black Leadership, Politics, and Culture in the Twentieth Century*. Chapel Hill: University of North Carolina Press, 1996.

Gates Jr., Henry Louis. "Introduction." In *The Classic Slave Narratives*, edited by Henry Louis Gates Jr., ix–xvi. New York: New American Library, 2002.

——. *Figures in Black: Words, Signs and the "Racial" Self*. New York: Oxford University Press, 1987.

Glenn, Evelyn Nakano. "From Servitude to Service Work: The Racial Division of Paid Reproductive Labor." In *History and Theory: Feminist Research, Debates, Contestations*, edited by Barbara Laslett, et al., 113-55. Chicago: University of Chicago Press, 1997.

Gordon, Lewis R. *Fear of Black Consciousness*. New York: Farrar, Straus and Giroux, 2021.

——. *An Introduction to Africana Philosophy*. Cambridge: Cambridge University Press, 2008.

Gupta, Sarita, and Erica Smiley. *The Future We Need: Organizing for a Better Democracy in the Twenty-first Century*. Ithaca: ILR Press, 2021.

Hong, Grace Kyungwon. *Ruptures of American Capital: Women of Color Feminism and the Culture of Immigrant Labor*. Minneapolis: University of Minnesota Press, 2006.

Horne, Gerald. *The Apocalypse of Settler Colonialism: The Roots of Slavery, White Supremacy, and Capitalism in Seventeenth-Century North America and the Caribbean*. New York: Monthly Review Press, 2018.

——. *Confronting Black Jacobins: The United States, the Haitian Revolution, and the Origins of the Dominican Republic.* New York: Monthly Review Press, 2015.

——. *The Counter-Revolution of 1776: Slave Resistance and the Origins of the United States of America.* New York: New York University Press, 2014.

——. *Negro Comrades of the Crown: African Americans and the British Empire Fight the U.S. Before Emancipation.* New York: New York University Press, 2012.

——. *Mau Mau in Harlem: The U.S. and the Liberation of Kenya.* New York: Palgrave MacMillan, 2009.

——. *The Deepest South: The United States, Brazil, and the African Slave Trade.* New York: New York University Press, 2007.

Howe, Leanne. "Embodied Tribalography: Mound Building, Ball Games, and Native Endurance in the Southeast." *Studies in American Indian Literatures* 26, no. 2, 2014, 75-93.

Howey, Meghan C. "'The question which has puzzled, and still puzzles': How American Indian Authors Challenged Dominant Discourse about Native American Origins in the Nineteenth Century." *American Indian Quarterly* 34, no. 4, 2010, 435–74.

Hunton, W. Alphaeus. *Decision in Africa: Sources of Conflict.* New York: International Publishers, 2021.

Hunter, Tera W. *To 'joy my freedom: Southern Black Women's Lives and Labors after the Civil War.* Cambridge: Harvard University Press, 1997.

Isani, Mukhtar Ali. "Far from 'Gambia's Golden Coast': The Black in Late Eighteenth-Century Imaginative Literature." *William and Mary Quarterly* 36, no. 3, 1979, 353–72.

James, Joy. "The Profeminist Politics of W. E. B. Du Bois with Respects to Anna Julia Cooper and Ida B. Wells-Barnett." In *W.E.B. Du Bois on Race and Culture,* edited by Bernard W. Bell, Emily R. Grosholz, James B. Stewart, 141-160. New York: Routledge, 1996.

James, Rashad L. "Du Bois' *The Quest of the Silver Fleece*: Sociology Through Fiction." *Sociation Today,* 10, no. 2, 2012, http://www.ncsociology.org/sociationtoday/v102/fleece.htm.

Janiewski, Dolores. "Making Common Cause: The Needle-women of New York, 1831-1869." *Signs* 1, no. 4, 1976, 778-786.

Jones, Peter. *History of the Ojebway Indians; with especial reference to their conversion to Christianity.* London: A. W. Bennett, 1861.

Jung, Moon-Ho. *Coolies and Cane: Race, Labor, and Sugar in the Age of Emancipation.* Baltimore: Johns Hopkins University, 2006.

Karamanski, Theodore J. *Blackbird's Song: Andrew J. Blackbird and the Odawa People.* East Lansing: Michigan State University Press, 2012.

Kelley, Robin D.G. *Freedom Dreams: The Black Radical Imagination.* Boston: Beacon Press, 2002.

Kessler-Harris, Alice. *Women Have Always Worked: A Historical Overview.* Old Westbury, NY: Feminist Press, 1981.

Konkle, Maureen. *Writing Indian Nations: Native Intellectuals and the Politics of Historiography, 1827-1863.* Chapel Hill: North Carolina University Press, 2004.

Lawson, John Howard. *The Hidden Heritage.* New York: Citadel Press, 1968.

Lee, Julia H. "Estrangement on a Train: Race and Narratives of American Identity." *ELH* 75, no. 2, 2008, 345-365.

Li, David Leiwei. "On Ascriptive and Acquisitional Americanness: The Accidental Asian and the Illogic of Assimilation." *Contemporary Literature* 45, no. 1, 2004, 106-134.

Little Traverse Bay Bands of Odawa Indians. "Our Land and Culture: A 200 Year History of Our Land Use." 2005. http://www.ltbbodawa-nsn.gov/Arch/Our%20Land%20and%20Culture%20for%20web.pdf.

Lowe, Lisa. *The Intimacies of Four Continents.* Durham: Duke University Press, 2015.

Lugo-Lugo, Carmen R. and Mary K. Bloodsworth-Lugo. *Feminism after 9/11: Women's Bodies as Cultural and Political Threat.* New York: Palgrave Macmillan, 2017.

Marx, Karl. *Capital,* Vol. I. New York: International Publishers, 1973.

McCaskill, Barbara. "Anna Julia Cooper, Pauline Elizabeth Hopkins, and the African American Feminization of Du Bois's Discourse." In *Souls of Black Folk 100 Years Later,* edited by Dolan Hubbard, 70-84. Columbia: University of Missouri Press, 2003.

McCoy, Isaac. *History of Baptist Indian Missions: Embracing Remarks on the Former and Present Condition of the Aboriginal Tribes; Their Settlement within the Indian Territory, and Their Future Prospects.* Washington: William M. Morrison, 1840.

McDuffie, Erik S. "Black and Red: Black Liberation, the Cold War, and the Horne Thesis." *Journal of African American History* 96, no. 2, 2011, 236-254.

Miles, Tiya. "Beyond a Boundary: Black Lives and the Settler–Native Divide." *The William and Mary Quarterly* 76, no. 3, 2019, 417–26.

Miles, Tiya, and Sharon P. Holland. "Introduction." In *Crossing Waters, Crossing Worlds: The African Diaspora in Indian Country,* edited by Miles and Holland, 1–24. Durham: Duke University Press, 2006.

Miller, Carey. *Ogimaag: Anishinaabeg Leadership, 1760-1845.* Lincoln: University of Nebraska Press, 2010.

Morrison, Toni. *Playing in the Dark: Whiteness and the Literary Imagination.* New York: Vintage Books, 1992.

Nash, Gary B. *Red, White, and Black: The Early Peoples of the Republic.* Englewood Cliffs, NJ: Prentice-Hall, 1992.

Noodin, Margaret. *Bawajimo: A Dialect of Dreams in Anishinaabe Language and Literature.* East Lansing: Michigan State University Press, 2014.

Omi, Michael, and Howard Winant, *Racial Formation in the United States,* 3rd edition. New York: Routledge, 2015.

Painter, Nell Irvin. *The History of White People.* New York: W.W. Norton and Co., 2010.

——. *Sojourner Truth, A Life, A Symbol*. New York: W.W. Norton, and Co., 1994.

Pecinovsky, Tony. *The Cancer of Colonialism: W. Alphaeus Hunton, Black Liberation, and the Daily Worker, 1944-1946*. New York: International Publishers, 2021.

Piatote, Beth H. *Domestic Subjects: Gender, Citizenship, and Law in Native American Literature*. New Haven: Yale University Press, 2013.

Powell, Malea D. "Sarah Winnemucca Hopkins: Her Wrongs and Claims." In *American Indian Rhetorics of Survivance: Word Medicine, Word Magic*, edited by Ernest Stromberg, 69-94. Pittsburgh: University of Pittsburgh, 2006.

——. "Rhetorics of Survivance: How American Indians Use Writing." *College Composition and Communication* 53, no. 3, 2002, 396-434.

Prashad, Vijay. *Washington Bullets: A History of CIA, Coups, and Assassinations*. New York: Monthly Review Press, 2020.

Ramirez-Shkwegnaabi, Benjamin. "The Dynamics of American Indian Diplomacy in the Great Lakes Region." *American Indian Culture and Research Journal* 27, no. 4, 2003, 53-77.

Ruoff, A. LaVonne Brown. "Three Nineteenth-Century American Indian Autobiographers." In *Redefining American Literary History*, edited by Ruoff and Jerry W. Ward Jr., 251–69. New York: Modern Language Association of America, 1990.

Said, Edward W. *Culture and Imperialism*. New York: Vintage Books, 1986.

——. *Orientalism*. New York: Vintage Books, 1978.

San Juan, Epifanio Jr. "Literary Studies in the Age of Empire's Collapse." *Danyag: Journal of Humanities and Social Sciences* 14, no. 1, 2009, 1-11.

——. *Working through the Contradictions, From Cultural Theory to Cultural Practice*, Lewisburg, PA: Bucknell University Press, 2004.

——. *The Philippine Temptation: The Dialectics of Philippines–U.S. Literary Relations*. Philadelphia: Temple University Press, 1996.

——. *Hegemony and Strategies of Transgression: Essays in Cultural Studies and Comparative Literature*. Albany: State University of New York Press, 1995.

Saxton, Alexander. *The Rise and Fall of the White Republic: Class Politics and Mass Culture in Nineteenth-Century America*. New York: Verso, 1990.

——. *The Indispensable Enemy: Labor and the Anti-Chinese Movement in California*. Berkeley: University of California Press, 1976.

Sun, Zhen. "Challenging the Dominant Stories of the Boxer Rebellion: Chinese Minister Wu Ting-fang's Narrative." *Chinese Journal of Communication* 1, no. 2, 2008, 196-212.

Slocum, Karla. *Black Towns, Black Futures: The Enduring Allure of a Black Place in the American West*. Chapel Hill: University of North Carolina Press, 2020.

Stansell, Christine. *City of Women: Sex and Class in New York, 1789-1860*. New York: Knopf, 1986.

Stark, Heidi Kiiwetinepinisiik. "Transforming the Trickster: Federal Indian Law Encounters Anishinaabe Diplomacy." In *Centering Anishinaabe*

Studies: Understanding the World through Stories, edited by Jill Doerfler, Niigaanwewidam James Sinclair, and Heidi Kiiwetinepinisiik Stark, 259-278. East Lansing: Michigan State University, 2013.

———. "Marked By Fire: Anishinaabe Articulations of Nationhood in Treaty-Making with the United States and Canada." In *Tribal Worlds: Critical Studies in American Indian Nation Building*, edited by Brian Hosmer and Larry Nesper, 111-140. Albany: State University of New York Press, 2013.

Stark, Heidi Kiiwetinepinisiik, and Kekek Jason Stark. "Nenabozho Goes Fishing: A Sovereignty Story." *Daedalus*, 147, no. 2, 2018, 17-26.

Takaki, Ronald. *A Different Mirror: A History of Multicultural America*. New York: Basic Books, 1993.

Taylor, Alan. *William Cooper's Town: Power and Persuasion on the Frontier of the Early American Republic*. New York: Vintage Books, 1995.

Teuton, Sean Kicummah. *Red Land, Red Power: Grounding Knowledge in the American Indian Novel*. Durham: Duke University Press, 2008.

Truth, Sojourner, and Olive Gilbert. *The Narrative of Sojourner Truth, A Northern Slave, Emancipated from Bodily Servitude by the State of New York in 1828*. Boston: J.B. Yerrinton and Sons, 1850.

Turbin, Carole. "Beyond Conventional Wisdom: Women's Wage Work, Household Economic Conditions, and Labor Activism in a Mid-Nineteenth-Century Working-Class Community." In *"To Toil the Livelong Day": America's Women at Work, 1780-1980*, edited by Carol Groneman and Mary Beth Norton, 47-67. Ithaca: Cornell University Press, 1987.

Tyler, Royall. *The Contrast*. In *The Heath Anthology of American Literature*, 3rd edition, edited by Paul Lauter, 1148–88. New York: Houghton, Mifflin, 1998 [1787].

———. *The Algerine Captive, or The Life and Adventures of Doctor Updike Underhill*. New York: Modern Library, 2002 [1797].

Vest, Jay Hansford C. "From Bobtail to Brer Rabbit: Native American Influences on Uncle Remus." *American Indian Quarterly* 24, no. 1, 2000, 19–43.

Vizenor, Gerald. *Native Liberty: Natural Reason and Cultural Survivance*. Lincoln: University of Nebraska Press, 2009.

Warrior, Robert. *People and the Word: Reading Native Nonfiction*. Minneapolis: University of Minnesota Press, 2005.

Washington, Booker T. *Up from Slavery: An Autobiography*. Garden City, NY: Doubleday and Company, 1901.

Washington, Mary Helen. "Introduction: The Enduring Legacy of Sojourner Truth." In *The Narrative of Sojourner Truth*, edited by Mary Helen Washington, ix-xxxiii. New York: Vintage Books, 1993.

Weaver, Jace. "Turning West: Cosmopolitanism and American Indian Literary Nationalism." In *Native American Renaissance: Literary Imagination and Achievement*, edited by Alan R. Velie and A. Robert Lee, 16-38. Tulsa: University of Oklahoma Press, 2013.

Wei, William. *Asians in Colorado: A History of Persecution and Perseverance in the Centennial State*. Seattle: University of Washington Press, 2016.

Wendland-Liu, Joel. "'Indifferent Commodities' and 'Abstract Labor-power': Angela Davis' Critique of White Supremacy and U.S. Racial Capitalism," *Peace, Land, and Bread*, No. 4, 2021.

——. "A Culture of Human Liberation: U.S. Communist Writers in the 20th Century." In *Faith in the Masses*, edited by Tony Pecinovsky, 249–87. New York: International Publishers, 2020.

——. *The Collectivity of Life: Spaces of Social Mobility and the Individualism Myth.* Lanham, MD: Lexington Books, 2016.

Wheatley, Phillis. "To the Right Honourable William, Earl of Dartmouth." In *The Complete Writings of Phillis Wheatley*, edited by Vincent Carretta, 39–40. New York: Penguin, 2001 [1773].

White, Richard. *The Burt Lake Band: An Ethnohistorical Report on the Trust Lands of Indian Village.* East Lansing: Michigan State University Press, 1980.

Wilson, Harriet E. *Our Nig: or, Sketches from the Life of a Free Black.* New York: Vintage Books, 1983 [1859].

Witgen, Michael. *An Infinity of Nations: How the Native World Shaped Early North America.* Philadelphia: University of Pennsylvania Press, 2012.

Womack, Craig. "Alexander Posey's Nature Journals: A Further Argument for Tribally-Specific Aesthetics." *Studies in American Indian Literatures* 13, no. 2/3, 2000, 49-66.

Wong, Edlie L. *Racial Reconstruction: Black Inclusion, Chinese Exclusion, and the Fictions of Citizenship Account.* New York: New York University Press, 2015.

Wu Tingfang. "The Causes of the Unpopularity of the Foreigner in China," *Annals of the American Academy of Political and Social Science* January 1910, 1-14.

Yung Wing. *My Life in China and America.* New York: Henry Holt and Co., 1909.

Zhang, Tao. "The Confucian Strategy in African Americans' Racial Equality Discourse." *Dao* 20, 2021, 309-329.

Zhou Xiaojing. "Introduction: Critical Theories and Methodologies in Asian American Literary Studies," in eds. Zhou Xiaojing and Samina Najmi, *Form and Transformation in Asian American Literature*, 3-29. Seattle: University of Washington Press, 2011.

Zinn, Howard. *A People's History of the United States: 1492–Present.* New York: Harper Perennial, 1995.

Zimmerman, Andrew. *Alabama in Africa: Booker T. Washington, the German Empire, and the Globalization of the New South.* Princeton: Princeton University Press, 2010.

About the Author

Joel Wendland-Liu teaches courses on diversity, intercultural competence, migration, and civil rights at Grand Valley State University in West Michigan. He is the author of *The Collectivity of Life: Spaces of Social Mobility and the Individualism Myth*, and a former editor of *Political Affairs*.